COUNTER-CARTOGRAPHIES

COUNTER-CARTOGRAPHIES

NEURODIVERGENCE AND THE ERRANCIES OF PERFORMANCE

LEON J. HILTON

UNIVERSITY OF MINNESOTA PRESS
MINNEAPOLIS • LONDON

The University of Minnesota Press gratefully acknowledges the generous assistance provided for the publication of this book by Brown University.

Portions of the Introduction were previously published in "Staging the Asylum: Javier Téllez's Disability Aesthetics," in *Sex, Identity, Aesthetics: The Work of Tobin Siebers and Disability Studies,* edited by Jina B. Kim, Joshua Kupetz, Crystal Yin Lie, and Cynthia Wu, 141–60 (Ann Arbor: University of Michigan Press, 2021); copyright University of Michigan Press; reprinted with permission of the publisher. Portions of chapter 3 were previously published in a different form in "'Avonte's Law': Disability Surveillance, Racial Schematization, Autistic Wandering," in "Blackness and Disability," edited by Therí Picken, special issue, *African American Review* 50, no. 2 (2017): 221–35; copyright 2017 St. Louis University and The Johns Hopkins University Press; reprinted with permission.

Published by the University of Minnesota Press
111 Third Avenue South, Suite 290
Minneapolis, MN 55401-2520
http://www.upress.umn.edu

ISBN 978-1-5179-0902-4 (hc)
ISBN 978-1-5179-0903-1 (pb)

A Cataloging-in-Publication record for this book is available from the Library of Congress.

Printed in the United States of America on acid-free paper

UMP BmB 2025

For my parents

and

for V., J., A., and M.

Contents

Introduction

Toward a Cartography of Neurodivergence

Bala Perdida

Arriving at the high border fence that runs the width of the main beach of Tijuana's Las Playas neighborhood, a crowd assembles before a stage facing an enormous, almost cartoonishly proportioned blue cannon, its long barrel angled ominously to point toward the U.S. territory that lies beyond the tall, pointed steel partitions that trail off like ellipses into the Pacific Ocean. The pack of spectators has been led to this site by a festive parade of colorfully attired performers, many wearing commedia dell'arte–style animal masks. Some play instruments; others hold demonstration-style placards with hand-painted messages: "Vivir sin frogar" (Live without building walls), "Los enfermos mentales tambien somos seres humanos" (Mental patients are also human beings), "No racismo intelectual!" (No to intellectual racism!). After a series of short performances and musical interludes comes the main event: David E. Smith, an American daredevil performer better known as the Human Cannonball, climbs a ladder and showily waves his U.S. passport to the assembled crowd before descending into the cannon's barrel. After a few moments, during which the crowd looks on with breathless anticipation, Smith is launched over the fence, landing triumphantly in a net that has been set up on the other side of the wall.

This performance, created by artist Javier Téllez and entitled *One Flew Over the Void (Bala perdida [Stray bullet])*, took place in 2005 as part of the Tijuana-based inSITE performance festival. The richly symbolic act that the event culminated in was not an idea that Téllez came to on his own. The cross-border launch of the Human Cannonball was proposed by his collaborators on the project, which was conceived, produced, and staged by patients of the state psychiatric hospital in the Mexican border city of Mexicali. These patients wanted their collaboration with the artist to reflect their experiences of psychiatric institutionalization within a hypermilitarized, intensely surveilled border region. The theatrical gesture at the heart of this performance, Téllez notes, "used the geopolitical border between USA and México as a metaphor for another boundary, the boundary between the normal and the pathological."[1]

Téllez has often worked in close collaboration with psychiatric patients in mental institutions in his native Venezuela, as well as in Mexico, Australia, Germany, and the United States, where he has lived since 1993.[2] This defining aspect of his artistic practice has, at least in part, autobiographical origins. Born in 1969 in Valencia, Téllez grew up on the grounds of the city's Bárbula psychiatric hospital, where his parents were members of the psychiatric staff.[3] His interest in producing forms of artistic collaboration that fracture taken-for-granted distinctions such as normal/pathological, ability/disability, artist/patient, and clinical/aesthetic calls attention to the role that contestations over mental health have played within larger histories of emancipatory social struggle. Téllez identifies himself with a tradition of radical thought that defines emancipation as a struggle over different forms of visibility and perception, and that understands aesthetics as a realm of action that obtains political force insofar as art has the potential to rip apart what Jacques Rancière describes as the "sensible fabric of experience."[4] The fabric of sensory experience, constantly woven and rewoven, that constitutes the common lifeworld of sense perception is a product of historical contingencies that are at once political and aesthetic. But aesthetics is also flush with potentiality, a site for the elaboration of practices that "intervene in the general distribution of ways of doing and making" to forge new configurations of the sensorium.[5]

Téllez makes it clear that the possibilities for flourishing afforded to people living with mental diagnoses are contingent on the discursive and representational systems that give their experiences social meaning and coherence in ways that also undercut their own rhetorical agency and autonomy. "Most 'objective' representations of the mentally ill have been made by the psychiatric institution," he observes, "in which the discourses of the patients are always categorized as mere illustrations of their diagnoses, not to mention stigmatic media constructions."[6] Addressing questions about the ethics of creating artistic work with collaborators whose diagnoses imply an impaired or diminished capacity to exercise rhetorical or expressive agency, Téllez says that he means for his work to "create a flexible space where those represented can intervene in their own representation."[7] Indeed, his works lay bare the ethical underpinnings of representation as a historical structure of modernity, inseparable from the larger histories of exclusion, confinement, and disqualification that are as spatialized and materialized in the art gallery, theater, or cinema as they are in the architecture of the psychiatric hospital, asylum, or prison.

Bala perdida makes ingenious use of la frontera—a tear made by history in the body of the earth that also has the power to mark and injure the bodies that traverse and are traversed by it, and even to warp their very consciousness—to render it a site of aesthetic invention and performative inversion.[8] In so doing, the performance enables new ways of sensing the contiguities between the powers of confinement associated with psychiatric institutions and the hypermilitarized surveillance and policing of movement that characterize the U.S.–Mexico border. The carnival-like atmosphere leading up to the cross-border Human Cannonball launch produced a momentary interruption in the administrative procedures that typically determine the flow of bodies at this most geopolitically charged zone. (Téllez and the festival organizers worked to obtain special clearance from both the Mexican and U.S. customs and immigration agencies, and even then, it is notable that Smith, a white U.S. citizen, was the one chosen and granted permission to perform the stunt.)

In disability studies and criticism that attends to questions of cultural representation, the use of disability as a metaphorical trope is often met with critical suspicion, particularly when the formal or aesthetic ends to which a disability metaphor is put diverts from or even undermines attention to the lived, material realities of disabled people. Yet *Bala perdida* seems to surpass the boundaries of its dominant metaphorical gesture, pointing beyond simple equivalences or parallels between racism and ableism by instead suggesting deep contiguities between the two forms of partitioning it references (normal/pathological, United States/Mexico). The performance invites us to ask how we might come to see this border as being produced and maintained by some of the same modes of rationality that partition the normative (healthy) subject from its (ill, debilitated, or pathologized) other. "How might we define a system of ethics capable of moving beyond the dichotomy of the normal and the pathological?"[9] Who watches? Who flies? Who moves? Who is made to move, and whose movement is constrained? How are we asked to imagine or reimagine what we mean by something like vision? These are questions that are at once addressed to the artist, the viewer, and the pathologized or institutionalized people who are both represented and active participants in shaping the formal dimensions of the works in which they appear.

At stake in the dichotomy between the normal and the pathological that modern rationality instantiates—and that enters our discourse via the diagnostic language of psychiatric and medical expertise—is nothing less than the expulsion of neurodivergence from the consolidation of modern subjectivity and selfhood as such.[10] Yet *Bala perdida* suggests that neurodivergence must be seen as a central site of struggle in the weaving of the sensory fabric of common experience, particularly as its meaning and embodied reality is shaped by modern contestations surrounding the medical pathologization and institutional confinement of unreason. The Human Cannonball launch in which *Bala perdida* culminated introduced a tear that temporarily ruptured the basic illusion that sustains the geopolitical reality of an international border bisecting an otherwise uninterrupted stretch of rocky beach.

Bala perdida is but one example of what this book will describe as counter-cartographic performances—however fleeting, contingent, or covert—that aim to dishabituate the neurotypical sensorium by deactivating the rules and logics that normally govern the terrain of the earth and the territories of the self.

The term *neurodivergence* suggests a spatial metaphoric of the aslant and askew, of that which deviates from the gridded space imposed by the regime of normalization and its disciplining logics. *Counter-cartographies* seeks to describe hidden practices, silent countermeasures, and overlooked insurgent strategies against the interminably shifting and unstable diagnostic taxonomies that classify, order, and regulate the distribution and modulation of life and death for those whose neurologies are pathologized under what Catherine Malabou describes as an emerging regime of neuronal ideology.[11] This book is interested in practical, concrete, and quotidian attempts at prying open the stranglehold of normalization and reconfiguring the world so that it might cultivate, rather than annihilate, the persistence and flourishing of neurodivergent forms of life. It is concerned with projects, experiments, and practices that follow neurodivergence along errant trajectories of doing, feeling, and being. It maps out long unseen pathways for thinking, watching, and responding to the forms of life called up and made visible through the apertures for thought afforded by the concept of neurodivergence. It attempts to both unearth and theorize the way neurodivergence has been mapped across a range of intellectual currents and discourses (from postwar cybernetics to contemporary disability studies), political formations (from the anti-psychiatry and the psychiatric survivor movements of the 1970s to present-day disability justice and mental health reform projects), and aesthetic forms (including documentary cinema, performance and experimental theater, and digital media art).

The critical aperture of performance studies is central to this project because it is not just, or not only, an idiom for thinking about aesthetic or expressive practices—though this is an important domain of my analysis—but also allows for a discussion of how social reality is actively produced, and reproduced, through an accumulation of doings, redoings, and undoings. *Counter-cartographies* thus endeavors to bring to light what seems to be a hidden or at least unacknowledged aspect of the critical interest, across disciplines, in concepts of performance and performativity, arguably two of the most influential terms of critical thought of the past half century. Efforts to describe social reality as performative make it a particularly apposite location for considering the specific disruption that autism represents to neurotypical expectations that the contiguity between subject and speech should be seamless or transparent. Some of the most interesting, meaningful, and consequential discussions on the stakes of these seemingly arcane or academic matters of language, speech, and power that belong to the act of naming have occurred in proximity to the emerging discourse of neurodiversity and neurodivergence. This growing body of scholarship and cultural production has set the parameters for the kinds of inquiry and modes of analysis that I offer here.[12]

The extent to which disability can be adequately accounted for through normative liberal conceptions of political action has been an ongoing subject of debate within disability studies. Feminist critic Cora Kaplan notes that disability "continues to trouble the rhetoric of liberal individualism, testing both its ethics of tolerance and its fetishization of autonomy and agency as conditions of human status and civic participation." Kaplan argues that disability's unruly status within liberal discourse points to long-standing contradictions and unresolved ambiguities within the liberal tradition itself: "the continuing debate about the rights of citizens, and the price of increased agency for them, is itself a legacy of liberalism's historically mixed messages about autonomy and social justice, an ongoing paradox that remains as radically unresolved in the liberalisms that characterize late-twentieth-century social democracies as it did in the 'classic' liberalism of the nineteenth century."[13] In place of the historically contradictory ethical constraints built into the liberal conception of autonomy—and what Kaplan calls its fetishization of agency—disability studies has put forth a range of alternative ethical models that rely on less rigidly individualized conceptions of subjectivity. These have involved attending to the forms of mutual care, collectivity, and assistive facilitation that emerge in proximity to disability, so that sociality is no longer conceptualized as a discrete, atomized exchange between autonomous individuals but rather as an entangled relational field that is always in process.

The contributions of feminist disability studies and the emerging field of mad studies have been especially significant, offering new resources for understanding concepts such as dependency and care within the context of an analytic attuned to gender as well as to bodily and cognitive forms of difference.[14] Sociologist Micki McGee, drawing from the work of feminist philosopher Eva Feder Kittay, suggests that neurological difference poses a test case that exposes the "limits of liberalism." Noting that neurodiversity makes claims for the political and social enfranchisement of individuals who in earlier historical moments would have represented the very antithesis of reason—the "mad," "insane," "deficient," "feebleminded"—McGee writes that "the idea of neurodiversity necessarily strains the very notion of the rational, choosing subject that is at the heart of the liberal ideal."[15] These positions, too, reveal neurodiversity and disability rights discourses to be caught in the incongruous position of making claims for access and autonomy that ultimately rely on a stable, binary opposition—between disabled and nondisabled, neurotypical and neuroatypical—whose terms remained firmly prescribed by modern liberal formations of personhood, autonomy, and rationality.

As a way of charting a new course through these questions, this book's interests can be formulated according to the perspectival reversal that is accomplished in the unclassifiable work of Fernand Deligny (1913–96), who insists that "it is not on the side of autism that one finds wildness [sauvagerie], but rather in civilization and in its most characteristic gestures."[16] Deligny finds many different ways of describing himself: primordial communist, nonviolent guerrilla, weaver of networks, cartographer of wandering lines. A fascinating but still somewhat overlooked and marginal figure, Deligny is situated in the crosscurrents of many trajectories of radical twentieth-century thought and culture: anti-psychiatry, the ecosocialism of the to back-to-the-land movement, experimental cinema, radical pedagogy, proto-disability theory. A partisan of the French Resistance to the Nazi occupation, Deligny resists the authority of psychiatric experts and institutions and refuses to identify conditions such as autism as pathological deviations from a norm. Early on he came to be totally opposed to the asylum system, a vast archipelago of state institutions first established in the nineteenth century alongside other projects of national and colonial consolidation, and whose very architecture reflects successive waves of psychiatric expertise as it became professionalized through the practice of "asylum medicine" as a medico-pedagogical project. (It is thus possible to make a case for Deligny as an important forerunner of the movements to deinstitutionalize and decarcerate the treatment and care of persons who live with mental disabilities.) In the 1950s he began to experiment with unusual new approaches for working with "delinquent" and other socially marginalized children and adolescents. With a few collaborators, he went on to pursue a series of nomadic, communal encampments—he called them "attempts" (or *tentatives*)—for living and working alongside children who would have otherwise spent their lives in psychiatric and other custodial institutions of the state. Together, he and his "network" set out "in search of a mode of being that allowed them to exist even if that meant changing our own mode."[17]

In turning to Deligny and the wider historical context in which his work took shape, we can see how intersecting perspectives from psychiatry, psychoanalysis, cognitive science, political theory, social policy, and aesthetics (drawing, painting, theater, cinema) contribute to what might be called the hidden histories of neurodivergent refusal and counter-action.[18] Revisiting an earlier historical moment and a different national context through the lens of Deligny's trajectories also yields new perspectives on the historical consolidation of modern taxonomies of what would come to be called neurodivergence.

Reframing Neurodiversity

Autism and autism spectrum disorders (ASDs) are currently classified by the American Psychiatric Association's *Diagnostic and Statistical Manual (DSM)* as pervasive developmental disorders characterized by impairments in social interaction, deficits in social communication, and restrictive, repetitive patterns of behavior, activities, or interests.[19] Yet this definition, as will become clear throughout the course of this study, sits perched atop a "surface of emergence" that conceals an enormously complex and ongoing history of fierce contestations across and within a range of communities, organizations, disciplines, and fields of knowledge.[20] Scholars from a variety of disciplinary perspectives have demonstrated how contestations over the meaning of autism have played out within an equally complex and wide-ranging set of historical processes, cultural contexts, and ideological coordinates. These have included dramatic transformations in scientific protocols and paradigms within the sciences of the mind—psychiatry, psychology, cognitive science, neuroscience, and so on—from the early nineteenth century through the present; shifts in public policy, legal codes, and clinical practice concerning the care and treatment of persons with mental disabilities, mental illness, and those deemed "mentally deficient" (a term still in use until late in the twentieth century); the appearance of well-organized groups made up of parents and others with autistic family members who advocated for further research, different treatment options, and improvements in care protocols; and, finally, the expansion of a diverse range of mobilizations for disability rights and disability justice organized around explicitly political, social, and cultural models of disability. These overlapping historical processes and trajectories have continued to shape the way autism appears as an object of concern that can be studied, measured, and quantified as much as they are embodied, experienced, and lived.[21]

It is clear that some aspects of the concept of neurodiversity existed before the word was coined in the late 1990s. Since the early days of the internet, self-identified autistic and neurodivergent people started to formulate alternative political and cultural accounts of the condition, often in ways that were critical of the dominant cultural and medical narratives through which it had been represented. In the early 1990s, largely facilitated by online message boards, a number of loosely organized networks and groups of autistic self-advocates and neurodiversity proponents began to form, including the Autism Network International (ANI) and the Autistic Self Advocacy Network (ASAN). In 1993, Jim Sinclair, one of the pioneers of autistic self-advocacy, wrote a manifesto for ANI's newsletter entitled "Don't Mourn for Us." Sinclair's text is addressed directly to parents of autistic children who, as Sinclair suggests, frequently relate to their children as if in mourning for the nonautistic child they did not have:

> Autism isn't something a person *has,* or a "shell" that a person is trapped inside. There's no normal child hidden behind the autism. Autism is a way of being. It is *pervasive;* it colors every experience, every sensation, perception, thought, emotion, and encounter, every aspect of existence. It is not possible to separate the autism from the person—and if it were possible, the person you'd have left would not be the same person you started with. This is important, so take a moment to consider it: Autism is a way of being. It is not possible to separate the person from the autism.[22]

A growing body of scholarly, literary, and cultural work about autism and the concept of neurodivergence has been following up on Sinclair's insight. The first use of the word *neurodiversity* has generally been attributed to Judy Singer, an Australian sociologist and disability activist, who began using it on an internet exchange forum in 1997 and elaborated on the concept in an essay published in 1999.[23] Later, Singer noted that her early use of the term was linked to her long-standing interest in biodiversity and the human ecology movement: "I came to the ND word from the Green Movement. . . . Environmentalists used the word *Biodiversity* to argue that the most stable ecosystems are those that are most diverse, from which it follows that all species must be conserved. I thought the same principle could be used by 'neurologically different' people who had traditionally been excluded, bullied and humiliated by mainstream society."[24] For Singer, "the role of the Neurodiversity Movement is to unite all the people with simple neurological variants behind the same advocacy banner: i.e., the syndrome formerly known as Aspergers, ADD, ADHD, Dyslexia, Dyspraxia, Stuttering, etc. All those Neurotribes who have not been appropriately catered to in education or health, all those whose skills and abilities are not recognised because of superficial behavioural traits, all those who have suffered active discrimination in employment—all can advocate for their specific tribe, while banding together under a common umbrella."[25] A similar analogy is made in an article by journalist Harvey Blume published in the *Atlantic* in 1998, although without crediting Singer: "Neurodiversity may be every bit as crucial for the human race as biodiversity is for life in general."[26]

But the metaphorical potency of both autism and neurodiversity (and neurodivergence) are rife with contradictions, as autism comes to be increasingly figured as alternatively—and sometimes simultaneously—a form of debilitation (of sociality and relationality) and a mode of being that is "super" capacitated in relation to the unique demands placed on workers under conditions of postindustrial, "informational" capitalism.[27] In October 2012, newsstand browsers in New York City found themselves confronted by a startling question emblazoned across the cover of *New York* magazine: "Is Everyone on the Autism Spectrum?" Noting the frequency with which diagnostic disorders of autism and Asperger syndrome are invoked in popular media—and contemporary discourse more broadly—to explain socially maladapted, emotionally vacant, and systematically obsessive behavior, journalist Benjamin Wallace's cover article suggests that autism might be the "defining psychiatric malady" of postmillennial America. Arguing that its increasing cultural prominence indicates something more general about the contemporary zeitgeist, autism, writes Wallace, has become "a conceptual gadget for processing the modern world."[28] In 1998, fourteen years before the publication of Wallace's article, an anonymous internet user named Muskie created a tongue-in-cheek website that he called the "Institute for the Study of the Neurologically Typical." Expressing an immense frustration with clinical and popular representations of the autistic experience of emotion and sociality as "flat," Muskie's first post notes: "This site is an expression of autistic *out*rage." Forcefully contesting the diagnostic terms in which Muskie's neurological and cognitive disability were described to him, Muskie counters: "My brain is a jewel. I am in awe of the mind that I have. I and my experience of life are not inferior, and may be *superior,* to the NT [neurotypical] experience of life."[29]

The contradictory figurations of autism in these two examples—as, alternatively, the reigning psychiatric metaphor of the historical present and the exclusive, jewel-like provenance of a lucky few—point to tension that has shaped clinical and cultural articulations of *autism* since the word first entered the psychiatric lexicon in the early decades of the twentieth century. The earliest clinical use of the word *autism* occurred in 1911, in an article by pioneering Swiss psychiatrist Eugen Bleuler, who used the word *autism* to describe children who "have no more contact with the outside world [and] live in a world of their own. They have encased themselves with their desires and wishes . . . ; they have cut themselves off as much as possible from any contact with the external world. This detachment from reality with the relative and absolute predominance of the inner life, we term autism."[30] For Bleuler and other psychological theorists in the early twentieth century, *autism* was a term to describe neurotic symptoms of a more general character, an evocative neologism from the Greek word autos, "self." It was not until pioneering child psychiatrist Leo Kanner's studies at his clinic at Johns Hopkins University in the early 1940s that autism was first proposed as a distinctive psychiatric disorder, which Kanner defines as an "inability to relate" to others, or to the world, "in the ordinary way."[31] Kanner was an Austrian-born physician who had immigrated to the United States from Vienna to escape Nazi persecution before World War II and essentially founded the field of child psychology. Through a series of clinical studies of a relatively small group of children at his clinic in Baltimore in the 1940s, 1950s, and 1960s, he identified the primary "phenomenological" hallmarks of autism as "obsessive aloneness and an anxiously obsessive desire for the preservation of sameness."[32] Kanner's early research was agnostic about whether the symptoms he grouped under the broad diagnostic category of "early infantile autism" were the result of ("emotional") psychological disturbance or ("organic") neurological pathology. For Kanner, as medical sociologist Gil Eyal notes, autism "represented a problematization of the distinction between mental retardation and mental illness."[33] The social, juridical, and institutional implications of this distinction were profoundly consequential during the decades that followed World War II. Mental retardation was understood to be temporary and rectifiable through treatment, while mental illness was thought to be a fixed and immutable condition requiring lifelong custodianship. In essentially inventing a new diagnostic category, Kanner's work on infantile autism challenged this bifurcated model by bringing a newly modern understanding of the multiple and heterogeneous potentialities that existed within the previously homogeneous category of "feeblemindedness."[34] The genealogical development of autism can thus be traced from its initial designation of a cluster of behavioral tendencies—profound aloneness, incommunicability, and radical self-enclosure—to its gradual solidification into a clinical or medical subject, pathologically bound to such tendencies.

In the decades after World War II, psychiatric researchers and clinicians principally located autism in the "psyche," as first proposed by Freud and then modulated by the subsequent establishment and growth of psychoanalytically informed therapeutic models. Controversial child psychologist Bruno Bettelheim used a modified Freudian paradigm to postulate that autism resulted from insufficiently developed capacities for the ego to differentiate itself from its surroundings. Autism was compared to "an empty fortress," the title of Bettelheim's infamous 1967 best-selling book about the condition and his controversial treatment methods devised at the University of Chicago's Orthogenic School. This phrase, and Bettelheim's account of the condition, quickly became associated in wider cultural contexts with tropes of pathological solipsism, aloneness, and isolation.[35] In the 1950s and 1960s, autism was also frequently described as a symptomatic condition of the technology-saturated, increasingly depersonalized, and automated modern age, as when Betty Friedan postulated in *The Feminine Mystique* (1963) that the rise in "atypical" or "autistic" children might be attributable to a "progressive dehumanization" that also limited women's opportunities to pursue careers and interests beyond the domestic sphere.[36]

By the early 1970s, new frameworks for understanding autism had begun to emerge that reflected a "cognitivist" paradigm, adopting a model of the mind as a kind of "modular" machine made up of discrete components assigned to specific mental tasks. Cognitive psychology relied on the metaphoric trope of the computer in its emerging accounts of mental processes.

This metaphor of the mind as computer was particularly consequential within discussions of autism.[37] These cognitivist approaches generated three broad hypotheses about autism. First, the hypothesis of weak central coherence posited that the symptoms of autism resulted from the mind's inability to generalize and make broader connections on the basis of local details. A second hypothesis related to the growing attention within cognitive psychological models to what came to be called the Theory of Mind (or, in the case of autism, Lack of Theory of Mind), which postulated that autistic people lacked the specific modular architecture responsible for the capacity to attribute thoughts, intentions, and emotions to others. (This is the origin of the widely disseminated credence that autistic people are "mind blind" and lack the ability to empathize with others.[38]) A third cognitive hypothesis proposed that the symptoms of autism resulted from deficits in "executive function," a term used to designate the mental capacity to direct mental focus and attention in consequentially ordered, functional ways.

By the 1990s, cognitive models began to be supplemented, and in some cases challenged, by rapid advances in both neurobiology and genetics research. Still, biological research into the neuroscience and genetics of autism has been notoriously fraught, with few uncontroverted breakthroughs to point to with any degree of certainty. Many of the most promising neuroscientific studies have sought to shift emphasis away from the cognitivist focus on modular "deficits" toward attention for the neurobiology of the senses. The recent emphasis on the neurological basis of sensory processing differences in autism has led to a number of provocative new hypotheses about the condition, including studies that have offered a new account of autism as "Intense World Syndrome," "a unifying hypothesis where the core pathology of the autistic brain is hyper-reactivity and hyper-plasticity of local neuronal circuits."[39] The growing attention to the distinctive sensory dimensions of autistic neurotypes has suggested that many of the behavioral hallmarks that were long believed to indicate cognitive, intellectual, or affective deficits might be better described simply as *differences* in the brain's sensory processing mechanisms.[40]

As the rate of autism diagnoses has risen since the 1990s, both in the United States and abroad, and as the condition has come to the forefront of public consciousness, often framed in terms of the crisis and threat that autism poses to the future of the nation, the autistic body becomes mapped as pathological according to the ambient cultural anxieties about health, security, and productivity that are projected onto it. Consider, as just one example, the increasing frequency with which the "autistic brain" is associated with a heightened, almost "unhuman" ability to perform informational or "systems-based" thinking outside the constraints of normative emotional investment.[41] The tendency to compare autism with machine- or computer-like thinking and behavior has been nearly constant since practically the beginning of its life as a medical diagnosis. As Julia Miele Rodas observes in her study of autistic poetics, "gestures of verbal collecting, ordering, listmaking, and delineating—generating formal order from verbal sign—have historically been interpreted in accordance with two common and dehumanizing tropes: autist-as-robot or autist-as-intellectual-acrobat."[42]

As this cursory overview would suggest, autism has been exceptionally difficult to define with any lasting degree of precision. The long-standing inability of medical and psychiatric science to isolate a single, identifiable cause of autism's symptoms has led some to suggest that *autism* must be understood as provisional and an overly generalized term, a holdover from an earlier era of medical science and diagnostic protocols that is inadequate for the range of conditions it attempts to subsume under a single label—or, with the emergence of the concept of the autism spectrum in the 1980s, at the height of the influence of cognitive psychology, a large and capacious diagnostic "umbrella."[43] To be clear, this is not to assert that the different neurotypes currently and historically associated with autism and ASDs are not real and consequential categories, or that these categories lack (neuro)biological correlates that might still someday be located in the body or brain. Rather, it is meant to indicate the provisional, contingent, and highly speculative grounds on which medical experts on autism have based their claims.

The efforts by researchers, funders, parent groups, and caregivers alike are steeped in martial metaphors that case the "fight" against autism in military terms. This process enables the autistic body, as Anne McGuire writes, to be narratively represented as "both the site and origin of its own disorder."[44] Autistic behaviors are not forms of voluntary communication; they are merely symptoms of a pathology that is out of the autistic subject's control. Social interactions are impoverished by "mindblindness," a cognitive deficit that is said to impede one's capacity to intuit that other people have states of mind that are different from one's own.

How all these metaphors confine neurodivergence to the status of demi-rhetoricity, Yergeau writes, reveals them to be "a horrifically useful strategy for denying the agency, rhetorical being, and personhood of autistic people."[45]

Recent studies have shown that mortality rates among persons with autism or ASD are twice as high as they are for the general population.[46] Autism mortality is in part higher because of frequent comorbid health conditions—including mental health conditions such as anxiety and depression—yet it is also linked to enhanced vulnerability to accidental and preventable causes of death. Most autistic people remain especially vulnerable to being abused, neglected, and killed by those who are responsible for their care, including state-employed and private care workers and family members. Other studies have drawn attention to the higher suicide rate of autistic people. In such a context, death—whether natural, accidental, or preventable—is inseparable from the forms of political power that organize and distribute life and death in aggregate through hierarchical schematization across and within the population. That is to say, neurodivergence emerges within a biopolitical paradigm that is inextricable from the exercise of sovereign power defined by the "right to 'make' live and 'let' die."[47] Queer disabled writer and activist Eli Clare argues that "the violence set in motion by diagnosis" is also a form of violence that is "made thinkable and doable" by diagnosis itself.[48] The task is to devise strategies to respond to how disability continues to be transformed into bare life in order to ameliorate the threat of injury, abuse, and death that autistic people confront as a quotidian fact of existence, built into the structures that bring disability within the structure of political sovereignty precisely by way of its attempted prevention and exclusion.

The stakes of political struggles over the forced institutionalization and confinement of disabled people are clear in the case of the Judge Rotenberg Educational Center, a Massachusetts institution for intellectually disabled minors where the use of techniques derived from applied behavior analysis (ABA) for over forty years has become the subject of litigation from mental health and disability advocacy groups only recently, over the past decade.[49] In a 2017 article published in *Punishment and Society,* disability studies scholars D. L. Adams and Nirmala Erevelles discuss expert testimony given at a 2014 hearing of the Food and Drug

Administration concerning the use of electroconvulsive shock devices in the context of "aversive conditioning" therapies at the Rotenberg Center. Noting how the official testimonies from medical experts persistently defended the use of electric shocks as behavioral aversives based on a presumption that intellectually disabled people do not experience pain as intensely as nondisabled people, Adams and Erevelles observe that "even though disability activists offer testimonies located within a rights-based discourse, the effectiveness of these testimonies in courts of law are mediated via the negative ontologies that construct disabled subjects as 'bare life' abandoned within the legal limbo of the 'the camp.'"[50] Invoking the term used by Giorgio Agamben to describe the core structure of sovereignty in Western politics, Adams and Erevelles show how psychiatric expertise conjoined with the regulatory power of the state to "include" disabled people within the structure of sovereignty by excluding them from the community of those whose lives have been given a meaningful form.

Biopolitics, Psychiatric Power, and Normalization

I have chosen to use the term *neurodivergence* in order to situate this project in relationship to a longer critical tradition that has been invested in unearthing the history of social difference more broadly. In her field-shifting 1991 essay, "The Evidence of Experience," historian Joan W. Scott defines this in elegantly straightforward terms as a history of "the designation of 'other,' of the attribution of characteristics that distinguish categories of people from some presumed (and usually unstated) norm."[51] This project endeavors to bring some existing critical perspectives on the history of difference, as Scott describes it, to the study of emerging discourses of neurodiversity and neurodivergence. It considers how contestations about autism and neurological difference have powerfully reformulated prevailing, neurotypical models of subjectivity, personhood, and autonomy, as well as the ethical dimensions of intersubjective concepts such as relationality, collectivity, and community.

As Scott indicates, the concept of difference as I use it here is inextricable from the idea of the norm. This project thus also takes seriously Michel Foucault's insistence on the productive force of power, and particularly the way it has been exerted by through regimes of normalization that have taken shape since at least the early nineteenth century alongside the development of psychiatric expertise. I am particularly attentive to his arguments about the essential part played by disciplinary institutions —schools, prisons, hospitals, psychiatric asylums—within the multifarious and proliferating techniques of surveillance and social control associated with what Foucault characterizes as psychiatric power.[52] Indeed, Foucault's work on psychiatric power concerns the relationship he elaborates between concepts of political sovereignty, the science of biology, and psychiatric techniques of normalization. Foucault offers a powerfully original account of the historical advent of the psychiatric sciences since the late eighteenth century, showing how disciplinary practices authorized by psychiatric expertise were formed in tandem with an emergent concept of normalization that was being concurrently advanced within the life sciences, as the "diffusion of psychiatric power takes place by way of this development of the concept of the normal."[53]

Foucault's discussion bears traces of the powerful influence of Georges Canguilhem, a prominent French philosopher of science who was also one of Foucault's most significant teachers. Canguilhem used a Nietzschean approach to study the history of the biological sciences, seeking to reveal how modern scientific discourses concerning the "normal" functioning of biological organisms have been inseparable from the broader ideological contexts in which they emerge. Canguilhem described how biological conceptualizations of error were transposed and assimilated within the emergence and transformation of certain moral and ethical norms, and the institutions dedicated to their regulation. In *The Normal and the Pathological* (a text expanded from his 1943 doctoral thesis in medicine), Canguilhem writes that "the introduction of the concept of error into pathology is a fact of great importance as much in terms of the change it reveals in what it brings to bear in man's attitude toward disease, as in terms of the new status which is supposedly established in the relationship between knowledge and its object."[54]

In view of such assertions, it is perhaps not surprising that Foucault would refer to Canguilhem in the course of his own work on the techniques of normalization that have been central to the expansion and diffusion of psychiatric power. Within the psychiatric sciences, as Foucault says in his January 15, 1975 lecture, "the norm is not simply and not even a principle of intelligibility; it is an element on the basis of which a certain exercise of power is founded and legitimized." Instead, he continues, "the norm brings with it a principle of both qualification and correction. The norm's function is not to exclude and reject. Rather, it is always linked to a positive technique of intervention and transformation, to a sort of normative project."[55] Foucault argues that the distinction between normal and abnormal psychological typologies formulated within the psychiatric sciences has at once depended on and generalized the biopolitical logic that linked the discovery of scientific laws regulating the life of biological organisms to modern political practices devised to govern human populations in accordance with the establishment and regulation of norms.[56] Psychiatric power, in other words, appears in Foucault's lectures as one of the most potent vectors that sutures Western liberal modernity's (political) techniques of discipline and social control to scientifically authorized principles of (biological) normalization.

The norm—a concept whose seemingly magnetic power to organize the political regulation of life constituted a core aspect of Foucault's expansive line of inquiry—has been a central category of analysis and critical scrutiny within disability studies for several decades, not least due to Foucault's influence on the field in the late 1980s. It is notable that much of the intellectual engagement with Foucault's thought in this regard has tended to focus on the body as the primary site of historical inscription while minimizing, or assigning a secondary role, to the issues of psychiatric power, mental illness, and mental deficiency that are addressed extensively in the 1973–75 lectures.[57] Significant examples here would include Lennard Davis's influential accounts of the ways in which the modern category of disability emerged in the nineteenth century in tandem with the nascent statistical sciences;[58] and Rosemarie Garland-Thomson's crucial elaboration of the concept of the "normate," the term she offers to describe the statistically determined and abstract standard of able-bodiedness and able-mindedness against which modern taxonomic classifications of disability have been defined—a "figure outlined by the array of deviant others, whose marked bodies shore up the normate's boundaries."[59]

From Psychopolitics to Neuropolitics?

Scholarly attention to the history of normalization, norms, and the normate has largely been formulated in relationship to physical disabilities and more immediately visible forms of disablement. Yet a key aspect of this book's argument is that neurodivergence must be understood in relationship to what might be described as a more general shift away from the mind and toward the brain as the primary locus of political concern. Recent work expanding beyond the historical analysis of biopolitics and psychopolitics as they were shaped by nineteenth-century techniques of normalization has sought to grapple with this shift toward the brain as a primary object of political concern in the late twentieth and early twenty-first centuries.[60] Scholars including sociologists Nikolas Rose and Joelle M. Abi-Rached, political theorist William Connolly, and philosopher Catherine Malabou have variously described the last half century as a "neurobiological era," one that has been defined by a series of interrelated developments through which the human brain and nervous system have become increasingly scrutinized objects of medical-scientific, political, and cultural concern.[61] To be sure, the brain has been a perennial source of philosophical and political fascination, an organ that has been studied and represented in ways that are deeply shaped by broader historical and technological developments. Writing in the early twentieth century, French philosopher Henri Bergson famously analogizes the brain to a central telephone exchange: "Its office," Bergson writes in *Matter and Memory,* "is to allow communication or to delay it," and not to transform sensory information into new representations on its own accord.[62] In their essay on the influence of cybernetics on midcentury American psychologist Silvan Tomkins's theory of affects, Eve Kosofsky Sedgwick and Adam Frank note that systems theorists and computer engineers working in the immediate postwar period conceived of the brain as a homeostatic machine—an "undifferentiated by differentiable ecology" that mirrored the automated, self-regulating mechanics characteristic of Fordist modes of capitalist production.[63]

Here, it may be useful to consider why assertions of neurodivergent selfhood have taken shape against the backdrop of what Malabou has termed an era of "neuronal ideology."[64] For Malabou, our ever-increasing knowledge about the brain's workings has only further displaced us from ourselves because this knowledge has immediately been put to use to explain human behavior, culture, and social worlds in terms of neurological processes, to fulfill the social command to maximize brain productivity, and to invent new treatments. These scientific and biomedical developments have, for the most part, been justified as being in the service of improving health and quality of life. Yet Malabou insists that "the neuronal revolution has revolutionized nothing *for us,* if it is just true that our new brains serve only to displace ourselves better, work better, feel better, or obey better."[65] Instead, she argues that the growing interest in retrofitting conceptions of selfhood and subjectivity on advances in neuroscience has not liberated us, the ostensible subjects of this research. Rather, it has provided the fodder for making us even more pliable subjects of the prevailing conditions of economic production and social reproduction. Malabou offers an account of the "plasticity" of subjectivity, which she in turn links specifically to the historical period of post-Fordist (otherwise called late) capitalism. She has also argued that the specific forms of alienation and social anomie endemic to this period can themselves be linked to the emergence of specific forms psychic and indeed neurological injury, pathology, and suffering.[66]

If Malabou has been the critical theorist who has most openly and uncritically incorporated neuroscience into her thinking on the contemporary politics of the brain as a subject of history, she is not the only thinker to have lately become interested in the neurological and cognitive dimensions of contemporary modes of production, including the production of subjectivity. Philosophers Jan Slaby and Shaun Gallagher observe that "the particular construal of self currently championed by social neuroscience—with a focus on social-interactive skills, low-level empathy and mind-reading—neatly corresponds with the ideal skill profile of today's corporate employee."[67] Sociologist Victoria Pitts-Taylor notes that the concept of neuroplasticity that has come to prominence within neuroscience research since the 1990s—the now widely prevalent view that cerebral structures are constantly forming and reforming in dynamic interaction with external environments—closely resembles the decentralized, flexible, and networked nature of contemporary "informational" capitalism. As Pitts-Taylor suggests, "the popular discourse on plasticity firmly situates the subject in a normative, neoliberal ethic of personal self-care and responsibility linked to modifying the body."[68] These more recent considerations of neural selfhood are not exactly replacing older conceptions of the self; rather, "neural understandings are being layered upon or mobilized flexibly alongside older, established ways of constructing identity and selfhood."[69] Thinkers working within the tradition of postautonomist Marxism have lately considered the neurological, and analogously the pre- or nonconscious scales of the production process that characterizes "cognitive capitalism." Maurizio Lazzarato has proposed to supplement the Foucauldian concept of biopolitics with the inelegant term "noo-politics"—a neologism that draws on both the Aristotelian designation of the noos, "intellect," and the brand name of an internet search engine—to describe the technological manipulation of the brain through interventions on the neurocognitive dimensions of memory, attention, sensation, and emotion within the modes of production and techniques of governance of contemporary global capitalism.[70] For Lazzarato and Tiziana Terranova, who expands on his concept of noo-power in her work on the political economy of information technology, the neurocognitive dimensions of contemporary capitalism are enabled and reinforced by rapid advances within communicational, neuroimagining, and artificial intelligence technologies that have made it possible to generate representations of the brain (and its functions) at ever more precise and microscopic scales.[71]

Social theorists and cultural critics have responded to this contradictory status of autism as a social-historical metaphor in a variety of ways. In *The Burnout Society* (2015), for instance, Korean German philosopher Byung-Chul Han writes of a "general positivization of the world," a slow but inexorable disappearance of what he calls "worldly negativity" that has come about with the shift to an increasingly depersonalized social reality whose contours are determined by the inhuman, programmed calculations of digital technologies like algorithms: a development that he argues "means that both human beings and society are transforming into *autistic performance-machines*."[72] In another recent example of this tropism, philosophers Hans A. Skott-Myhre and Christina Taylor propose that autism "became a central focus of psychiatric control and concern under the previous regime of industrial capitalism and is now the focus of behavioral and psychiatric attention under the new regime of global capitalism."[73] Their argument extends the influential (if not uncontroversial) idea proposed by Gilles Deleuze and Félix Guattari that schizophrenia was not simply an organic disease but a type of pathology whose conceptualization corresponded with particular stages in the development of industrial capitalism. As such, Skott-Mhyre and Taylor move on to characterize the neurodiversity movement as "the *unintentional* development of a minoritarian voice for autism that has begun to call for its self-valorisation as a viable alternative form of consciousness and subjectivity."[74]

Moreover, neurodiversity has become an especially contentious site within the contemporary politics of scientific and medical knowledge—one that is defined by a frequently antagonistic relation between expert investigators, care-workers, and family members and the subjects of their concern. This argument is in accordance with the historian of science Roger Cooter's urgent call for a "historically informed critique of the neuro-turn" that has taken place across the humanities, social sciences, and increasingly in policy discussions and popular discourse over the past several decades.[75] If, as Cooter argues, "our neuro-times [. . .] are epiphenomenal of our economic and ideological times" (151), then it is especially crucial to remain vigilant against reductive acceptance of neuroscientific explanatory paradigms that lock us "into an *ahistorically* conceived neurobiological representation of ourselves that can only articulate being human *in* neurobiological terms."[76] Yet for all of the critical attention that has been devoted to the role of the neurological in contemporary thought, there has been less direct consideration of the place of disability within these debates. The era of neuronal ideology has been one of profound transformation in the meaning and lived reality of disability, yielding new diagnostic categorization, techniques of intervention, and protocols of surveillance and control targeting those identified as deviating from increasingly granulated norms of embodiment and cognition. How can we elaborate a concept of neurodivergence that is capable of accounting for the many clashing scales, temporalities, and spatial imaginaries bound up with ideas about the neuronal? How does neurodiversity fit within the noo-political mechanisms of control that theorists of technology and digital media have described as a networked ecology of proliferating speeds, rhythms, and affects that encompass but also exceed the human subject?

Counter-cartographies builds on these insights alongside recent developments in the field of disability studies that have sought to excavate the historical and political limitations of disability itself as a category of analysis as well as an axis of political or social identification. On the one hand, disability rights movements premised on a politics of liberal cultural recognition—put forth alongside, and in tandem with, a range of social mobilizations arising in the 1960s and 1970s demanding the expansion of political rights and state-supported resources to disenfranchised groups—would seem to have achieved considerable success in entering and transforming the institutions and infrastructures of liberal governance. This has occurred at both the level of the state itself and within the array of bureaucratic, nonstate organizations that reproduce and imitate its procedures, including nonprofits, NGOs, universities, and research centers. On the other hand, the same period has witnessed a systematic dismantling of the postwar social welfare state, whose functions are increasingly relegated to the sphere of private, free-market enterprise.[77] The politics of disability thus confronts a paradoxical situation, one in which disabled people are compelled to seek political recognition and accommodation as disabled from a state whose social welfare infrastructures are being increasingly dismantled and privatized.[78] Moreover, cultural recognition claims made on the basis of a political or social model of disability are more complex to articulate and sustain because the very apparatuses of security and disciplinary surveillance that define liberal modes of governance were themselves devised as a way of managing the aggregate health of the population and maximizing its productive capacities.

Such accounts point to the limitations of the late liberal politics of recognition in the context of neoliberalism, forcing us to ask, as legal theorist Dean Spade writes, "why legal change in the form of rights has not brought the deep transformation" sought by the emancipatory social movements of the 1960s and 1970s, and "why disparities of life chances have increased during a period when we have seen the elimination of formal segregation and the advent of policies prohibiting discrimination on the basis of sex, race, and disability."[79] On closer inspection, it becomes clear that the "expansive" politics of cultural recognition and the economic mandates of neoliberalism have been far from oppositional or contradictory historical developments. Rather, they have often been complementary, even mutually constitutive, processes—two sides of the same coin. The assertion that disability is an explicitly social category that necessitates legal accommodation, protections, and rights—a position that has long been identified as a signal achievement of the modern disability rights movement—emerges in historical contiguity with a period when the state-supported institutions of social welfare that disabled individuals depend on have been under increasing assault.[80] The modern politics of disability, then, run up against the contradictions of rights and recognition-based claims for the inclusion of people with disabilities within a liberal social order that premises its conception of political personhood on an able-bodied and able-minded capacity to work. Indeed, disability politics from this perspective becomes primarily a matter of how to grapple with the "problem" of what David Mitchell and Sharon Snyder have termed nonproductive bodies: "inhabitants of the planet who, largely by virtue of their biological (in)capacity, aesthetic non-conformity, and/or non-normative labor patterns . . . [are] not merely excluded from—but also resistant to standardized labor demands of human value."[81] When followed to its logical end, contemporary disability politics requires confronting what disability activist, artist, and theorist Sunny Taylor has called "the right not to work"—an ideal that is "worthy of the impaired and able-bodied alike" because it points toward the extent to which normative conceptions of moral value, worth, and personhood are tied to "a complex system of historical, cultural, and geographical discrimination that has evolved inside and alongside capitalism and that we now simply regard (and too frequently dismiss) as disability."[82]

Such perspectives are useful for considering why autism has increasingly been figured as either a form of hypercapacitation or radical incapacitation, depending on whether or how an individually identified neurodivergent person is considered "high functioning" or "low functioning." Indeed, economist Tyler Cowen published an article in 2011 describing how autism has begun to be seen as an advantage for workers in tech industries. Danish entrepreneurs started a firm, Specialisterne, that employs autistic people and markets their services, often to high-tech firms. This is a for-profit venture that endorses the quality of its workers, especially when it comes to performing detailed tasks in information technology, such as writing software.[83]

With the emergence of autistic self-advocacy and the advent of neurodiversity discourses in the 1990s, the distinction between so-called low-functioning autism (LFA) and high-functioning autism (HFA), which is largely (though by no means exclusively) made on the basis of an individual's perceived or assessed capacity for verbal communication, has itself come under increasing scrutiny. Many neurodiversity proponents have criticized this distinction as a false representation of the true range of abilities and impairments that characterize the spectrum of neurotypes that are currently subtended within contemporary neuropsychiatric diagnostic protocols. Even as the concept of the autism spectrum has, since the early 1990s, gradually come to dominate psychiatric, biomedical, and cultural discussions of individual variations within autistic symptomology, the distinction between low and high functioning persists as a distinction that reiterates earlier frameworks. Like other contemporary diagnostic protocols related to the assessment and treatment of ASD, the distinction between high and low functioning is not grounded in the detection of any specific biological or neurochemical pathology; rather, it is developed and reiterated on the basis of behavioral observation and assessment.[84] The persistence of the diagnostic distinction between HFA and LFA, neurodiversity proponents have argued, unwittingly marginalizes and disempowers individuals who have been placed on the low-functioning end of the spectrum and effectively serves to divide autistic people from one another on the basis of an (allegedly) arbitrarily imposed criterion of functionality.

The critique of the HFA/LFA distinction has taken a variety of forms within the writing of autistic self-advocates and their allies. In a 2013 blog entry, autistic self-advocate Cynthia Kim writes that functioning labels "assume a uniform set of competences" that do not correspond to the experiential variety and inconsistency that most people diagnosed with autism experience. Rather, Kim argues, autistic functioning is "fluid, nonlinear and nonuniform."[85] Similarly, in a 2007 online interview with autistic writer Donna Williams, Mel Baggs responds to a question about the concept of function by noting, "I don't like the idea of functioning levels because I don't think you can measure everything about a person and assign them a single level, people are more complicated than that. [. . .] I think people come up with a 'functioning level' when they think of a particular ability as more important than others and then they measure a person's entire 'functioning' by that ability."[86] Baggs calls attention to the fact that the limited set of behavioral criteria used by both psychiatric experts and laypeople to determine on which side of the functioning divide an individual falls are more reflective of social and cultural values than they are accurate indicators of an underlying ontological reality.

It seems necessary to work toward new and more capacious conceptualizations of autistic "functioning" that are not constrained by hard distinctions separating low from high, but that do not inadvertently minimize or fail to account for the more difficult and painful dimensions of autistic lifeworlds. Stuart Murray argues that "the worrying aspect is that an idea of autistic functioning equates with an idea of disabled human value."[87] Murray suggests that the word *function* has become a kind of shorthand that "allows for processes of assessment and judgment that fix those with autism into inflexible ontological categories." And it is the categories of HFA and LFA that "themselves then pass for the norm."[88] Indeed, the concept of function has been pervasively defined according to strictly maintained epistemological, ethical, and even moral economies that are in turn sanctioned through the performative force of expert assessment and diagnosis.

What if, taking off from educator and writer Fernand Deligny—whose ideas and work with autistic people (and others whose existence was caught up in the turbulent instability of that term) anchor this book—we imagine a mode of relation that would be nonfunctional, or rather "outside of function" ("un mode de relation hors function")—one that would not bear the traces of a desire to make autistic people and others who live outside or in the margins of language conform to the shape of the "thought-out-project," the neurotypical subject, the human that we are?[89]

Deligny's work took place through the elaboration of a series of nomadic, communal encampments with a small network of collaborators from the worlds of the militant student movement, avant-garde film, and a milieu of politically minded mental health clinicians drawn to the emergent ideas of anti-psychiatry, "institutional analysis," and therapeutic communities. These small, deliberately obscure projects, which took place away from cities, were always on the verge of running out of money, although their work eventually attracted the attention of a number of the era's notable figures, including filmmakers Chris Marker and François Truffaut, as well as the rock band Pink Floyd, which donated 80,000 francs in 1973. Eventually moving to the sparsely populated Cévennes region, Deligny and his collaborators understood these encampments as attempts to forge radically new, noninstitutionalized modes of living and working alongside children who would have otherwise spent their lives confined to mental asylums or other custodial institutions of the state.

At a time when the normal course of therapy and treatment for autism and other kinds of intellectual or developmental disabilities was marked by inhumanity and cruelty, Deligny scorned the authority of psychiatric institutions and refused to pathologize children diagnosed with autism or autistic symptoms like stimming (the clinical term used to describe the perseverative bodily motions characteristically linked to the condition), perseverating, or not speaking. Rejecting the predominance of psychoanalysis and its reliance on depth-based models of human subjectivity in the French understanding of autism at this time, Deligny turned instead to discourses like ethology and the anthropological study of ritual to understand autism instead as a distinctive mode of being and doing. Together with the children who came to spend time with the group, Deligny and his collaborators set out "in search of a mode of being that allowed them to exist even if that meant changing our own mode."[90]

Perhaps Deligny's most original contribution emerged through the act of tracing the wandering trajectories of the autistic people who came to stay in his network's encampment, which he came to term *lignes d'erre,* a phrase that might be translated as "wander lines," "errant lines," or "lines of drift." The concept of the lignes d'erre is arguably the most significant and original formulation in Deligny's thought. It condenses, in a single stroke, his distinctive determination to disrupt traditional ways of conceptualizing the relationship between language, human subjectivity, and political community. Turning to the dictionary, as Deligny often describes himself doing in his writing, one might follow an etymological pathway leading from the French *erre* to the Latin word *errare,* meaning "to wander," "to go astray," to English cognates such as *errant, errancy,* and *error.* Yet Deligny is careful to distinguish his use of *erre* from morally inflected connotations regarding the act of deviating from a predetermined code of action or system of norms. He distinguishes between the act of *tracing* (or perhaps *describing,* as one might describe the arc of a curve) the movement of a body through space and the act of interpreting, analyzing, or diagnostically evaluating that movement and that body. "We did not take the children's ways of being as scrambled, coded messages addressed to us," Deligny notes. The maps, he writes, were created "in order to make something other than a sign."[91] They emerged within a liminal zone between drawing and writing, thereby resisting the categorical distinctions that language imposes on the world.

Deligny's writings on the lignes d'erre persistently associated the concept with an attenuation of conscious intentionality. In his descriptions of the lines, Deligny often uses the verb *vaguer* (typically translated as "to drift"), a word that also shares a root with the French noun for "wave" (*vague*). Like *vaguer,* "drift" carries with it some residual sense of the movement of bodies of water, as one *drifts* down a river, a figuration that also recalls Deligny's occasional comparison of his attempts at anti-institutional collective living with "rafts."[92] In an intriguing passage in his 1976 text "The Arachnean," Deligny writes, "Que vaguer n'ait pas d'objet défini à l'avance peut faire penser que le sujet, alors, est dans le vague."[93] In their English translation of this essay, published in 2015, Drew Burk and Catherine Porter render this line as follows: "The fact that drifting has no predefined object can make one think that the subject, then, is adrift."[94] The play on the double sense of *vague* evokes a state of entering into a kind of sensory current with smaller and larger nonhuman forces. As the traces of gestures, Deligny's maps and the other counter-cartographies discussed in this book are a kind of prefigurative experiment in occupying a mode of relation that would be "outside of function"—one that would not bear the traces of a desire to make autistic people conform to the shape of the thought-out project of the human as neurotypical subject.

Performance and Destituence

My efforts here are in dialogue with a growing body of scholarship that has sought to consider autism in relationship to performance.[95] Throughout the book, *performance* is meant to signal an engagement with specific performances, performance theory, and concepts of the performative and performativity. In its responsiveness to questions of gesture, movement, behavior, and social practice, performance studies offers powerful analytical resources for understanding efforts to contain and control inscrutable, unaccountable, or undetectable forms of expression, communication, behavior, and movement.[96] This is in large part due to the field's interdisciplinary attention to, in the words of performance theorist Dwight Conquergood, "the whole realm of complex, finely nuanced meaning that is embodied, intoned, gestured, improvised, coexperienced, covert—and all the more deeply meaningful because of its refusal to be spelled out."[97]

I am surely not the first to be drawn to rubrics of performativity as a way of thinking through the dilemmas of self-definition posed by psychiatric or neurodivergent diagnoses. In an insightful reflection on autism itself as a performative speech act, James McGrath looks back through the intellectual genealogy of performance theory to offer an account of the way autistic and other subjects of psychiatric power are "both caught between and free between the performativity of a diagnosis and the performance of a self"—a paradoxical and contradictory state of being that McGrath argues also applies to "orthodox psychiatry itself."[98] Other scholars have attended to how the performativity of the diagnosis contains within it the kernel of violence—a violence often deployed by the state that seizes hold of, constrains, and attempts to discipline the neurodivergent body and subject—even as, in the words of Julia Miele Rodas, it may also "open up unintended aesthetic avenues."[99] Writing of the drawings by children in Bruno Bettelheim's autism clinic at the notorious Orthogenic School at the University of Chicago in the 1950s, J. J. Kahn has identified the existence of a much longer tradition of historical evidence of autistic and neurodivergent resistance to institutional, diagnostic, and representational enclosure, decades before the emergence of the neurodiversity movement per se in the 1990s.[100]

Yet this book also seeks to add something about the genealogy of performance studies that we did not know to look for. Many theorists have turned to the performative as a way of understanding the productive and regulatory power of speech, and of describing how specific properties of language itself come to be imbued with a force and consequence that allows those who speak it to act upon and transform the world in addition to describing it. In order for a performative to be "felicitous," it must be spoken by "someone in authority" in order to bring into being the act performed as it is spoken.[101] Yet where does the force said to be effectuated by the performative originate, and on what authority is it exercised? Some critics who have taken up the performativity of speech acts, such as Shoshana Felman, understand the speech act as the place where the materiality of the body and the signifying, meaning-making processes of language meet and even blur into one another. The speech act, Felman writes, is "an enigmatic and problematic production of the *speaking body*" that "destroys from its inception the metaphysical dichotomy between the domain of the 'mental' and the domain of the 'physical,' breaks down the opposition between body and spirit, matter and language."[102] Felman's discussion of the speech act as breaking down the distinction between signifying, conscious, and linguistic intentionality and material bodily action is indicative of the ways in which the performative has been understood as a radical intervention in the production of social reality.

We might recall that the etymology of *function* can be traced to the Latin word *functiō,* which denoted the performance or execution of a task.[103] Variants of the word, such as *malfunction* (typically associated with the technological breakdown of machinery) and *dysfunction* (associated with the breakdown of a biological process or system) start to appear in the early twentieth century. More recently, with the emergence of autistic self-advocacy and the advent of neurodiversity discourses beginning in the 1990s, these terms have been especially contested within the ongoing debates over the diagnostic distinction between LFA and HFA, which is largely (though by no means exclusively) made on the basis of an individual's perceived or assessed capacity for verbal communication. As Stuart Murray has argued, "The worrying aspect is that an idea of autistic functioning equates with an idea of disabled human value."[104] Murray suggests that the word function itself has become a kind of shorthand, one that "allows for processes of assessment and judgment that fix those with autism into inflexible ontological categories." And it is these categories—HFA/LFA—which "themselves then pass for the norm."[105] The very concept of function has been pervasively defined according to strictly maintained epistemological, ethical, and even moral economies that are in turn sanctioned through the performative force of expert assessment and diagnosis.

How, then, do the politics of neurological difference involve not only assertions about ways of being but also about ways of doing—to invoke the critical inflection point that we have come to associate with the politics of the performative? The account of the performative I put forth in the chapters that follow puts pressure on our conceptualization of *function* as such, but it does so in a very particular way. By expanding outward from recent projects relating to the aesthetics and politics of neurodivergence, I approach the conversation about autistic and neurodivergent selfhood as performative slantwise. I use the example of thinking about autism found in Deligny's writing and experimental modes of living to elaborate a distinctive investment in expanding the theoretical purview of performativity in light of the claims of neurodiversity by adopting what can be characterized as a destituent stance and set of strategies.

Now is the title of a short pamphlet published in 2017 by the Invisible Committee, an anonymous collective of authors who have issued a series of theoretically dense missives about the political situation of contemporary France.[106] *Now* provides a blueprint for grappling with the crises of social democracy in the time of digitization through the embrace of a political and ethical stance of destituence. They introduce this somewhat obscure concept by turning back to the word's Latin roots: "Destituere in Latin means: to place standing separate, raise up in isolation; to abandon; put aside, let drop, knock down; to let down, deceive. Whereas constituent logic crashes against the power apparatus it means to take control of, a destituent potential is concerned instead with escaping from it, with removing any hold on it which the apparatus might have, as it increases its hold on the world in the separate space that it forms. Its characteristic gesture is *exiting*, just as the typical constituent gesture is taking by storm."[107] The Invisible Committee goes on to propose that an institution can be destituted by a gesture that "neutralizes it, empties it of its substance, then steps to the side and watches it expire."[108]

In a chapter entitled "Let's Destitute the World" (lifted from a slogan that began to appear as graffiti in the mid-2010s), the Invisible Committee turns to an unexpected source: a passage that quotes from Fernand Deligny. One way that Deligny's project exemplified what the Invisible Committee will call destituent power is in his efforts to "destitute" not only the power of language and of institutions (psychiatric asylums above all) but also the apparatuses of power that cluster around the word *autism* itself. When uttered by a medical expert as a diagnosis, *autism* or *autistic* can be understood to function as performative speech acts that have particular material consequences, with the power to shape the lives of those who are assigned it. "In order to fight *against* language and the institution, the right phrase is perhaps not to fight against, but to take the most distance possible, even if this means signaling one's position. Why would we go and press ourselves against the wall? Our project is not to take and hold the square."[109] These words from Deligny were first published in *Cahiers de L'immuable (Notebooks of the Immutable)*, which appeared as three special issues of the psychoanalytic journal *Recherches* from 1975 to 1979. The *Cahiers de L'immuable* works consist of excerpts from the voluminous notebooks that Deligny and his collaborators kept, documenting the group's daily life as different members arrived, stayed for a while, and departed, although a core group of participants in the Delignian project indeed stayed on long term—indeed, a few of them are still around today, retaining the basic structure of their communal living arrangements. These notebooks contain illuminating reflections on the development of Deligny's theories on the various forms of exclusion, dehumanization, and even incarceration that await children who do not speak, behave, or communicate in ways that they are expected to.

Not surprisingly, one of the preoccupations that runs through the notebooks concerns the role that language plays in defining the human as a subject. Deligny is specifically interested in how language functions in and as an institution that has the capacity to distribute the privileges of personhood and, crucially, to determine who belongs to the category of the human and who does not. Deligny would come to be totally opposed to the asylum model, finding himself in disagreement even with Guattari's efforts to revolutionize the site of psychiatric clinic. If, for Deligny, "the human is a gesture, and a form, before it is a being of language,"[110] then it is in the act of tracing the lignes d'erre that a different way arises of understanding what the human itself might be. Deligny and his network began investigating cartography as members of the group started to experiment with trailing alongside their autistic counterparts as they made their way across the Cévennes' rocky terrain, making rudimentary line drawings to indicate their direction of movement across the rural encampment and into the surrounding wilderness. The tracings soon became a central aspect of the group's activities, and the maps steadily grew more detailed and elaborate. They established visual systems for designating the various sounds and gestures encountered along their pathways and started to use transparent wax paper to trace the children's daily routes. No attempt was made to interfere with their movements or to explain or interpret them. The focus remained on the process of tracing itself. Over time, distinct patterns began to emerge: certain trajectories tended to be repeated from one day to the next, and the group noted that some of the lines seemed to correspond to the conduits of underground waterways. The focus remained on the process of tracing itself. Deligny writes of the project of making maps that "are nothing other than the trace of a gesture."[111] As the traces of gestures, the maps are a kind of prefigurative experiment with occupying a mode of relation that would be "outside of function"—one that would not bear the traces of a desire to make autistics conform to the shape of the "thought-out-project," the neurotypical subject, the human-that-we-are.

At certain moments, Deligny objected to the characterization of his work as primarily concerned with "destitution." In a text from 1978, he takes issue with how his work with autistic children is described in Guattari's book *The Molecular Revolution* (published the year before). Guattari writes that Deligny's project is an example of the development of a "collective agency of utterance" that is able to "deprive [destituer] speech of its function as imaginary support to the cosmos."[112] But, Deligny asks, "destitute—the spoken—does this not implicate the necessity of instituting 'something else?'"[113] Deligny leaves this question open, but I have come to believe that what he asks here is in fact the most important question that any consideration of destituence as a viable or desirable position or strategy must grapple with. The call for destituence is sometimes received as a mere call for lawlessness, anarchy, and disorganization in ways that are at best naive and at worst actively destructive. Yet in this reception or critique of destituence there is also a tendency to overlook the necessary corollary, which is the positive, worldmaking, and even perhaps utopian possibilities that glimmer within destituence. Deligny's project can be read as an important historical precursor to some of the ideas about autism and neurological difference as modes of being that have emerged alongside the growing discourse of neurodivergence. Amit Pinchevski invokes Deligny's work in relationship to a larger consideration of the challenge to communicational disabilities such as autism involve and a curious reading of Herman Melville's story "Bartleby, the Scrivener." Pinchevski, in a reading inspired by Deligny's work, suggests that "Bartleby is not a figure of refusal but of undoing—the undoing of identity, order, and language—and as such epitomizes the plea for alternative constellations of the social bond." Thus, Pinchevski insists, Bartleby's "preference 'not to' does not signal the end of the relation but rather its beginning; his 'line of flight' is not terminal to liberatory possibilities but rather inherently generative of them."[114] From this, Pinchevski concludes that "it is the undoing of the common that makes the common; it is the interruption of communication that breeds communication."[115] Pinchevski suggests that Deligny's work prefigures recent philosophical efforts to "rethink community in terms of difference (rather than sameness) and away from essence, telos, and logos

—that is, beyond the traditional (ethnic, religious, ideological) notions of community."[116]

In an intriguing passage of his essay "A for Asylum," discussed extensively in chapter 2, Deligny observes that one of the young autistic residents of his network would never be seen "flick[ing] away a wasp that lands on the skin of his arm." Rather, Deligny continues, the boy, Janmari, "grasps it in such a way—which seems to be the only way—that causes the wasp to go out of order, so to speak, making its sting inoperative, no matter how much it wriggles, and then throwing it far away, still intact."[117] Whereas a neurotypical response to having a wasp land on your skin would be to instinctively swat it away, most likely with no immediate concern for the wasp's well-being, Deligny observes a difference in Janmari's approach: handling the insect's tiny body with care and precision in order to temporarily deactivate its sting, allowing him to release it unharmed. Deligny's thought often proceeds by way of analogy: this small, seemingly trivial observation about Janmari's treatment of the wasp hints at something more consequential. If there is an image that holds together the errant cartographies of neurodivergent performance that I attempt to describe in this book, then perhaps it is the one evoked by Deligny's account of Janmari's attitudes, gestures, and actions taken in relationship to the wasp that lands on his arm, whose stinger Janmari renders inactive. Perhaps in the same way, the performances, films, maps, drawings, installations, and other artistic projects described here render inoperative the sting of the world on neurodivergent personhood and ways of being.

A Map of the Book

Chapter 1 looks at the figure of the wild child, exemplified by Victor of Aveyron as described by his physician-teacher, Jean-Marc Itard, and later depicted in Truffaut's film *L'enfant sauvage*, with a focus on how the forms of medico-pedagogical intervention on the body's nervous sensibilities would come to constitute the regime of moral treatment as an early technology in the effort to discipline the proto-autistic body. The second part of the chapter turns to Fernand Deligny, with whom Truffaut had a series of exchanges that returned a number of themes that had preoccupied Itard in his work with Victor a century and a half earlier. Focusing on Deligny's radical ideas about pedagogy and cinema, I discuss Deligny's film *Le moindre geste (The Slightest Gesture)* and suggest that his observations about autistic movement and gesture open up an important alternative to the behaviorist legacy of Itard. Chapter 2 takes up the figure of the asylum in relationship to its dual meaning as place of confinement and place of refuge. It uses Deligny's writings on asylum alongside dramaturgical models of the self that arose in the 1960s and 1970s by, respectively, the Living Theatre, documentarian Frederick Wiseman, and Marxist philosopher Louis Althusser, before turning to Deligny's reflections on the practice of mapping wander lines as a activity that makes nonsense of the usual distinction between drawing and tracing. Chapter 3 considers mapping and cartography as counterstrategies responding to the increasing surveillance and policing of neurodivergence in societies of control after deinstitutionalization, and particularly the appearance of increasingly sophisticated forms of digital mapping and tracking used to surveil and police neurodivergent people and populations. A reading of a drawing by performance artist William Pope.L alongside the case of Avonte Oquendo brings attention to the imbrications of race, disability, and neurodivergence in the efforts to enhance the surveillance of autistic wandering. Chapter 4 looks at the question of voice as it is mediated through several aesthetic works, including Jonathan Berger's installation *An Introduction to Nameless Love,* autistic activist Mel Baggs's famous video manifesto *In My Language,* and artist Wu Tsang's full body quotation of Baggs's words. To consider the possibilities and limitations that performance brings to the intersections of body and voice, language and gesture, and sensation and identity, the discussion in this chapter also borrows a concept from dramaturgical theory, the gestus, in order to propose a neurodivergent politics of the voice in the wake of facilitated communication—that is, techniques and technologies through which autistic and other verbally disabled people have found ways of voicing and speaking in ways that are recognizable in neurotypical terms. The coda asks how shyness enters the repertoire of neurodivergence as a counterdiscourse that emerges when the subjects of medical diagnosis begin to speak back in the language used to diagnose them. By way of a brief discussion of *Shy Radicals,* an ongoing project undertaken by London-based writer, artist, and activist Hamja Ahsan, the coda suggests that drawing on the destituent inflections and possibilities of Deligny's radical thought about autism can shed light on these more recent artistic articulations of neurodivergence as a mode of being.

Like many of the philosophical, theoretical, and aesthetic examples discussed in what follows, this study can be citationally unruly. At various points, it seeks to draw connections between performance theory and the history of science and medicine; theater history and ethics; dance studies and political theory; and media art and biopolitics. In attempting to weave these disparate areas of inquiry into a cohesive critical idiom, it has partly emulated the idiosyncratic methodological approach of Deligny himself, who frequently invoked the image of a spider weaving its web as a metaphor for his vigorously anti-pathologizing views on autism as a distinctive mode of being. He described his methods as Arachnean, a word he coined in order to evoke a different mode of social organization, and an entirely new political ethos. For Deligny, the Arachnean mode is always provisional, perpetually in danger of either falling apart or rigidifying into an institution. Like the industrious arthropod from whom it takes its name, the Arachnean traces provisional threads of connection and association that link diffuse outcroppings of thought to one another, allowing new singularities to emerge like the shimmering outline of a spider's web. Eschewing the dominant modern hermeneutics of suspicion and symptomatic interpretation, with their implicit faith in exposure and depth-based methods of analysis, Deligny's Arachnean is defined instead by a quietly attentive, patient, and slow practice of cartographically tracing the trajectories of the autistic people alongside whom he and his collaborators lived for several decades, in relative isolation and obscurity.

In a similar way, this book is invested in a certain horizontality that might be positioned in alliance with certain strands of recent critical work in the humanities that have sought to prioritize the minor over the major; everydayness, the quotidian, and the sheer duration of the ordinary above the spectacular or cataclysmic; and surface or planar understandings over depth-based models of power and subjectivity. The web that the following chapters weave can perhaps best be understood as an attempt to emulate Deligny's Arachnean approach, weaving, tracing, and mapping the lines and forms that begin to emerge, if you are patient enough to watch for them.

1

Feral Performatives

On January 8, 1798, residents of the small village of Saint-Sernin-sur-Rance in the Aveyron region of southern France caught sight of a mysterious figure emerging from the surrounding forest. Naked, caked in mud, and covered with scars, he appeared to be about twelve years old and was unable to speak. First brought to the attention of local church authorities, who were unable to locate any family members in the region, he was soon transported to the National Institute for Deaf-Mutes in Paris and entrusted to the supervision of Jean Marc Gaspard Itard, a young medical student enrolled in the institute. Itard christened him Victor (he seemed to respond best to the long "o" phoneme contained in the second syllable of that name) and kept scrupulous records of his quest to work toward Victor's "physical and moral development," a process that he describes in his journals as a civilizing educational mission.[1] Reflecting Enlightenment-era preoccupations with the conditions of natural, primitive man and the role of culture in the constitution of the human species, Victor became a celebrated test case, a real-world specimen who might enable researchers to advance scientific debates concerning the concept of sauvagerie—a word that, conveniently for the purposes of Victor's case, derives from the Old French expression for that which materializes "from the woods." As more recent critical assessments of Victor's legacy have noted, the popular and scientific fascination with wild or feral children that took hold of the European cultural imagination in the early nineteenth century was deeply shaped by the ideological context of European colonialism, especially with regard to the scientific discourses of racial differentiation that developed in tandem with its contemporaneous imperial ventures.[2]

The crucial question that motivated Itard and the other experts who studied Victor when he was brought to Paris, including Roch-Ambroise Cucurron Sicard, the renowned instructor of deaf children who was the first to examine Victor, was whether he could be taught to speak. Itard believed that if they could coax Victor to learn how to use and respond to spoken language, he might then be able to advance to a "higher" state of humanity, learn how to exercise moral judgment, and even fall in love. Yet according to Itard's journals, Victor remained impervious to all efforts to coax him into language. While Itard was able to instruct him in the basics of domestic behavior, such as setting the table for a meal and using utensils, the boy only ever managed to learn to use a few rudimentary words and phrases. Victor eventually moved in with Itard's housekeeper and continued to live in relative isolation until his death in 1828, when he was estimated to be forty years old.

Victor, the Wild Boy of Aveyron, is a ubiquitous, ghostly presence throughout the vast clinical, historical, and sociological research literature on autism. O. Ivar Lovaas, the controversial child psychiatrist who devised the techniques of ABA as an approach to the therapeutic treatment of autistic behavior in the 1970s, traced the origins of his methods to Itard's descriptions of his work with Victor.[3] As Remi Yergeau notes, "Lovaas appears to have remained either unaware or unconcerned that one of Itard's aversive techniques involved dangling Victor head-first out of a fifth-story window."[4] More recently, cognitive psychologist Uta Frith, one of the most influential scientific researchers on autism since the 1980s, has suggested that Victor was autistic before the advent of the diagnostic category.[5] In a less prescriptive register, journalist Paul Collins, father of an autistic child, revisits the story of Victor to uncover a lost prehistory of the condition that would not be named as such until the 1940s.[6] Indeed, it is possible to view the entire psychiatric-clinical history of autism—from early articles on the condition by Leo Kanner and Hans Asperger in the World War II era to more recent controversies over revision to the clinical definition of autism adduced in present-day manuals of psychiatric diagnoses—as a series of encounters with the intractable problem that stymied the young doctor's best efforts to civilize his test subject. The feral state from which Itard attempted to rescue Victor was itself a fantasy, one sustained by the same ostensibly therapeutic techniques that he used to discover it—an illustration of Donna Haraway's observation that within the history of science, "myth and tool mutually co-constitute each other."[7] The wildness ascribed to Victor and other feral children was in fact the product of apparatuses—pedagogical, medical, therapeutic, psychiatric—designed to eradicate it. In being subjected to Itard's civilizing treatment, as disability theorists David T. Mitchell and Sharon L. Snyder suggest, Victor was trained not only "in the manners and customs of the moderns but also was being taught his savagery—a barbarism that he had not recognized before his ingestion in the classification of 'feral.'"[8]

How else might this story be told—or rather, how might its elements be repurposed and retrofitted to be put to a different use? Might we understand debates over neurodiversity as an outgrowth of older and lasting conflicts over the boundaries that separate savagery from civilization, wildness from rationality, danger from security, the instinctual from the learned? In pursuit of this question, this chapter and the ones that follow chart a course that veers sharply away from the pathways laid out by Itard and well traveled by his inheritors. Instead, it asks how Victor might be understood as one of the first of a long and continuing line of wanderers who have found ways to resist, elude, and reshape the categories imposed on them by diagnostic institutions and the many forms of enclosure they deploy.

For Itard, the ability to acquire verbal speech emerges within an ascendant discourse of psychiatric expertise. Indeed, insofar as modern psychiatry continues to make recourse to biological—and increasingly neurobiological—concepts in its determinations of psychological normality and pathology, Victor and Itard are with us still. This chapter thus maps out a trajectory for navigating contestations over wildness and civilized reason as they have materialized within ongoing efforts to discipline the autistic and proto-autistic body. The first part of the chapter discusses Itard's published account of his efforts to educate Victor in the context of the genealogy of psychiatric power that provides the background for any later consideration of neurodivergent selfhood. It then considers *L'enfant sauvage* (*The Wild Child,* 1970), François Truffaut's assiduous film adaptation of Itard's report on Victor. The second part of the chapter turns to the work of Fernand Deligny, with whom Truffaut had a series of exchanges that returned a number of themes that had preoccupied Itard in his work with Victor a century and a half earlier. Focusing on Deligny's radical ideas about pedagogy and cinema, I discuss the film *Le moindre geste (The Slightest Gesture),* which Deligny worked on with a small group of collaborators, and which I argue offers an attempt—characteristic of Deligny's overall method and philosophical approach—at a feral mode of cinematic poeisis that would be on the side of wildness rather than civilization (as articulated first by Itard and later again by Truffaut). Finally, I examine how Deligny's observations about autistic movement and gesture suggest a radical alternative to the behaviorist legacy of Itard, which I explain through the rubric of the feral performative.

Feral enters our lexicon by way of Homo ferus, a designation that appears in a book by Swedish naturalist and botanist Carl Linnaeus (1707–78), who included this term in the tenth edition of his *Systema Naturae,* published in 1758–59 and considered to be the inaugural work of modern scientific taxonomy. Linnaeus's first efforts to taxonomize the species of nature in this book were limited to the world of plants. It was not until the tenth edition that he had a go at categorizing the animal kingdom, which he divided into six classes, including mammals, birds, amphibians, and invertebrates. This book began the zoological scientific tradition of Linnaean classification, or classifying living species using two Latin words in a scheme now known as binomial nomenclature: Homo americanus, Homo europaeus, Homo asiaticus, Homo africanus, Homo monstrosus.

The feral is a category produced by the ambivalent interplay between myth, fantasy, repression, and scientific documentation. It is anxiously policed and pathologized. Historian Hayden White observes the existence of the strange persistence of the "myth of the Wild Man" in the Western imagination, which often functions as a "projection of repressed desires and anxieties" endemic to particular social and historical formations.[9] This myth takes shape across transitions "from myth to fiction to myth again, with the modern form of the myth assuming a pseudoscientific aspect in the various theories of the psyche currently clamoring for our attention."[10] The wild *child,* in particular, figures as humanity's past, its immaturity, the unformed, insensate and unrefined naiveté from which the mature, human adult is established as an individual within a social world. This process finds its echo in how the historical Enlightenment defined itself as the overcoming of and emergence of man "from his incurred immaturity"—that is, his "inability to make use of one's intellect without the direction of another."[11] In the shadow of the Enlightenment's sciences of man, as well as the crises and anxieties about human freedom they represented, the notion of the feral bequeathed to us through accounts of wild children, as Adriana Benzaquén observes, also indexes "the many ways in which a community relates to someone resisting it, and the many ways in which the community strives to understand, know, classify, and transform the unknown being into a member or an outcast."[12]

Itard's diary of his observations of Victor—published in French in 1800 and in English in 1802—sits at the edge of the historical appearance of new taxonomies of medico-pedagogical personhood, in particular revealing how "idiocy" was coming to be understood as a proto-medical category defined by the stunted development of organic, nervous sensibilities of the body. Indeed, Itard presents his work with Victor as a pedagogy of the nervous body, producing a narrative of his attempt to "train" Victor's sensibility that parallels the developmental trajectory of human civilization, culminating in the enlightened, modern citizen governed not by nervous sensibility but rationality. At the same time, as Stacy Clifford Simplican notes, for "Itard and medical practitioners after him, their own burgeoning field could answer this possibility by crafting idiots into citizens. But these medical men needed more than a promise to gain public support; thus, they also sought to manufacture a deep anxiety about idiots' impulsivity, sexuality, and criminality as a central tactic to gain capital for their nascent field."[13] A key theme across Itard's account of his work with Victor concerns his observation that "moral superiority which has been said to be *natural* to man, is merely the result of civilization, which raises him above other animals by a great and powerful stimulus."[14] For Itard, the stimulus of man's moral superiority "is the predominant sensibility of his species; the essential property from which flow the faculties of imitation, and that unintermitting propensity which forces him to seek, in new wants, new sensations."[15]

Several aspects of Itard's fascinating book are especially germane to the discussion here. The first is the extent to which Itard characterizes his work with Victor as following the enlightened and "humane" methodology of "moral medicine," what he terms "that sublime art created by the Willis's and the Crichtons of England, and lately introduced into France by the success and writings of Professor Pinel" (32).[16] Itard writes that when he first encountered Victor, the boy was in a "deplorable situation." His "petulant activity of mind had insensibly degenerated into a dull apathy, which produced habits still more solitary" (35).

> In this deplorable situation he was seen by some people from Paris, who, after a very short examination, adjudged him to be only fit to be sent to Bedlam; as if society had a right to take a child from a free and innocent life, and dismiss him to die of melancholy in a mad-house, that he might thus expiate the misfortune of having disappointed public curiosity. I thought that a more simple, and, what is of still greater importance, a much more humane course should be taken, which was to treat him kindly, and to yield a ready compliance with his taste and inclinations. (36)

Itard suggests that his "moral treatment or education of the Savage of Aveyron" (32) entailed a pedagogy of the body, and the nervous system in particular. He describes Victor's initial appearance as a "a disgusting, slovenly boy," whose behavior was made up of "spasmodic motions" (17) and whose senses were in a "state of inertia" (20); his existence was "purely animal" (22). He explains that his goals with Victor were to "attach him to social life" and "awaken nervous sensibility," so as to "lead him to the use of speech" (33). Itard proceeds to narrate his attempts to educate Victor's "nervous sensibilities" with what appears to be the dutiful assistance of a woman named Madame Guérin, "to whose particular care the administration had entrusted this child," and who "acquitted herself, and still discharges this arduous task, with all the patience of a mother, and the intelligence of an enlightened instructor" (36–37)—though whose opinions and perspective on the matter is, needless to say, otherwise wholly absent from Itard's chronicle. Itard takes many approaches to the task of awakening Victor's sensibilities: observing that Victor's hearing seems dulled and inattentive, Itard fires pistol shots near his head and is surprised that the sound "merely made him turn his head with indifference" (47). He finds more "success" by placing Victor in a hot bath for several hours a day, which eventually leads Victor to become more sensitive to cold and eventually he seems to want to start to wear clothes to protect himself from the weather. He also begins to prescribe the "application of dry frictions to the spinal vertebrae and even the tickling of the lumbar regions," which Itard soon finds the necessity to forbid when the effects of the tickling "appeared to extend themselves to the organs of generation, and to indicate some danger of awakening the sensations of puberty" (50–51). He soon proceeds to attempt to convert the awakening of the boy's nervous sensations to specific emotions and desires, a process that Itard describes as the task of "converting pleasure into want" (68).

In turn, as Itard advances from the stimulation of Victor's nerves toward attempts at cultivating feelings (joy, sorrow) and the expression of desire—even if still wordless—Victor begins to increasingly express his frustration and even erupt in angry tantrums. As Victor's "paroxysms became more frequent, and liable to be renewed by the least opposition, often even without any evident cause," Itard finds himself searching for a way to inhibit Victor's outbursts, and thus stumbles on a tactic that constitutes an early version of the use of aversive means to modify undesirable behavior, an approach that will in turn find renewed attention in the twentieth-century paradigm of behaviorism. Itard narrates how he came through necessity to invent "a treatment that was calculated to awaken horror."

> I suddenly opened the window of the chamber, which was on the fourth story, looking down upon a rough pavement. I approached him with every appearance of fury, and seizing him forcibly, I held him out of the window, his face directly turned towards the bottom of this precipice; when, after some seconds, I withdrew him from this situation, he appeared pale, covered with a cold sweat; his eyes moistened with tears, and still agitated with a slight trembling, which I attributed to the effects of fear: I then took him again to his boards; I made him gather up his scattered papers, and insisted that they should be all replaced. (128)

The final sections of Itard's account are devoted to an explanation of his halting and largely unsuccessful (at least to date) attempts to move beyond the conversion of "pleasure into want" and toward the moral clearinghouse of language, communication, and writing. Though Itard does report that he achieved some success in teaching Victor how to use metallic blocks of letters to spell out rudimentary words (much effort is devoted to teach him how to spell out the word *lait,* to express his desire for milk), the chronicle of Victor's course of instruction ends on a cliffhanger, with the question of Victor's acquisition of language unresolved. Nonetheless, Itard does not hesitate from declaring victory, at least on certain accounts: "we have a right to conclude, from our observations," he writes, "that the child known under the name of the *Savage of Aveyron*, is endowed with the free exercise of his senses; that he gives continual proof of attention, reflection, and memory; that he is able to compare, discern, and judge, and apply in short all the faculties of his understanding to the objects which are connected with his instruction" (139). It is on this more or less triumphant note that Itard offers his concluding reflections drawn from his observations of his experiments with Victor. Perhaps the most stirring of these is Itard's conviction that his work with Victor reveals that "the progress of teaching may, and ought to be aided by the lights of modern medicine, which of all the natural sciences can co-operate the most effectually towards the amelioration of the human species, by appreciating the organical and intellectual peculiarities of each individual; and by that means determining what education is likely to do for him, and what society may expect from his future character" (146). Still, in spite of Itard's attempt to close the story on a positive, even inspirational note, it is hard to read Itard's *Historical Account* and not come away with the sense that there remains something fundamentally unresolved at the heart of the story. This is what Mitchell and Synder describe as an essential impasse that opens up, over the course of the narrative, as "the considerable distance between Victor's desires and those of the diagnostic institution."[17]

This fundamental impasse can perhaps be better understood by considering Victor and Itard's encounter within the historical context in which it occurred, and particularly as a transitional moment in the scientific surveillance of modern childhood. The project of instituting a generalized system for the surveillance of childhood by way of an apparatus of medical-psychiatric expertise is a key historical innovation of what Michel Foucault has identified as "psychiatric power."[18] By tracing the elaboration of modern psychiatry's understanding of the distinction between mental illness and developmental or intellectual disability, Foucault unearths how, beginning in the eighteenth century, psychiatric power consolidated itself as a scientific discourse with a double function: as "power over madness and power over abnormality."[19]

A decisive period in this historical process occurs in the early nineteenth century, precisely the moment when case studies of Victor of Aveyron and other feral children are gaining widespread popularity. Foucault is particularly interested in how, during this period, the emergent psychiatric profession produced "the notion of imbecility or idiocy as a phenomenon absolutely distinct from madness."[20] Until the end of the eighteenth century, imbecility was merely understood as one among many different kinds of madness; it was "defined as a particular form in a series in which one could find mania, melancholy, and dementia."[21] Yet Foucault reveals that in the first four decades of the nineteenth century, a new understanding of "idiocy, of mental retardation, of imbecility" began to take shape. Researchers such as Itard and Jean-Étienne Dominique Esquirol—a protégé of Pinel's who would oversee the reforms that led to institutionalization of the modern asylum as a national project following Pinel's principles of moral treatment—increasingly put forward an understanding of imbecility as a problem of stunted or retarded nervous sensibilities, which in the idiot "have never been sufficiently developed."[22] One of the long-standing consequences of this shift, Foucault writes, is that "the therapy for idiocy will be pedagogy itself." Indeed, it is by way of "these practical problems raised by the idiot child," Foucault proposes, that "you see psychiatry becoming something infinitely more general and dangerous than the power that controls and corrects madness; it is becoming power over the abnormal, the power to define, control, and correct what is abnormal."[23] This generalization of the idea that treating idiocy simply by pedagogy, and that feral children can be fixed or cured of ferality and idiocy by imposing education on them—indeed, the same education that ought to be imposed on *every* child, albeit in perhaps a more intensified form—comes through strongly in Itard's continual insistence that Victor's education is itself a kind of analogy, in microcosm, for the universal (and unidirectional) development of both individual human subjects and civilization itself.

Pedagogy, Civilization, Cinema (Truffaut's Victor)

Over a century and half after Itard's account of his efforts with Victor were published, François Truffaut's film *L'enfant sauvage* (*The Wild Child;* 1970) offered a cinematic restatement of the feral child's therapeutic pedagogy as an allegory for education as a universalized, necessary progression from savagery to citizenship. Truffaut not only wrote and directed the film but also cast himself in the role of Itard, the paragon of the doctor-educator. Truffaut assiduously follows the narrative sequence established by Itard's account and includes many scenes from the *Historical Account.* But in the film, the early nineteenth-century debates about idiocy as a problem that can be solved through a certain kind of education are grafted onto a struggle that plays out on an aesthetic level. The film is studiously classical and harmonious in its narrative construction and formal composition, from its use of black-and-white film stock to the excerpts from Vivaldi concertos that accompany the scenes of Itard attempting to teach Victor how to behave.

L'enfant sauvage operates through a kind of formal and narrative containment of the wild child's haptic embodiment. The unruly, unpredictable movements and indiscernible gestures of Victor (played by Romani French child actor Jean-Pierre Cargol) at the beginning of the film do not seem to mean anything; they cannot be read as symbolically or semantically charged. As the film proceeds, Victor's movements are methodically subject to an inescapably domesticating force of that gradually imbues them with significance. Indeed, the film treats Victor's sauvagerie as the primary disturbance that both its narrative sequencing and its mise-en-scène finally succeed in controlling. As a number of critics have recognized, Truffaut's film concerns itself formally with how cinema itself can function as an apparatus that produces its own "education of the senses."[24]

Many of the key scenes of the film's depiction of Victor's education take place against the smooth, dark planar background of the chalkboard. There is perhaps no better encapsulation of the film's aesthetic and narrative trajectory than a sequence of two shots that occurs near the end of the film. In the first, Victor is shown from the waist up standing alone, turned away from us and facing the blackboard, which takes up the entirety of the background of the frame. He grips a piece of chalk in his fist and begins to trace a circle on the board, then another one, slightly bigger, making a white spiral appear as his hand moves in a continuous circular motion; the only sound is the friction of the chalk as it moves across the rough surface of the board. The shot seems to last a long time—or at least far longer than it should. (It is about seventeen seconds long.)

Figure 1. Jean-Pierre Cargol as Victor in *L'enfant sauvage,* directed by François Truffaut, Les Films du Carrosse/United Artists, 1970.

Figure 2. François Truffaut as Jean Marc Gaspard Itard and Jean-Pierre Cargol as Victor in *L'enfant sauvage,* directed by François Truffaut, Les Films du Carrosse/United Artists, 1970.

Any slight anxiety produced by the sustained shot of Victor's hands making a chaotic spiral on the board, though, is immediately leavened by a sudden cut to a new shot. Now we see what seems to be the same blackboard, from the same eye-level position, but now it is a few feet further back. The rectangular blackboard is now framed by the white wall behind it and edged by an elegant border of white molding. Truffaut-as-Itard now appears in the shot next to his young pupil. Both face the blackboard and each holds a piece of white chalk, though now Victor, in imitation of his teacher, holds his chalk not with his fist but between his thumb and forefinger, gripping it like a pen. As the sound of a harpsicord begins and the opening bars of Vivaldi's jaunty Mandolin Concerto in C Major swell, Itard methodically starts to draw a (remarkably straight) vertical line down the board, and Victor, eyes trained attentively on his teacher's hand, imitates him by drawing his own wobblier line in parallel. This is followed by a series of subsequent shots of Victor, again alone at the blackboard, first drawing a circle much more slowly, and then tracing the rudimentary lines of the letters A and E next to the more confidently written examples that have been outlined (presumably by Itard) for him to imitate.

Through a remarkably elegant and simplified economy of means, this sequence exemplifies the way *L'enfant sauvage* depicts the methodically ordered domestication of Victor's wildness through the pedagogical training of his body. Such sequences reveal Truffaut's brilliantly effective visual and sonic rendering of the process by which Victor comes to gradually internalize the moral discipline that is embodied by the severe yet ultimately sympathetic figure of Itard. In this respect, the film has also been read as an allegory of Truffaut's own biography, having been de facto adopted and "civilized" by influential film critic André Bazin when he was a teenager after having spent his troubled childhood years in and out of institutions reserved for socially delinquent youth. The film itself takes on the role first played by Itard in his efforts to train, orient, and direct Victor's untamed nervous sensibilities toward proper objects and aims. As Anne Gillain perceives, in the film, Truffaut "mimicked the act of attention with the use of the iris, reinventing the language of cinema in pristine black-and-white."[25] It is therefore not surprising that shortly after its release, one critic expressed the unblinking commitment to the inevitable victory of Enlightenment values that the film conveys by writing, "One emerges from *L'enfant sauvage* feeling proud of knowing how to read."[26]

In 1968, as he was in the midst of writing the screenplay for *L'enfant sauvage,* Truffaut had a number of interesting exchanges with Fernand Deligny, who had written seeking support for a cinematic project that Deligny and a small group of collaborators had been working on to document their experiments in noninstitutional social work with young people diagnosed with autism and other mental disabilities. Deligny included in his letter to Truffaut a vivid description of Janmari, an autistic boy who had recently joined Deligny's group in the Cévennes:

> A kid 12 years old who hasn't said a word his whole life. He is neither deaf nor dumb, agile as a chimpanzee. One thing makes him shiver and vibrate: that's running water whether from a well, fountain, or tap. . . . By instinct, he refuses to talk. From the cretin that he was constantly swaying, throwing himself on the ground, knocking his head against the wall, he has become a nice little guy [bête] who sets the table, gets water, washes the dishes; he doesn't leave us wherever we go, having adapted himself to our savage life [la vie sauvage]. . . . Here [in the Cévennes] he goes naked when he can in the sun [. . .] He dances in front of the fire . . . he sniffs for a long time what he eats. He's beautiful, except when he scowls, just like a young orangutan.[27]

Truffaut was immediately struck by the degree to which Deligny's descriptions of Janmari's behavior corresponded with the descriptions of Victor found in Itard's diary, which he had been reading in preparation for filming *L'enfant sauvage.* In response to Deligny's letter, Truffaut wrote:

> Your description of [Janmari's] behavior is so similar to what Itard described in his writings and to what we want to achieve in the film that I find it extremely disconcerting. In any case, I think your boy should serve as our model in selecting the boy who will actually play the part and should inspire us for his style of bodily comportment.[28]

Truffaut's frequent collaborator Suzanne Schiffman visited Deligny's encampment in the Cévennes, obtaining footage that Truffaut would use as a reference point for filming *L'enfant sauvage* later that year, particularly when directing Jean-Pierre Cargol on how to play Victor in Truffaut's film. In response to Truffaut's interest in using Janmari as the basis for the performance of the actor playing Victor in his film, Deligny wrote the following letter:

> I have read and reread Itard's memoirs (and all sorts of writing concerning wolf-children and others) and it's precisely this that has left me perplexed for a year. [. . .] Speech is for [Janmari] what algebra was for me in high school. Can he be filmed? It all depends on the mode of filming.[29]

Truffaut's idea that Janmari's "style of bodily comportment" could serve as the model for the performance of the actor playing Victor in his film—and Deligny's response that filming Janmari "all depends on the mode of filming"—suggest a point of divergence that will be considered in the second half of this chapter, which introduces Deligny's background and then considers how his own distinctive interest in cinema as a "pedagogical tool," as well as his writing about autistic gesture and ritualized behavior, might offer an alternative trajectory to the one followed by Itard and Truffaut, thereby turning away from the ultimately unachieved effort (despite the optimistic endings both attempted to spin) "to bridge a gap that Victor refuses to cross."[30]

In an interview with writer and critic Émile Copfermann, Deligny explains that his life's work has consisted of what he calls "attempts" (tentatives) that have been defined by institutionalization: "An *attempt* is for me to make a common cause with: kids, teens, the others with whom we live. An attempt can also be said to be that which is intolerable in an institution. [. . .] There is an allergy between the institution and what I call an attempt."[31] Born to a middle-class military family in the northern French town of Bergues in 1913, Deligny was educated in psychology and philosophy at the University of Lille before securing a position as a special education teacher at the psychiatric hospital in Armentières in 1938.[32] He was mobilized into the French army in August 1939 and assigned to serve as liaison officer in the 43rd Infantry Regiment, which was initially sent to the Netherlands. He was decommissioned in June 1940 after the French armistice with Germany. Having had to illegally cross the no-man's-land of the new border back into German-occupied territory to return to work at Armentières, Deligny found the asylum besieged by the deprivations of the war. Deligny was assigned to be a special education teacher in the asylum's Third Pavilion, which was reserved for "profoundly retarded and ineducable" teenagers.[33] The Third Pavilion would become the site of Deligny's first attempts to shift the standard way of doing things within the context of an institutional asylum. He eliminated the harsh system of penalties under which the ward's adolescent residents had been living; organized excursions, workshops, sporting events, and games for the residents with local artisans and unemployed textile factory workers; and created short plays for residents, guards, and others to perform together in the asylum. These experiments would become the basis for the attempts at "making asylum" otherwise that Deligny would pursue for the rest of his life in different forms.[34]

In 1948, Deligny and Huguette Dumoulin (his wife at the time) along with several other colleagues, most of whom were, like Deligny, members of the French Communist Party, founded La Grande Cordée (The great rope), an organization that François Dosse describes as "the first experiment in outpatient treatment designed to keep adolescent delinquents out of psychiatric hospitals."[35] La Grande Cordée came into being with the assistance of Henri Wallon. A physician and psychiatrist by training whose early specialization was in the origins and treatment of the so-called turbulent child, Wallon (1879–1962) would come to occupy the highest echelons of France's intellectual and political institutions. Appointed to the faculty of the Collège de France in 1937, where he chaired the departments of childhood psychology and education for a dozen years, it was Wallon's involvement in the wartime resistance movement and his rise within the ranks of the French Communist Party that led to his appointment as secretary of national education by de Gaulle's provisional government in 1944. After the Liberation, Wallon was placed in charge of the national commission that would radically reshape France's postwar education. As Marlon Miguel has shown, Wallon's interest in models of pedagogical experimentation provided an important opening for Deligny's own development of an approach to working with delinquent teenagers, and then increasingly with mentally disabled and later autistic children—one defined in opposition to the (implicitly Christian) moralism that had long predominated in the environment of special education from its nineteenth-century roots.[36]

La Grande Cordée was a collectively run, loosely organized group made up of disenchanted professional educators as well as university students and everyday workers whom Deligny recruited, often at informal gatherings that would take place after his public readings or lectures. Its first location was an abandoned Parisian theater, which Deligny turned into a kind of drop-in center for marginalized youth. Until 1962, La Grande Cordée would pursue a series of what they called "attempts" in collective living with and alongside individuals who had been excluded and marginalized, for various reasons, from mainstream educational institutions. From an initial focus on youth who were designated socially delinquent by virtue of their inability to conform to the behavioral norms of mainstream educational institutions, the group increasingly concentrated its efforts on cognitively disabled children and adolescents, especially those with language difficulties who had been labeled autistic.

Deligny's interest in the pedagogical promises of cinema can be dated to the earliest period of his intellectual formation.[37] In the years immediately after the Liberation, Deligny had found work first as an extracurricular teacher and eventually as a regional director with Travail et Culture (Work and culture), an organization affiliated with the French Communist Party whose mission was to offer educational and cultural activities for proletarian factory workers and their children throughout the country. His emerging convictions about the pedagogical possibilities afforded by cinema can be traced to his early friendship with Bazin and Marker, who were then in charge of Travail et Culture's film bureau. Bazin and the generation of filmmakers and critics he mentored as the editor of *Cahiers du Cinéma* were convinced that filmmaking had entered a new phase of expressive possibility. In an influential 1948 essay, film critic Alexandre Astruc argued that the rise of auteur cinema demonstrated that film had "gradually become a language . . . a form in which and by which an artist can express his thoughts, however abstract they may be, or translate his obsessions exactly as he does in the contemporary essay or novel."[38] Indeed, the idea of cinema as a distinct language became perhaps the key theoretical contribution of the generation of critics and filmmakers that came to be known as the French New Wave.

Deligny's conviction that the tools of filmmaking could be put to use in his work with socially delinquent and mentally disabled children reflected his more general interest in accessing a mode of being that could exist outside, or perhaps beyond, the strictures of either verbal or written language—an interest that he shared with Bazin. If auteur cinema had shown that film could function like a language, then it did so in ways that were *nonlinguistic* but still subjectively expressive. Bazin and Deligny would each pursue the implications of this insight along different paths: Bazin through his critical writing and editorial work at *Cahiers du Cinéma* and Deligny by focusing his efforts on working with children and adolescents who, of necessity, forged ways of being that were not anchored in the sensus communis that language helps to both form and mediate.

It is worth lingering for a moment on the specific ways Bazin and Deligny came to view cinema as an aesthetic medium that was uniquely able to access the pre- or extralinguistic dimensions of experience. Noting the confluence of Deligny's and Bazin's ideas, Andrew writes that Deligny "shared Bazin's fascination with children and with animals, a fascination at once moral and philosophical. For both men language, which names everything it touches, may let us forget that human beings act and react in a world that is only partly human. The child's gestures, hesitations, instincts, and screams are there to be comprehended; and cinema is an instrument of both expression and comprehension."[39] Deligny and Bazin's shared interest in devising a phenomenologically grounded, subjectively expressive cinematic practice built around the nonlinguistic gestures of children and animals might be understood as a kind of cinematic transposition of Antonin Artaud's call for a theater of cruelty. Their account of such a cinema echoes Artaud's dream of eliminating the rift between embodied performance and written dramatic text—to "heal the split between language and flesh," as Susan Sontag puts it in her discussion of Artaud's theater.[40]

The subtitle of Astruc's essay, "La caméra-stylo" (The camera-stylus), resonates with a short text that Deligny published in 1955 entitled "La caméra, outil pédagogique" (The camera: A pedagogical tool).[41] In it, Deligny elaborates on his conviction that providing intellectually and rhetorically impaired children and adolescents with the technological tools of filmmaking could lead to powerful, pedagogically liberating modes of creative expression that would be otherwise foreclosed by the conservative educational establishment. He opens the essay with a direct reference to the idea that cinema is a language and goes on to assert that this fact alone makes it an important resource for educators working with students grappling with difficulties with spoken or written language. Yet while Astruc used the writing stylus as a productive analogy for the camera (and consequently film as an analogy for literary text), Deligny's article offers an intriguing account of the film camera as a *prosthetic* for the instruments of writing. In a typed manuscript revision of this essay sent to Guattari in the mid-1970s, Deligny writes:

> Imagine someone who is slightly tormented by the desire to write. This is, of course, quite common: anyone might feel that they need, and have the right, to express themselves; and to view those who manage to publish a book as the most privileged. Yet some who would like to achieve this privilege feel maimed and disabled, by either spelling or grammar. The [writing] instrument fails them, yet the camera reassures them through the internal clockwork thanks to which film alone is made. This is the bargain. The camera used as *a prosthetic for uncertain (or shaky) writing* is its strongest current usage.[42]

Here the notion of the film camera as prosthesis is one example of the pervasive evocation of what is never quite called disability in Deligny, Bazin, and their contemporaries' discussions of language, gesture, and cinematic expression during this period. Artaud's madness—including the arresting series of drawings he produced while confined to a psychiatric hospital in the final years of his life—serves as an exemplary instance of what Merleau-Ponty calls the "voices of silence" that phenomenological inquiry attempts to hear,[43] as well as what Deligny describes as the "language other than speech" that the camera/prosthesis facilitates among the autistic children alongside whom he worked and lived. Thus Deligny came to think of and write about his cinematic experiments not as a practice of filming, but rather one of *camering*: "Camering would consist in respecting what does not mean anything, does not say anything, does not address. In other words, camering escapes the symbolic domestication without which there would not be a story, since stories require a consciousness—whether it is an individual or a collective one."[44]

In these accounts, it is arguably what we can now identify as neurodivergence—described as a largely mysterious, seemingly internal or intrinsic disorder that alienates human subjects from their capacity for rational, linguistic self-expression—that serves as a kind of impenetrable limit to aesthetic representation, one that can disrupt what art critic Craig Owens has called Western modernity's "entrenched theatrical representationalism" precisely by closing the gap "between language and flesh" (as Sontag would have it).[45] Deligny, Bazin, and Merleau-Ponty seemed to share the belief that the nonlinguistic, gestural repertoires that characterized Artaud's madness as well as the autism of Deligny's young collaborators could provide access to some extrarepresentational, materially immutable, and objectively real ontological ground—a ground that seems to both precede and condition the emergence of self-consciously rational human subjects marked by language.

Deligny's work and writing served as an important touchstone for Truffaut's treatment of the themes of education, vagabondage, and delinquency in his early films, especially his 1959 debut feature, *Les quatre cents coups (The 400 Blows)*. In 1948, Bazin hired Truffaut, then sixteen years old, as an assistant at Travail et Culture. He eventually adopted Truffaut as a foster child after he was arrested for stealing money from his mother and stepfather (an incident that is recreated in *The 400 Blows*). Just as Bazin consulted with Deligny when determining how best to help Truffaut as a troubled adolescent, so too did Truffaut seek out Deligny's help in the course of making his first feature-length film. In 1958, Truffaut consulted Deligny while writing the final pages of the script; the two would continue to correspond intermittently until 1975.[46] According to their written correspondence, Deligny was especially influential in Truffaut's construction of the closing sequence of *The 400 Blows*, which would go on to become one of the most indelible closing sequences in the history of cinema. In the film's final moments, the troubled adolescent protagonist, Antoine Doinel (played by fourteen-year-old Jean-Pierre Léaud), having escaped the institutions of confinement that have made up the majority of the narrative's environment, arrives on the shore of a beach and runs unabashedly into the rolling waves of the ocean. Running through the landscape toward the beach, with the camera in tracking pursuit, Doinel careens into an aesthetically vague environment along the sandy shore. In its closing sequence, the film loosens itself from the shackles of fictional narrative representation and approaches something closer to both documentary record and imagistic painting. As Doinel runs into the ocean, waves splashing against his legs, he turns around for one last glance toward the shore. The final shot of the film is in a freeze-frame: Doinel's gaze directly meets the camera's. The frame zooms in on his face, which wears an inscrutable expression, and freezes into a static shot as the word *fin* (end) appears on screen. Summarizing the critical consensus that has developed around the film's closing moments, Tom Conley writes, "The sequence was taken to mark a moment of liberation from the worlds of confinement, incarceration, punishment, and surveillance in which the child had been living."[47]

This final image has typically been interpreted as a formal invocation of the aesthetic conventions of the case study genre of documentary film. By shifting registers from narrative fiction to something like cinema verité, the film's viewers in this instant are confronted by a presentational directness that frames Doinel's body in order to present it as an object of scrutiny. The final image offers viewers a constrained image of juvenile delinquency for sober reflection. In this sense, this moment can be understood as one of Brechtian alienation that disrupts, or at least places us at a remove from, the protocols of identification in narrative film. At the same time, the final freeze-frame is ambiguous because it can also be interpreted as an indication of Doinel's eventual recapture, so it may thus ultimately signal the futility of his attempting to escape.

The Slightest Gesture

In 1962, Deligny, along with La Grande Cordée members Josée Manenti, Guy Aubert, and his companion Anita (or Any) Durand, began to shoot footage on 16mm film that would eventually be edited into the film *Le moindre geste (The Slightest Gesture).* The film depicts the lightly fictionalized journey of Yves, portrayed by Yves Guignard, who had joined Deligny's entourage as part of La Grande Cordée in 1957 after a five-year institutionalization. Yves, described as "profoundly disabled," was in his early twenties at the time of filming.[48] The film follows Yves as he escapes from an asylum, meets up with a thirteen-year-old boy from a local village, and proceeds to wander through the desert landscape, encountering a variety of personalities in a series of loosely linked scenes.

Le moindre geste reflects the extended and never fully completed process of its creation. Deligny and Josée Manenti began collecting footage for the film in 1962 and continued to do so, with frequent interruptions, until 1965. The footage languished in storage, however, until around 1970, when at the encouragement of Chris Marker, Jean-Pierre Daniel, a young filmmaker, began to edit it and construct the film's extraordinary non-diegetic soundtrack, which serves, in its "completed" version screened at Cannes in 1971, as a kind of aural thread that weaves its elliptical narrative structure together.

Despite the haphazard process of its creation, the film traces the outlines of a more or less cohesive story. Its central character is Yves, who escapes from the psychiatric asylum where he resides into the rocky Cévennes countryside. Along the banks of a shallow stream, he soon encounters Richard, a thirteen-year-old boy who also seems to have absconded from school in a village nearby. Together, they wander through the stream and across a series of deserted landscapes. These scenes are periodically intercut with several long shots of a black-caped figure in a policeman's hat speeding along a country road on motorbike, presumably in pursuit of the runaways. Climbing to the top of a steeply craggy hill, the pair soon comes across an active quarry; we see its workers drilling into the mountainside and using large bulldozers to move around the crushed-up piles of rock. Spotted by one of the workers, Yves and Richard continue their trajectory, passing through another small mountain village before coming across the sun-drenched, crumbling ruins of a large stone structure. Richard briefly tries to trap Yves inside by closing a dilapidated wooden door, but Yves escapes by sliding underneath it. Climbing among the ruins, Richard discovers the entrance to an underground cistern and climbs inside to hide. Here, the narrative thread becomes more difficult to follow. The film next cuts briefly to a domestic scene in what seems to be a nearby house; a young woman (played by Any Durand) is asleep in bed; an older man enters her room, then leaves, and next is seen lathering his face for a shave. An intertitle explains that they are a laborer at the quarry and his daughter. The woman leaves the house, calling for her father. Yves hides from her, but not before pulling down a length of rope tied to a tree in their yard.

Having lost sight of Richard, Yves ventures further into the wilderness. He is shown wandering alongside a pair of railroad tracks stretching into the mountainous distance, then kneeling beside a creek and sipping water from his cupped hands, and finally sitting in front of a wall of piled stones while trying, and repeatedly failing, to tie two ends of rope together (perhaps in order to pull Richard from the cistern, though this is never fully clear). These scenes of Yves are intercut with brief scenes of the quarry, including several sequences depicting heavy machinery breaking down rock into gravel and a scene in which the quarry worker's daughter runs up a high stony ridge to deliver something to her father. Soon the daughter catches sight of Yves on the nearby hillside, but he avoids her company. Standing on a hilly ridge, he emphatically motions her away; after she is gone, he sits alone in the grass, the sunlight striking his face. The film then cuts back to the yard of the laborer's house, where we see the father molding a clay sculpture of his daughter's head while she sits in front of him, modeling.

We then return to sequences of Yves in the Cévennes wilderness. We see Yves navigating his way through tangled thickets of tall desert grass; using a stone to pound on the thin metal bars protruding from the walls of the abandoned stony structure; beginning to reconstruct a fence from some wooden slats he finds abandoned in a grassy patch nearby. Next, we see Yves arrive at the edge of the quarry itself, seemingly absorbed by the dramatic site of bulldozers moving around large piles of rock, a wrecking ball smashing into the quarry's walls, and dump trucks depositing the debris into a stone-crushing machine to make gravel. Leaving the quarry behind, Yves wanders back toward the hillside. On a road nearer to town (signaled by the presence of a more inhabited-looking building), he encounters a middle-aged woman carrying two suitcases, who looks at him warily before running off when he stomps on the ground in her direction. He continues along his path, coming across another large tangle of rope, which he again attempts to unfurl and drag behind him—perhaps again in the direction of Richard in the cistern.

Eventually he encounters Any again. He follows her along the road that leads back to the village. Haltingly, he follows her into a seemingly deserted town and then back into the countryside along an unpaved road, with her eventually taking him by the arm. In the closing minutes of the film, Any leaves him in front of the entrance to the clinic from which he had originally escaped; an attendant comes to fetch him and brings him inside a classroom with maps of the world posted on its walls. The final shots show Yves hunched over a schoolroom desk, painting the outlines of a rudimentary human figure. *Le moindre geste* is dominated by images

Figure 3. Yves Guignard wanders through a ruined building after having escaped from a nearby asylum, in *Le moindre geste,* directed by Fernand Deligny, Josée Manenti, and Jean-Pierre Daniel, Iskra Films, 1971.

of the austere natural grandeur of the Cévennes. Made using 16mm black-and-white stock, the film's many long, static exterior shots capture the region's primordial vastness and elemental severity. The wind-battered structures through which Yves and Richard wander are filmed in a series of static long takes of almost Beckettian desolation. By lingering on a crumbling wall, one shot transforms the entire plane of the screen into a bright stone surface pocked with holes and crevices. Sequences depicting the industrialized activity at the quarry—the inhuman scale and exertions of force that are involved in its operation—further intensify the harshness of the film's visual rendering of the environment.

But viewed closer in and lower down, *Le moindre geste*'s images bristle with life—a life in artful counterpoint to the shots of hard sunlight on stone. There are, for instance, three brief but notable close-ups of animals that occur over the course of the film. Two rabbits surround a small bowl of water, viewed through the gaps in the wire fence that encloses them. A single, tiny black ant crawls along a segment of rope, traversing the frame in a gentle horizontal curve. A lizard, tied by its neck to a stick planted in the ground, twitches and jerks in response to the grasping motions of Yves's hand. Above all, the film seems most visually preoccupied by the behavioral repertoires of its protagonist. These are the "slightest" or "least" gestures that give the film its title. Like that of the rabbits and the lizard, the horizon of Yves's world has been unnaturally curtailed; his life is defined by the physical and psychological constrictions imposed by the institution in which he resides. By escaping from the asylum into the limitless and often brutal environment that exists beyond its walls, Yves's gestures attain a new kind of resonance.

The film's sonic components present an equal challenge to interpretation. The soundtrack that Jean-Pierre Daniel assembled several years after the main part of the filming was completed is radically spare. Whole stretches of the film take place with almost no sound at all. Images of Yves and Richard wandering through the countryside are sometimes accompanied by the sound of a softly bubbling creek, the rustling of dry desert grass, and the slow, rhythmic *thwap* of rocks thrown against a hard surface. These are punctuated by an occasional sonic assault: the buzzing whir of the policeman's motorbike signals his pursuit of Yves even before coming into view, and the montaged shots of the quarry's machine in operation are matched with the suitably assaultive sounds of drills, motors, and industrial-grade stonecutting.

Perhaps the most elusive and unsettling aspect of the film's sonic composition is the use it makes of human voices. *Le moindre geste* contains almost no dialogue in the sense of the language that characters use to converse with one another. With several notable exceptions, the voices that we hear are extradiegetic; they do not appear to be emanating from the figures depicted on-screen. Rather, they seem overlaid, collage-like, onto the scenes. Mostly we hear the voice of Yves himself. Gravelly and low, his speech is effortful, frequently perseverative, and only sporadically intelligible. In the early part of the film, when Yves and Richard are wandering around together, we also hear Richard's voice—speedy, chipper, and much more high-pitched. Yet Yves's distinctive voice on the soundtrack provides a kind of sonic undercurrent that lends the entire film an intensely perceptible, almost guttural sense of bodily materiality. At certain moments, when Yves's voice crescendos into a shout, the sound evokes Artaud's famous vocalizations in his radio plays of the 1930s. Deligny had long been interested in Artaud, having included an imaginary exchange between the dramatist of cruelty and Vincent van Gogh in his 1948 book *Les vagabonds efficaces*.[49] The vocalizations heard on the film's soundtrack recall an Artaudian conception of theater that would turn away from its reliance on spoken dialogue and toward "a communication represented as a vibrational exchange among bodies, and away from the word toward the gesture."[50] This aspect of Artaud's thought, coupled with his forceful critiques of institutional psychiatry, makes him a particularly important antecedent for Deligny's writings and films.

If the machines required to make a movie—above all the camera and the microphone—are technological apparatuses that mimic the perceptual faculties of human consciousness by recording the sensory data that a particular camera/subject encounters as it moves through the world, then the principal aesthetic achievement of *Le moindre geste* perhaps lies in the alternative model of cinematic subjectivity that it proposes. To support this assertion, I would like to consider two brief segments of the film in greater depth. The first occurs at roughly the midpoint of the ninety-minute film. The sequence begins with a series of static, exterior shots depicting the crumbling walls of an abandoned stone edifice. The images center on the building's ancient doorways and window frames; the occasional bony branch of a tree sprouts from fissures in its walls. There's a close-up of a curiously round gap in a pitted stone surface that opens into an unseen, darkened interior; another shot shows a ruined doorway in front of which a few thin tree branches tremble in the wind. The soundtrack during this sequence is rough and seems only obliquely related to the images. There's a gritty, almost rhythmic sound, as if someone is digging a hole, pounding on the ground, or pulling at the crumbling exterior walls of the structures that appear on-screen. Perhaps we are meant to imagine that Richard is making these noises, still hiding (or maybe trapped) deep inside the cistern.

These static shots are followed by a medium-shot image of Yves sitting in an open, sunny field, a scrabble of overgrown grass visible in soft focus in the background. Then there is a close-up: Yves's head and collar fill up much of the left side of the screen as he brings the side of one hand to his mouth and gently waves his index finger in front of his nose. His eyes are half closed against the brightness of the sun falling on his face, and he blinks a bit erratically. Next there is a cut, and then Yves's face is shown again in close-up, lying still, his head now resting in the shadow created by his folded forearms. In this three-minute sequence, images of the decaying building are directly counterposed with close-up shots of Yves's face and body, creating a halting yet unmistakable relation between them. The manner and rhythm of the editing produces a connection via a sort of line of sensation that links the pocked surfaces of the building's walls with the figure of Yves himself. This sequence calls attention to the porous boundary between exterior and interior that exists in both the ruination of the building's physical exterior and our voyeuristic encounter with the human figure on-screen. Yet this cinematic association is not, I would suggest, an instance of "narrative prosthesis": it does not seem like the crumbling building and desolate landscape "materialize the metaphor" of Yves's own crumbling cognition or desolate subjectivity.[51] By linking the gestural movements of Yves's body with the textured boundary separating the building's exterior surface from its hidden depths, the film stages a refusal of the conventions of psychological identification.

Figure 4. Yves Guignard wanders through the countryside of the Cévennes, in *Le moindre geste,* directed by Fernand Deligny, Josée Manenti, and Jean-Pierre Daniel, Iskra Films, 1971.

It is tempting to place *Le moindre geste* in relationship to minor cinema, a category that Félix Guattari proposed to describe a number of films made in the 1960s and 1970s, many of them documentaries, that reflected the alternative and anti-psychiatric movements associated with figures such as David Cooper and R. D. Laing in the United Kingdom and Franco Basaglia in Italy.[52] Guattari was particularly interested in how films such as Frederick Wiseman's *Titicut Follies* (1967; discussed in the next chapter) and Peter Robinson's *Asylum* (1972) used the tools of cinema to create powerful cinematic critiques of mainstream psychiatric practices and institutions by representing madness on its own terms. Guattari also saw a connection between these films and contemporaneous developments in militant Third World cinema, particularly in Latin America, which sought to foster the creation of a revolutionary cinematic idiom by providing filmmaking equipment directly to proletarian workers.[53] The idea, in the words of Third Cinema proponents Octavio Getino and Fernando Solanas, was to "have the worker film *his way of looking at the world just as if he were writing it.*"[54] Guattari's and Getino and Solanas' formulations of Third Cinema and minor cinema resonate with certain aspects of *Le moindre geste,* as well as Deligny's efforts to radically reformulate what a filmmaker is or might be. Yet *Le moindre geste* resists easy alignment with these movements. It is clear that the film is not a work of militant or revolutionary cinema of the kind advocated by Getino and Solanas. *Le moindre geste,* like Deligny himself, resists being identified with any single political group, party, or position.

Critic Serge Daney offers a more compelling account of the significance of *Le moindre geste* within the context of its moment. In a discussion of different approaches to representing madness on film, Daney proposes that *Le moindre geste* represents a radical departure from the more common, and more familiar, tropism adopted by films made in the wake of the social upheavals of the late 1960s that attempted to analogize the world to a psychiatric asylum as a way of suggesting that "we are all mad." Instead, Deligny's film belongs to a less grandly universalizing tradition of representing madness that does not take "madness" for granted but rather consists in "relentlessly dynamiting *both* the word [i.e., madness] *and* the thing, in blowing up the material cage of madness, by connecting the camera to another space, one that is even less feasible, of all the *real* experiences that rescind the 'walls of the asylum.'"[55]

Deligny sought Truffaut's support and advice in his desire to edit and release *Le moindre geste* as a complete feature-length film. In his revealing account of Truffaut's exchanges with Deligny, film historian Dudley Andrew observes the ultimately incommensurate positions held by these two figures on the aesthetic consequences of attempting to represent the wild child on film.[56] Truffaut was apparently "baffled" when he saw the footage that Deligny and his group had recorded over several years in the early 1960s. He encouraged him to edit the footage into a coherent narrative and include voice-over narration so that the audience might follow the story the film attempted to tell. Deligny, however, rejected Truffaut's suggestion, and it is not surprising that he would do so, considering the rest of his work. Deligny, as Andrew writes, "would never let any *voice,* be it authoritative or childlike, limit *images,* such was his animus when it came to language."[57] Truffaut's bafflement can also be read as a refusal or inability of the increasingly establishment filmmaker to recognize Deligny's position as a viable one: "Their gestures are not like ours. Their gestures speak another language, one that isn't a complement to words; those gestures are closer to those of a chimpanzee than to those of a child. This is a question neither of deformation nor retardation; they are different because what controls them is not verbal thought.[58]"

Truffaut's *L'enfant sauvage* and Deligny's *Le moindre geste* could be said to follow opposite trajectories. Truffaut's film serves as a pointed rejection of the "savage cinema" *(cinema sauvage)* that appeared in French and international avant-garde filmmaking in the 1960s (most influentially in the increasingly fragmented and politically radical work of Truffaut's New Wave frenemy, Jean-Luc Godard). Deligny's approach to filming the autistic children alongside whom he lived rejected the "civilizing," pedagogical mandates that Itard represented, and that were in turn adopted and embodied by Truffaut in his direction of the film and his performance as the Enlightenment's doctor-pedagogue. Truffaut's *L'enfant sauvage* operates via a kind of formal refusal, containment, and foreclosure of the wild child's haptic embodiment, which the film treats as the principal aesthetic disturbance that vibrates at the heart of both its narrative and theme. By contrast, the experience of viewing Deligny's *Le moindre geste* is entirely defined by its haptic impartiality and open-endedness. *Le moindre geste* deactivates the civilizing apparatuses of medico-pedagogy exemplified in Itard's account of his attempts to transform Victor into a functionally civilized and acculturated subject.

This incommensurability—perhaps like the bridge Victor "refuses to cross"—is the key aspect, to conclude this chapter, of the conceptual aperture of feral performativity I have attempted to outline. As Andrew observes, "Deligny believed that Itard had headed in the wrong direction at the outset, when he determined to bring the boy into language. [. . .] Itard should have followed the boy, not led him; he should have trusted the boy's behavior as the proper reaction to the hazards of experience rather than forcing him to learn lessons laid out in advance."[59] The ongoing ramifications of this definitional errancy for Itard's legacy are evident in contemporary contestation around the behaviorist paradigm in the treatment of autism: O. Ivar Lovaas, the Norwegian child psychiatrist who developed the methods of ABA that have become the most widely accepted clinical standard of early childhood autism intervention therapy. Lovaas observes that the core of the method, which revolves around the use of "aversives," could be traced back to Itard's descriptions of his work with Victor.[60] As Remi Yergeau writes, "For Lovaas and other behaviorists, [. . .] aversives represented (and still presently represent) one among many mechanisms that sought to modularize, manipulate, and ultimately predict instances of rhetorical behavior, or the many motions required to constitute a normatively rhetorical action."[61] The feral performative suggests a different route through this history, charting a pathway that belongs to the counter-cartographies of neurodivergence collected in this study.

The examples that have been considered in this chapter arrive at different conclusions about the consequences of overcoming or extinguishing wildness through the moralizing therapeutic pedagogy of civilization (often signaled by being taught how to speak), suggesting other possible approaches to this divide by undoing, disassembling, or remaking the meaning of the wild child or ferality as such. The feral performative is not just, or not only, an idiom for thinking about aesthetic or expressive practices—though this is an important domain of analysis. It also allows for a discussion of the ways in which social reality is actively produced, sustained, and reproduced as an accumulation of doings, redoings, and undoings.

2

(Un)making Asylum

In summer 1968, the actors of the Living Theatre, including company founders Judith Malina and Julian Beck, were preparing to perform at the Avignon Festival. In July, the festival would present the world premiere of the company's play *Paradise Now.*

After some initial success in the New York avant-garde theater scene in the 1950s, Beck and Malina's decision to put art before money led the theater to temporarily cease operations in 1964. Reconvening in Europe, Beck, Malina, and new members of the company spent the next four years traveling throughout France, Italy, and Spain, living nomadically in artist's residences and collectives as they attempted to create new productions. During their European sojourn, the company began to experiment with new ways of integrating their anarchist and pacifist political beliefs into the form and structure of the plays they were creating. They worked to develop a process for making plays that would come to be called collective creation, an example of what Beck called an "Anarcho-Communist Autogestive Process which is of more value to the people than a play."[1] Many of the actors who joined the company were untrained performers having their first experience onstage, which meant that the process of devising and rehearsing was painstakingly slow, and often tortuous.

Paradise Now would go on to become the Living Theatre's best-known and most controversial play from this important period of its development. The play is now considered by many critics to be one of the most significant works of American experimental theater from the 1960s. Improvisatory, ritualistic, at times orgiastic, *Paradise Now* was also highly participatory. The play is organized as a series of "ladder rungs," each of which has an abstract theme and ritual action associated with it. The staging featured the actors in various states of undress, who exhorted audience members to disrobe. The play culminates by reaching "paradise," at which point the performers lead the audience out of the theater into an exuberant protest-cum-"be-in" in the streets. At Avignon, the festival organizers canceled subsequent performances after the unexpected ending caused scenes of chaos in front of the theater; when the company presented the play's American premiere at Yale the following year, several audience members and actors were arrested on charges of indecent exposure.

In an essay discussing the Living Theatre's plays of the late 1960s, Norman James describes *Paradise Now* as the most ritualistic and intensely physical of the company's productions from this period. "Like other forms of communion ritual," James writes, "the physical contact in which players and spectators engage is meant to draw the individual out of the passive, uncreative, and even uncommunicating isolation that the role of spectator usually implies, whether at the theater, in church, or in life outside. And, like other forms of communion ritual, this physical contact is meant to transform what is being acted out into a reality that is no longer pretended."[2]

Before the work's Avignon premiere, the Living Theatre was based at Gourgas, a sprawling, dilapidated estate (formerly a silkworm farm) in the Cévennes that Félix Guattari had acquired and was hoping to establish as an atelier for students and intellectuals. Beck and Malina had become acquainted with Guattari and his circle through their presence at the beating heart of the May demonstrations in Paris. Protests were initially sparked at the beginning of the month in response to a police crackdown on the occupation of several campuses of the University of Paris by student activists protesting the educational policies of Charles de Gaulle's Fifth Republic. For a fleeting moment, the crackdown had managed to unite students and workers into a fragile alliance. Mass demonstrations quickly spread throughout the country, which culminated in a general strike in the middle of the month. Beck and Malina were present at and participated in the demonstrations, including a takeover by students and workers of the Odeon Theater for several days.[3] During the occupation of the Odeon, which began on May 15, students, political agitators, actors, artists, and ordinary citizens—including Beck—took to the theater's stage to give rousing political speeches to the assembled crowd. Beck later remarked of the Odeon takeover, "It was pure theatrical forum and it was pure revolutionary."[4]

In June, the company left Paris and took up temporary residence at Guattari's house in Gourgas to prepare for their Avignon performances. With many students reeling from the events of the previous month, Guattari decided to turn his property into a gathering place for activists and students to cool off and regroup, far from the heat of Paris.[5] Journalist Jean Sagura, who spent time at Gourgas during this period, describes the atmosphere:

> The house is large and has two floors. We sleep at ten or twelve in vast dormitories, with mattresses on the floor; and those who are lucky enough to have a single room only have to because they are the first to arrive. No sexual border, and everyone sleeps as they want, alone, or in pairs, in fours, and not always with the same person from one night to the next. Collective nudity does not seem to bother anyone. We are in the aftermath of May 68, the images and the music of the film *Woodstock* come to give a soft flavor to the wind of freedom that reigns: the revolution begins here and now.[6]

While the Living Theatre was stationed at Gourgas and its members (presumably) rehearsing *Paradise Now,* they would have crossed paths with Fernand Deligny and a twelve-year-old autistic boy named Janmari, recently released from a long stay at the Salpêtrière Hospital. Janmari's mother, a friend of Deligny's landlady, had sought out Deligny's help when the hospital's chief of pediatric psychiatry had finally declared her son to be "untreatable" and "ineducable," and discharged him.

Little scholarship on the Living Theatre, of which there is a considerable amount, has discussed the group's temporary sojourn at Gourgas that summer; nor is there any mention by Malina or Beck of the presence of Deligny or Janmari in their writings from the period. For his part, Deligny apparently felt stifled by the post-May euphoria of the motley group of militants, students, and artists who suddenly arrived in Gourgas that summer.[7] To escape the commotion, Deligny soon took Guattari's suggestion to move out of Gourgas to join Any Durand and her sister,

Gisèle Durand, in a cabin about a kilometer away, in the tiny village of Graniers.[8]

What might be made of the curious historical happenstance that Deligny's network briefly lived alongside the members of the Living Theatre that summer? This chapter investigates some of the underlying implications that are at stake in the question of why the activities of Deligny and his circle on the one hand, and those of the Living Theatre on the other, set each collective on pathways that intersected at the particular time and place that they did. Even more in *Paradise Now,* the Living Theatre sought to demolish the social hierarchy that separated performers from spectators, and to awaken them from their usual state of passivity and isolation. This is why the frenzied collective exodus from the theater at the end of *Paradise Now* became so crucial to the play's success with audiences. For their part, Deligny and his small network were experimenting with ways of living alongside people diagnosed with profound disabilities, including autism, that frequently meant they would come to be labeled ineducable and even deemed unsuited to institutional asylums.

To Make Asylum, As a Tree Makes a Shadow

The etymology of the word *asylum* can be traced via Latin *asȳlum* to the Greek word ἄσῦλον (asilos, "refuge" or "sanctuary"). *Asylum* is the neuter form of the adjective ἄσῦλος, which designates a place or state of being inviolable to the right of seizure by the political authority of the state. The term's modern meaning—as a sanctuary or place of refuge from political, legal, and moral intrusion or violation—dates from the early fifteenth century. The more narrow use of *asylum* to designate a specific type of "benevolent institution to shelter some class of persons suffering social, mental, or bodily defects" is from the late eighteenth century, when it was first used to refer to a home for female orphans.[9] However, *asylum* as an institutional form for the large-scale management of populations deemed incapable—mentally or otherwise—of working to support themselves came to predominate only in the nineteenth century, with the appearance of moral treatment as the key conceptual innovation behind the asylum system.[10] What historian of psychiatry Andrew Scull has called the asylum's moral architecture consisted of "buildings designed as therapeutic instruments."[11] The moral machinery of the asylum's physical presence was understood by its proponents as a method of intervening into the troubled minds of its inmates in a way that would be analogous to the role assumed by the invisible hand of the market in the regulation of civil society under the emergent economic model of industrial capitalism. As it reached its institutionalized maturity with the generalized adoption of the "moral treatment" paradigm across the nineteenth century, the asylum came to be seen as a paragon of the modern liberal state's reasoned beneficence: as Foucault writes in *The History of Madness,* the modern asylum "was no longer a cage for man abandoned to his savagery, but a dream republic where relations were only ever established in a virtuous transparency."[12]

Asylum was a word of enduring fascination, even obsession, for Deligny, and was perhaps one of the primary preoccupations of his life's work. Though he would come to be totally opposed to the asylum system, he also always remained attached to the concept of asylum. The rethinking and remaking of *asylum* beyond all institutionalizing and institutionalized parameters became one of the grounding objectives of his life's work. In a fascinating text entitled "A for Asylum," Deligny offers perhaps his most compressed and evocative account of his work as a sort of lived rebuke to the historical processes by which *asylum* came to designate the kind of place that a society reserves for those who go off the rails it sets for itself. In this essay, Deligny proclaims himself a lifelong "being of [the] asylum"—être d'asile—and attempts to describe a mode of activity that he calls *asyluming,* a verb of his own invention (asiler, "to asylum").[13] He declares that asyluming was what he had been doing—or perhaps making—for fifty years, likening the making of asylum to the way "a tree makes a shadow."[14] (Deligny's writing is thick with such figurative details, at once poetic and mystifying.)

How might this evocative notion of asylum as an action that is done, a thing that is made—that is, as a performance—help illuminate how institutions that came to be known as asylums became understood as crucibles for the shaping of subjectivity as such? How might performance be implicated in the kinds of subjectivity that asylums produce? Why is the asylum becoming represented in specifically performative terms—at an historical moment when both the theater and the asylum, two heterotopic spaces, are encountering crises of definition and viability? To address such questions, this chapter considers Deligny's attempt to unmake, and remake, *asylum* in relationship to a number of other key sites from roughly the same period, including the experimental psychiatric clinic La Borde, the theatrical interludes that punctuate Frederick Wiseman's infamous asylum documentary *Titicut Follies,* and a disagreement that Deligny expresses with the model of subject formation proposed by Marxist philosopher Louis Althusser. I conclude by considering how Deligny's turn toward a practice of collectively tracing wander lines offers a complement to the unmaking of asylum and the performative construction of the self as it is produced and conditioned by ideology and institutions. These examples illuminate how a *dramaturgy of subjectivity* becomes visible via forms of formally experimental aesthetic procedures that sought new and—crucially—newly *politicized* modes of representation adequate to tracking the experience of institutionalization as it is lived in the shadows of increasingly prevalent and diffused apparatuses of psychiatric power, particularly as its institutional templates are in the midst of undergoing profound transformation, an historical process that is now designated under the general term *deinstitutionalization. Neurodiversity* is a concept that would not have become thinkable without a highly specific set of histories regarding the institution, in particular the historical tendency that has come to be known as deinstitutionalization. Yet deinstitutionalization is a somewhat misleading shorthand used to describe the reasons for this dramatic reduction in psychiatric institutionalization. Deinstitutionalization, however, is better understood as a series of local psychopolitical conflicts—perhaps a micropsychopolitics—whose different causes cannot always be resolved into a coherent historical narrative.[15]

By the mid-1960s, Deligny and his collaborators in La Grande Cordée found themselves in precarious financial straits. In 1965, Deligny and several of his collaborators were invited to live and work at La Borde, the radical psychiatric clinic where the psychiatrists Jean Oury and Félix Guattari attempted to revolutionize the treatment of mental illness, insisting on the integration of the political and psychic dimensions of the group dynamics of institutional life. A sprawling complex of buildings located in the rural Cour-Cheverny region in the Loire Valley, a two-hour drive from Paris, La Borde was founded by psychiatrist Jean Oury in 1951 as an experiment in applying Marxist principles to the domain of mental health, working to develop an approach to the treatment of mental disorders that came to be called institutional psychotherapy, which might best be understood as a form of psychotherapy for the *institution,* insofar as it is intended to transform the milieu—that is, the social and physical environment in which patients, staff, and clinicians live and work. Oury had been a protégé of François Tosquelles, a Catalan-born psychiatrist whose ideas about the relationship between the psyche and the social were shaped by his years as a political prisoner after his involvement with anti-fascist Republican forces in the Spanish civil war. As director of the Saint-Alban psychiatric hospital in Lozère, Tosquelles fostered links between the clinic and the French Resistance movement. After the end of World War II, St-Alban became an important training ground for figures including Franz Fanon, Oury, and Félix Guattari.[16]

After his time at St-Alban, Guattari joined the staff of La Borde in 1953. He retained a close affiliation with the clinic for the next several decades, until his death in 1992, and for large periods was its director. Particularly in the late 1960s and early 1970s, largely because of Guattari's presence, La Borde also served as a refuge and occasional hideout for various factions of the student left. It was at La Borde that Guattari experimented with the practice that he would come to call *schizoanalysis,* and that would form a crucial basis for his collaborations with Gilles Deleuze. Schizoanalysis attempts to develop a method of understanding the *psychic* dimensions of subjectivity—that sphere, "mental life," that we have all come to experience as a private interiority belonging to no one but ourselves—in relationship to the broader historical development of capitalism as an economic system—and of the social relations that are necessary in order for capitalism to sustain and reproduce itself (above all, the bourgeois nuclear family and the Oedipus complex that Freud identified as its universal core). Schizoanalysis is an attempt to introduce Marxist concepts of *production* "into considerations of the problem of desire": "The order of desire is the order of production; all production is at once desiring-production and social production" (296), to quote from *Anti-Oedipus.*[17]

The use of theatrical games and productions became a key feature of the therapeutic process elaborated at La Borde. As historian Flore Garcin-Marrou notes, for Oury, "the theater facilitates the formation of the collective, the decompartmentalization of the insane, the creation of a virtual space where psychiatry can experience a new distribution of roles."[18] Garcin-Marrou reveals that Deligny, at Oury's invitation, directed several theatrical texts with patients at La Borde.[19] In a 2007 interview, Oury discusses the concept of heterogeny and the importance François Tosquelles had placed on cultivating a heterogenous milieu within the space of the psychiatric institution. Tosquelles, Oury recalls, "often said that the milieu needed to be heterogeneous, even the educational milieu of children. He made clear that in order for things to be alive, for there to be exchanges, groups, inter-groups, initiatives, chance and encounters, there must be heterogeneity. Fernand Deligny also always spoke of heterogeneity. When Deligny left Armentières, for example, after his experience with dissident minorities and marginalized communities (les marginaux), he highlighted that in order to harness an approach enabling these people to remain even slightly interested in something, it was necessary to constitute an unexpected heterogeneous environment, for objects as much as spaces and different people. This was one of the essential conditions that guaranteed the effectiveness of the milieu."[20]

Though he would maintain contact with and allegiance to the group at La Borde, Deligny's work from this moment forward would largely take its own path. Rejecting both the reigning Lacanian doxa that emphasized the linguistic dimensions of the unconscious and the increasingly pervasive tenets of Guattarian schizoanalysis, Deligny continued to develop his ideas and techniques in relative, self-imposed obscurity beyond the mainstream channels of French intellectual and political life. The "attempt," prompted by Janmari's arrival, marked a meaningful rupture with the orientation of Deligny's earlier therapeutic activities with disabled or delinquent children because of how decisively it turned away from all "programs of adaptation and normalization" that, as Igor Krotlica perceives, were the inheritance of nineteenth-century psychiatric power, which Deligny increasingly found to be in "need for a new approach to care."[21] Defying the weighty pronouncements of asylum psychiatry and its therapeutic protocols, Deligny refused to accept the necessity of institutional confinement. Rather, Deligny maintained that it was Janmari's distinctive mode of acting and being that the Monoblet *tentative*—described occasionally as a kind of "raft"—was itself "built" around—or perhaps it is better to say that it was woven.

Asyluming is a practice that creates a space for a different mode of relation and existence, one that does not take for granted the subject as the only endpoint but instead becomes the occasion for making a refuge for what is ordinarily called "insignificant": "the sound that is heard when close-up to a trickle of dripping water, the fly that runs across the plaster, the light."[22] For Deligny, "the search for a 'solution' to autism and 'the advent' of the subject as a horizon . . . were both fundamentally (and inappropriately) teleological, insofar as they assign a meaning to a process underway, giving it both a significance and a direction."[23]

Deligny's activities from the late 1960s and throughout the 1970s might be placed in the context of the acute interest during this period, spanning developments in the social sciences, science and technology, and aesthetics, in how cultural practices could be understood according to such "behavioral" rubrics as system feedback, ritual, and performance. Art historian Judith Rodenbeck has characterized a distinct current of interest within postwar intellectual and aesthetic movements in what she calls "the problem of behavior"—a tendency exemplified, in the American context, as much by the emergent sociology of social interaction of Erving Goffman and the psychological "behaviorism" of B. F. Skinner as by the Happenings of Allan Kaprow and the systematic interrogation of the mechanisms of social behavior undertaken by performance art pioneers including Vito Acconci and Adrian Piper.[24] The social scientific *and* the aesthetic preoccupations with social behavior of this moment shaped the emergent field of performance studies as it was then being formulated at the juncture of theater, ritual, and anthropology by figures like Goffman, Richard Schechner, and Victor Turner.[25] Interestingly, Deligny read Turner's work from the late 1960s when preparing to write *Cahiers de L'immuable* (Notebooks of the Immutable). His handwritten notes contain quotations from Turner's anthropological writings. At one point, he quotes Turner's assertion that "symbolic gestures that correspond to certain movements of the body are adaptations from the point of view of selection. The meaning of these movements varies considerably from one culture to another."[26] Deligny aligns his observations with contemporaneous developments in anthropological thought concerning the ways in which geographic territories are inhabited and given meaning through ritual actions. Deligny's preoccupation with animality and the methods of animal ethology, as well as anthropological studies of the place of ritual within what were characterized as "primitive" human societies, are particularly notable in light of his career-long interest in shifting away from psychoanalytic, structuralist, or Marxist interpretations of human action in favor of less hermeneutically driven modes of observing social behavior. Deligny's handwritten quotations from Victor Turner's observations on the culturally variable meanings that can be assigned to different gestures and bodily movements are indicative of his interest in moving away from inherited models of human subjectivity that pivot around the capacity to create meaning through language and other processes of symbolization. Instead, Deligny focuses on gestures, bodily trajectories, and provisional arrangements of acting and living alongside those deemed to be living "in the infinitive mode."[27]

It is precisely around the question of the self-declaring subject that Deligny's mode of thinking reveals his irritation and impatience with the reigning orthodoxies of Marxism, psychoanalysis, and structuralism during the height of their influence in French thought and politics. A refrain that runs throughout Deligny's writings is a concern about the role attributed to language as a structure in and by which the individual human being is produced as a subject. Deligny was critical of theoretical frameworks in which language functions as an institution that has the power to distribute the privileges of personhood, to determine who belongs to the category of the human and who does not. "A for Asylum" is an especially fascinating entryway into the singularity of Deligny's mode of thinking. Despite considerable proximity to leading figures associated with these currents of thought, Deligny pursued a dissenting position on one of the key questions facing intellectuals on the political left during this period. Was the human subject utterly determined by the structuring force of language (which Jacques Lacan would evoke in his conceptualization of the symbolic order) or does the subject retain a degree of freedom that allows for the possibility of escaping the determinative nature of structure? The latter position, associated with the account of ideology and interpellation put forth by Althusser, is sometimes characterized as a break from the more strictly structuralist direction taken by Lacan, developed through the influence of Claude Lévi-Strauss.[28]

In fact, Deligny and Louis Althusser exchanged several letters in the mid-1970s, and it appears that Althusser and his wife came to visit Deligny's group at Monoblet in 1977. In a letter to Althusser dated September 1976, Deligny specifically addresses terms used by Althusser in "Ideology and Ideological State Apparatuses."

> But the individual, this "individual always already subject"? If the individual and the subject are "the same thing," why two terms? [. . .] the opposition between the individual and society that has had its day and its use is in a way relayed by a human–subject "opposition" that would account for this stubborn resistance of each to be resorbed as a perfect subject, the "gaps" of each in relation to the ideal line—ideologically ideal—having two foci of essential causes: the very contradictions of ideology—to which saint to devote—and this unconscious attraction towards an indistinct human.[29]

This essay, arguably Althusser's best-known and influential theoretical contribution, was first published in French as "Idéologie et appareils idéologiques d'état" in *La Pensée* in June 1970.[30] In it, Althusser seeks to explain how "*all ideology hails or interpellates concrete individuals as concrete subjects,* by the functioning of the category of the subject."[31] To give this abstract idea more concrete form, Althusser suggests that the reader imagine someone—anyone—who is walking down a street and who suddenly hears a police officer shout from behind, "Hey, you there!" Althusser continues:

> Assuming that the theoretical scene I have imagined takes place in the street, the hailed individual will turn round. By this mere one-hundred-and-eighty-degree physical conversion, he becomes a *subject.* Why? Because he has recognized that the hail was "really" addressed to him, and that "it was *really him* who was hailed" (and not someone else). Experience shows that the practical telecommunication of hailings is such that they hardly ever miss their man: verbal call or whistle, the one hailed always recognizes that it is really him who is being hailed. And yet it is a strange phenomenon, and one which cannot be explained solely by "guilt feelings," despite the large numbers who "have something on their consciences."[32]

Althusser offers what he calls the "theoretical scene I have imagined" to explicate how "all ideology hails or interpellates concrete individuals as concrete subjects" (173). The account of ideology he offers grows out of his long-standing engagement with how Marx's writings grapple with the contradictory relationship between the historical production of the self-aware human subject and the material determinations of social structure.

In *Reading Capital,* Althusser observes that Marx "defines for the capitalist mode of production the different forms of individuality required and produced by that mode according to functions, of which the individuals are 'supports' [Träger], in the division of labor, in the different 'levels' of the structure."[33] In proposing the concept of interpellation through this "scene" of the hailing police officer, Althusser sought to dramatize the process by which mere individuals get "recruited" or "transformed" into subjects. These various "forms of individuality" (which could just be called subjectivity) are themselves determined and shaped by the different needs of the capitalist mode of production. It is this act of hailing that in turn comes to define for Althusser the way that ideology itself "acts" or "functions": "The existence of ideology and the hailing or interpellation of individuals as subjects are one and the same thing."[34]

Étienne Balibar has identified in Althusser's writing on ideological interpellation an "intrinsic relationship between the structure of ideological processes and the dispositifs of theatrical representation."[35] This observation in turn explains Althusser's interest in the materialist dramaturgy most associated with the Brechtian tradition of epic theater, which he considers capable of exposing, disrupting, or at least short-circuiting the workings of ideology for potentially liberatory ends. In conversations with Brecht, Althusser in a number of key places illustrates the ideological formation of subjectivity as a kind of dramaturgical scene. In an earlier essay, written in 1964, Althusser analogizes the philosophical revolution of Marx to the dramaturgical revolution of Brecht, arguing for the revolutionary potential of theater in terms that the Living Theatre's *Paradise Now* would come to realize in practice: "The theater is like a mirror where the spectators come to see what they have in their head and body; they come to recognize themselves."[36] "Materialist theatrical practice," Bargu explains, "is marked by the capacity *to stage*" the dissociation "between reality and consciousness." Epic theater thus "enables the spectators to become aware of how ideology works, as it were, behind the backs of the actors onstage and, by extension, of the spectators themselves."[37]

One of the most important theoretical innovations to emerge from Althusser's "theoretical scene" of the police officer's hail has been the use of the concept of interpellation to understand the performative force of language itself, as in the work of later poststructuralist and deconstructive critics who propose that subjects are formatively constituted through language. In *Excitable Speech,* for example, Judith Butler invokes the Althusserian concept of interpellation to ask, "Is our vulnerability to language a consequence of our being constituted within its terms? If we are formed in language, then that formative power precedes and conditions any decision we might make about it, insulting us from the start, as it were, by its prior power."[38] The "initial insult" that constitutes subjects in language creates a "linguistic field" (Butler's term) that precipitates both a bodily vulnerability to violence, which asserts itself at the level of language, *and* the necessity to conceptualize violence in linguistic terms: "it is being interpellated within the terms of language that a certain social existence of the body first becomes possible" and, at the same time, vulnerable.[39] Indeed, the hail becomes merely one instance of what Butler calls "a long string of injurious interpellations" that "accumulates the force of authority through the repetition or citation of a prior and authoritative set of practices."[40] But this vulnerability does not *preclude* the possibility for play; nor, as will be seen, does it immediately annihilate any attempt to mobilize language's vulnerability to incursion in order to expose, acknowledge, and ultimately work through the causes of social injury.

Documentary as Mapping of Subjectivity: The Case of *Titicut Follies*

Althusser's dramaturgical model of ideological interpellation has been central to many critical defenses of the social function of documentary cinema as a political praxis aimed at intervening into and perhaps transforming the social reality it attempts to document. Documentary film, in this account, is understood to play a function akin to Brecht's (and in turn Althusser's) dream of a "materialist theatrical practice," one that would be "marked by the capacity *to stage*" what Bargu calls the dissociation "between reality and consciousness" that ideology imposes as the very condition of subjectivity.[41] The stakes (and perhaps limits) of this line of argument when considered in relationship to the political history of *asylum* (as both an institution and an idea)—and in turn to the politics of mental health and the genealogy of neurodivergence being traced in this study—are interestingly put to the test in one of the most important cultural representations of the asylum as a space of terrifying confinement from this period: Frederick Wiseman's asylum documentary *Titicut*

Follies. The film was released in 1967 but shortly thereafter was banned from public exhibition in the United States as a result of legal controversies about whether the filmmakers had received permission to film the patient-prisoners who appear in it. *Titicut Follies* exposes in shocking, graphic detail the everyday brutalities and dehumanizing procedures that characterized life inside a Massachusetts psychiatric prison. In 1964, Wiseman brought the students from a class he was teaching on punishment at Boston University's law school on a field trip to the Bridgewater State Hospital. While there, he decided the facility would make an interesting subject for a film.

After ostensibly obtaining the institution's superintendent's permission to film the inmates, Wiseman worked with ethnographic filmmaker John Marshall to film scenes of everyday life inside Bridgewater. He spent a year editing the raw footage into a roughly cohesive narrative structure, and with this film, he started to develop the utterly distinctive (if much imitated) style to which he has remained remarkably faithful over dozens of subsequent films. Despite their disturbing content, the images in Wiseman's film possess a stark beauty, enhanced by Wiseman's handheld camera. One of the most closely, and exhaustively, analyzed nonfiction films ever made, *Titicut Follies* exemplifies the unique approach to the "observational documentary" that Wiseman developed out of his interest in understanding how the social function of documentary cinema emerges from the conditions of its production. This question has continued to preoccupy Wiseman in his now five decades (and counting) of documentary filmmaking.[42] The observational style that Wiseman uses in *Titicut Follies* is deeply embedded in a "direct" or "pure cinema" tradition of nonfiction filmmaking that can be traced back to the Kino-Pravda newsreels made by Dziga Vertov in the 1920s and the innovations of cinema verité (a term the Wiseman has always disavowed) developed by Jean Rouch and Edgar Morin, which seeks to cultivate an unconscious, trancelike state of sensory openness that enables the camera to "discover meaning as embodied in the surface of things within the realm of visible phenomena."[43] Wiseman's approach to documentary filmmaking is as informed by the montage and cut-up techniques of the modernist avant-garde as it is by the observational ethos of ethnographic filmmaking and reportage, forging a unique visual and sonic vocabulary that has enabled him to create a series of critical examinations of institutions.

Beginning with *Titicut Follies,* Dan Armstrong writes, Weisman's documentaries pursue "a critical line" that investigates "subjectivity as it is processed (and sometimes resists processing) by the institutional and ideological machinery of the state and marketplace."[44] That is, Wiseman's films map not only the institutions they depict but also the production and regulation of subjectivity that takes place within these institutions. His films eschew voice-over narration and avoid direct-address interviews with experts, favoring instead a mosaic-style representation of reality as it unfurls at a low-level, mundane pace that might simply be called administrative time. In a 2007 interview reflecting on the circumstances that led him to decide to make *Titicut Follies,* Wiseman observes, "The idea of making a movie about one place, from my point of view, was useful because it provided a boundary."[45] The walls of the Bridgewater prison hospital thus become a kind of container for Wiseman's depiction of grinding, dull bureaucracy, which is then layered and collaged with images of startling vibrancy and violence. Multiple aspects of the form of the film—its roughly discernible narrative structure, its rigorously framed shot of Bridgewater's rigid partitioning of space via the rational multiplication of forms of enclosure, isolation, and surveillance—seem to exist in mimetic relation to the institution that it documents, and above all to Bridgewater's rigid organization of space and time. The film can be viewed as its own kind of cinematic cartography of the institution itself, a diagram that gradually reveals the architecture and spatial layout of the prison/hospital/asylum as Wiseman's handheld camera makes its way through its hallways, offices, examination rooms, and courtyard.

Titicut Follies is structured around two time spans laminated on top of one another: the first corresponds more or less to the length of a single day inside the walls of Bridgewater, beginning with the inmates waking up and eating breakfast and culminating in evening and eventually nighttime scenes. The second time span roughly follows an inmate's "career" in the institution, from conviction to commitment to death. (One of the last images of the film is a coffin carrying a deceased inmate's body.)

The film's title foregrounds the importance of its theatrical framing device. *Titicut Follies* is the name of a Christmas pageant that the wardens and inmates performed together each year in the hospital's mess hall—and to which they invited the neighbors and residents from the surrounding area. (Titicut is the Wampanoag word for the river that flows near

Bridgewater, a ghostly reminder of an eradicated Indigenous presence on the land where the hospital was first constructed, in the mid-nineteenth century, as an almshouse.[46]) The words "Titicut Follies" appear in the film itself, on a sign behind the stage of the Christmas pageant. The term *follies* recalls early twentieth-century American musical revues, the most famous of which were produced by Florenz Ziegfeld on Broadway and eventually as Hollywood films in the 1910s, 1920s, and 1930s. This is itself an Americanization of the music-hall revue format that originated in nineteenth-century Paris (the Folies Bergère), famous for large musical numbers featuring a chorus of female dancers. "Follies," of course, also points to the origins of music-hall "follies" in the French word for madness. (In a 2009 interview with French cinema journal *Positif,* Wiseman points out that the film's title has at least a double meaning for audiences aware of the French term la folie.[47])

As the film juxtaposes the events of a single day inside Bridgewater with key moments representing the longer arc of an inmate's institutional life cycle, the Christmas pageant interludes intertwine these time spans. The snippets of theatrical and musical performances are not narrative dramas but crude musical numbers, often focusing on a showboating warden. It depicts the prisoners as awkwardly assembled into presentational, forward-facing configurations. They jerkily mouth along as the guards sing and dance to the tinny accompaniment of an unseen upright piano. Wiseman has repeatedly insisted in interviews over the years that *Titicut Follies* is above all a musical comedy.[48]

The interludes from the pageant are key to the documentary's multiple layers of performance and dramatization, which in turn structure its kaleidoscopic depiction of how Bridgewater functions as a total institution—a concept that had been recently popularized by the Canadian-born sociologist Erving Goffman's surprise best seller *Asylums: Essays on the Condition of the Social Situation of Mental Patients and Other Inmates,* published in 1961. Drawing from fieldwork conducted at St. Elizabeth's psychiatric hospital in Washington, D.C., *Asylums* describes the mechanisms by which psychiatric wards enact forms of mortification on the patient's sense of self. Goffman argues that a defining feature of the total institution is the way that it violates the "territories of the self" and "objects of self-feeling—such as his body, his immediate actions, his thoughts, and some of his possessions." In total institutions, Goffman observes, "the boundary that the individual places between his being and the environment is invaded and the embodiments of self profaned."[49] *Titicut Follies* viscerally renders the constant profanations of the self to which the inmates are subjected.

Wiseman plainly states that "the idea of the movie came out of the absolute sense of shock about what Bridgewater was about."[50] The film itself seems engineered to transmit that palpable sense of shock from the filmmaker to the viewer's body through the intermediary of the camera. The intensity of sensation the film arouses was crucial to the significant role it came to play within the burgeoning anti-psychiatry movement and the push to close large state-run asylums such as Bridgewater. At issue in the legal judgment against *Titicut Follies* was the question of consent. Although Wiseman had received verbal agreement from inmates and staff to film them, the fact that he had not obtained signed release forms became grounds for the film to be banned from public exhibition. The film poses the question of whether and to what extent those depicted would have been "capable"—legally or otherwise—to grant their consent. Because they are both imprisoned and psychiatrically diagnosed, the inmates depicted in Bridgewater have "the right not to be filmed."[51] But

Figure 5. Still from *Titicut Follies,* directed by Frederick Wiseman, Zipporah, 1967.

Figure 6. A theatrical interlude features a Christmas pageant performed by patients and wardens in *Titicut Follies,* directed by Frederick Wiseman, Zipporah, 1967.

Wiseman has consistently maintained that this merely functioned as a pretext to prevent the film from exposing the conditions of Bridgewater, a state-run facility, to public scrutiny.

Wiseman's shots evoke the cruel reality of what is happening in frequently oblique ways, lingering on peculiar details that resonate contrapuntally with the larger context of what is going on around them. A little more than halfway through the film, there is a famous sequence of shots centered around a silent inmate, Malinowski. This sequence begins with a brutal, noisy scene in which one of the prison hospital's doctors and a group of wardens make the naked Malinowski lie down on table and forcefully insert a feeding tube up his nose while holding down his legs with cloth restraints. The shot casually ranges across the bored faces of the men assigned to carry out this task and close-ups of Malinowski's face and body, capturing the small gulps of his emaciated throat as liquid is poured into a funnel at the end of the feeding tube; at one point, a single, glistening tear appears in the corner of his squinting eye and rolls down his cheek. Suddenly there is a cut to a different, much quieter scene. Malinowski's gaunt face and body are again seen in vivid close-up, but something is different. To our dawning horror, it becomes clear that Malinowski has died, and we are witnessing a warden preparing his body for burial by placing cotton balls beneath the lifeless eyelids with a pair of medical pliers.

The editing of this sequence, which cuts back and forth several times between the force-feeding scene and the mortuary preparations, has been discussed by a number of critics as exemplary of the film's use of irony to critique the institution that it documents: Malinowski's body is treated with more dignity in death than when he was alive.[52] After the force-feeding is complete, the camera follows Malinowski as he is brought back to his cell and the door slammed shut behind him. Wiseman then cuts to a shot of an open coffin containing Malinowski's corpse being rolled into a mortuary chamber before a warden flips it closed. This sequence is immediately followed by a close-up of a birthday card ("Congratulations and Happy Birthday! To-day you are one year older!") and then cuts to a scene showing a group of inmates seated around a long dining table as one of them blows out the candles of his birthday cake, to the applause of several nurses who have gathered around them.

The Malinowski sequence is significant for the way it exposes the institutional "processing" (as Andrews puts it) experienced not just by the patient-prisoners but also by the wardens, doctors, and other staff members. What is shocking about the feeding tube scene is not just the images but their juxtaposition with the inane chatter of the doctor and wardens (who joke about pouring whisky in the funnel attached to the end of the feeding tube). Like Goffman, Wiseman is interested in the extent to which those subjected to disciplinary and institutional power find ways of asserting (relative) autonomy and resistance to the violations imposed on them. In *Asylums,* Goffman observes the constant, low-grade forms of resistance asserted by the individuals caught up in institutional mechanisms. However, a necessary corollary of the asylum system's attempt to impose complete control is the fact that it is always and inevitably doomed to fail. In this small distance, however miniscule, Goffman sees a tiny, glimmering possibility of defiance, of holding on to the "embodiments of self" that the institutional machinery otherwise denies. As Goffman contends, "The practice of reserving something of oneself from the clutch of an institution is very visible in mental hospitals and prisons but can be found in more benign and less totalistic institutions too. I want to argue that this recalcitrance is not an incidental mechanism of defense but rather an essential constituent of the self."[53] Often, watching *Titicut Follies,* one feels that the recalcitrance Goffman described is in fact the film's most precious and elusive subject—glimpsed only elliptically, in the slightest flicker of the not quite gestures of the not-quite-right attempts by the people recorded by Wiseman to fulfill the roles that the institutional architecture has set out for them to play.

What relationship are viewers meant to draw between the (intended, if forced) levity of the theatrical sequences and the brutal, often deeply unsettling scenes of everyday life at Bridgewater? From one perspective, the scenes of the music-hall revue challenge the institution's totalizing enclosure. The Follies performances might seem to hold out the promise of a utopian space, contrasting with the harsh reality depicted in the other scenes. Yet this distinction does not really hold over the course of the film: garish footlights illuminate the faces of the inmates in the Follies numbers from below, rendering their expressions uncannily impassive, and there is a pervasive sense of unsettled eeriness that seeps over from the way the scenes onstage are filmed to the scenes depicting the ordinary goings-on of the institution. Wiseman's blunt use of editing—Grant compares it to Sergei Eisenstein's "kino fist"—cuts harshly between the Follies songs and various brutal scenes of institutional degradation visited by the guards and medical staff on the inmates, underlining that it is not only when they are on the Follies stage that the Bridgewater inmates are performing. They are indeed always under potential inspection, subjected to the virtuous transparency that the therapeutic architecture of moral treatment was designed to cultivate. Instead, the theatrical interludes are responsible not only for the film's enduring fascination but also its potential capacity to incite action, to awaken new forms of political consciousness among its spectators.

To Err, to Drift . . . : Wander Lines and the Remaking of Asylum

Suggestions about Deligny's motivation for writing an account of himself as a "being of the asylum"—and for the peculiar constellation of philosophical interlocutors he engages in it (Marx, La Boetie, and Pierre Clastres, among others)—can be found in his correspondence from around the time of its composition in the early 1980s. In a July 1982 letter to his friend, writer and drama critic Émile Copfermann, Deligny discusses a reference to his work at Monoblet that he had recently come across in a book about the history of psychiatric asylums by philosopher Marcel Gauchet and psychiatrist Gladys Swain. In *La pratique de l'esprit humain: L'institution asilaire et la révolution démocratique* (1980, published in English as *Madness and Democracy: The Modern Psychiatric Universe,* 1990), Gauchet and Swain identify Deligny's Monoblet attempt as a piece of the larger mosaic of what they describe as the democratic revolution of institutional psychiatry. Yet Deligny evidently objected to Gauchet and Swain's characterization of his approach to working with children who (in their words) have "refused speech."[54] He forcefully contests this manner of describing his work at Monoblet: "Our method that we've developed has become singular because of the singularity of those beings who find themselves here, who are said to live in a refusal of language. Refusal? This is a very decisive term, and one that we have a choice about using. Has Janmari ever refused to understand—and to speak—language? And if he has not, who has denied him the capacity for understanding?"[55]

In a letter to Gauchet from November 1982, Deligny attempts to clarify matters: he describes himself as having spent about fifty years in "close presence with those who have not responded to the interpellation of the (democratic) State, [but] have turned their backs, closed their eyes and ears, and so thus have found themselves enclosed in a place made for them." He goes on to describe the brief but pivotal exchange he'd had with Louis Althusser—at the time arguably the preeminent Marxist intellectual in France—during the mid-1970s:

> Contrary to what K. Marx supposes in the writings of his youth, I do not believe that "the savage" [le sauvage] has disappeared [from the human species], having been made useless by the establishment of the reflexive subject. [Marx] had, moreover, noted in the margins to return to [this point]. Now is always the time. And it was on this topic that Althusser, traveling on vacation and having made a detour here [to Monoblet], left when I told him that, viewed from here, individual and subject were not

> the same thing. If there was a split, he chose [the side of] Lacan. Language was enough, and he proposed to go and seed the Soviet Union with this science.[56]

Deligny balks at how Althusser describes the production of subjectivity as a matter of interpellation; he is equally critical of the positions articulated by the second major proponent of a structuralist view of the subject as effectively a back projection of linguistic structures, psychoanalyst Jacques Lacan. Despite his occasional intellectual proximity to the most famous psychoanalytic theorist in France at the time, Deligny's objections to the Lacanian system when it came to its approach to autism were profound and fundamental. In Janmari, Deligny thought that he had found "the sign for the permanency of the species": a human existence whose wordless yet deeply engaged manner of relating to his environment was evidence of a mode of being human that was, contra Lacan, "without lack, released from the bullying reciprocity of desire."[57] (Lacan's influence on the practice of psychiatry in France and elsewhere outside the United States has continued to be inescapable; even today, psychoanalytic touchstones remain dominant in the institutionally sanctioned views of autism as a failure of symbolization.[58]) "What does the psychoanalyst say in the grip of a child said to be 'autistic'?" he asks in the 1982 letter to Gauchet. "If the child doesn't speak, it's because he <u>keeps</u> silent [il se tait], he doesn't <u>want</u> to say anything. Always refusal."[59] Althusser, in turn, would come to describe as "unabsorbable" Deligny's "thinking of a non-subject individual, existing beyond the reach of ideology."[60] Yet "the originality of Deligny's theoretical and practical position consists precisely in what can be called a 'suspension of interpellation,'" as Bertrand Ogilvie writes.[61]

The cartographic—indeed, *counter*-cartographic—practices that accompanied the development of Deligny's thinking and writing alongside Janmari and other neurodivergent individuals are thus perhaps best understood as attempts to evoke in visual form the modes of living that take shape in this state of suspended, paused, or perhaps deactivated interpellation. Deligny is careful to distinguish between the act of tracing the movement of a body through space and the act of interpreting, classifying, diagnosing, or pathologizing that movement and the body from which it emanates. He writes of his group's maps as works of art that "are nothing other than the trace of a gesture."[62] It is precisely this capacity of ritualized acting, of repetitive gestures or actions, that the cartographic tracings record:

> On transparent paper, we set ourselves to transcribing their pathways, wander lines, and then we held onto these lines, these traces, and looked at them and still do, through transparency; some of them date back ten years and others were made last week. For the most part, we have long since forgotten the *by whom* of these traces. This forgetting allows us to see "something else": the remainder, resistant to any comprehension.[63]

Consider a map of the small village of Graniers that was traced in 1975 by Gisèle Durand. In black pastel, Durand has indicated the artificial water routes created to bring water to the surrounding farms. The thinner lines of black India ink indicate Janmari's wander lines. Durand has marked her own trajectory in red pencil. The wander line that traces Janmari's perambulations has its own distinctive shape and direction, yet it is one line among an ensemble of lines that together produce something like, although not quite, a drawing. Another map, made up of a lamination of a series of transparent layers, is labeled "Le Serret" and dated June 1976. This map is the accumulation of several different trajectories. There is a large, thick line in black pastel designating the trajectory of Jean Lin, an adult. A layer beneath, in China ink, indicates the trajectory of Ann, an autistic child. A description of the map also informs us that both Jean Lin and Ann were accompanied in their wanderings by a flock of goats, whose footprints are also indicated throughout the map. Perhaps even more interesting, the map also contains visual indications of the sounds that the cartographers encountered during the period that the drawing records: ringing cowbells attached to the goats are indicated by brush-strokes; the sound of flutes and the clock are indicated by different strokes of ink. This map, which condenses the geospatial, temporal, and sonic registers of the day it was recorded, is a remarkable document that points to the complexity and sophistication of this cartographic practice.

The cartographic drawings are made up of many individual sheets of transparent wax paper layered on top of one another, producing composite images that condense weeks, months, and perhaps years of tracing. He insists that the wandering, drifting, and errant trajectories he and his

Figure 7. Map of the small hamlet of Graniers traced by Gisèle Durand-Ruiz in 1975. The fine curlicue lines retrospectively record the wander lines of Janmari from 1968. Background map on cardboard, 63 × 52 cm. Copyright Archives Gisèle Durand-Ruiz. Photograph by Anaïs Masson. Reproduced in Fernand Deligny, *Œuvres, L'Arachnéen,* 2007, www.editions-arachneen.fr.

colleagues sought to trace should not be mistaken for a representation of a "drifting" or "errant" mode of subjectivity. While Aline Wiame has suggested that these maps "produce a non-personal, performative subjectivity that makes a claim for emancipation in a reshaped common,"[64] it is clear that they are working toward a model of the human that is not encumbered by what Deligny objected to in Althusser's account of the ideological production of subjectivity through interpellation. Deligny and his network refuse to accept making any moral or political distinctions that would separate living beings "with" language from those "without" language, offering instead a performative model that unearths the "species memory" of the human individual from the encumbrances of the constrained and ultimately deadly exclusions of the subject. Thus for Deligny, "autistic children might be individuals, but they are not quite subjects: neither subjects through their suffering, nor subjects in formation, and above all not deficient subjects."[65] In place of depth-based models of the speaking human subject, Deligny offers cartographic surfaces and hand-drawn lines.

When shuffling through the browning, transparent pages, the maps, drawings, and handwritten manuscripts collected in Deligny's archive feel as fragile and precarious as a spider's web. Lines of pencil, ink, and charcoal register the haptic pressure once exerted by the hands that traced them decades earlier. The maps must be seen not just as purely two-dimensional visual images but also as ephemeral objects—material repositories that preserve residual traces of the bodily force with which the pages were marked. Such a reading offers the possibility of viewing Deligny's maps dynamically, even performatively, as documents of the pressurized force of a body on the page, existing in mimetic or imitative relation to the way the map drawings themselves were pursued. These cartographies can be understood as ephemeral remainders of the acts of drifting, wandering, erring, dwelling, and tracing alongside which they were created. José Esteban Muñoz writes that the material ephemeral left behind in the wake of an event long past can offer "a kind of evidence of what has transpired but certainly not the thing itself." Unlike more conventional forms of documentation, be they written, photographed, recorded, or filmed, the study of ephemera "does not rest on epistemological foundations but is instead interested in following traces, glimmers, residues, and specks of things."[66] As ephemera, they resist being contained within "dominant systems of aesthetic and institutional classification."[67]

The gridded organization of space through maps and diagrams has been inseparable from the operations of power in modern disciplinary societies.[68] Yet the wander line maps are antithetical to this form of cartography, tuned as it is to the keys of the state and the interests of circulation, exchange, and accumulation. Deligny insists that the mapping techniques of his network elaborate ways of "acting" or "doing" that are delinked from production in its proper sense. The maps—created "in order to make something other than a sign"[69]—do not offer a method for interpreting the behaviors or actions of the autistic individuals whose movements they record.

In "A for Asylum," Deligny writes: "There remains that which the transcribed trajectory tracings reveal, to know that a good number of them seem to us as being without an aim: the reiterated trajectory of a young girl goes here, each day and several times a day, and from day to day; even here, always stubbornly the same: the stubborn girl 'who attaches herself with energy and with a durable manner to a way [or manner] of acting.'"[70] In this passage, Deligny offers a striking account of the counter-cartographic project that unfurled through and alongside his practices of writing and living "alongside" autistic people, emphasizing concepts of *tracing* and *transcription,* quotidian *reiteration,* and modes of *acting* (agir). Deligny and Janmari together elaborated a mode of thinking, doing, and acting that involved intensified and reconfigured practices of attention, care, copresence, moving alongside, and looking out, offering what might be understood as performative model that opposes *doing* (faire) and *acting* (agir), and insists on distinguishing the autistic "individual" from the preformatted, institutionally and ideologically processed "subject." This performative model—so different from the kind of dramaturgy of subjectivity found in in Althusser's writing on ideological interpellation and Wiseman's documentary of the institutional processing and formatting of subjectivity in the Bridgewater prison hospital asylum—is exemplified by the practice of tracing and poetically invoked in relationship to the spider's tattered silken thread.

At times Deligny's evocations of autistic modes of being veer toward what literary critic James Berger has described as the tendency to represent verbal or communicational impairment attributed to cognitive disability with the promise of access to a wonderous alternative reality that is otherwise forbidden to the neurotypical, and hence as a "disarticulate" figure loaded with the representational weight of all forms of otherness—with, indeed, otherness itself.[71] Relatedly, Deligny's account of Janmari as an example of human existence free from "lack"—and hence exempt from the tribulations of desire that define the subject as an effect of historical structures and forces—echoes romanticized and infantalizing understandings of autism and risks reiterating age-old tropes that have figured the autistic child as a magical being endowed with special powers. Yet in calling attention to the correlation between *spatial* practices of institutionalization—above all confinement and surveillance—and *categorical* and even *existential* designations of mental pathology and deficiency, Deligny anticipates many of the ways in which disability activists and scholars of disability would come to think about the social construction of disability in ensuing decades. Deligny's writings on asylum have prompted theorists of education Jan Masschelein and Pieter Verstraete to formulate a critique of the ideology of "inclusion" within contemporary debates over education policy for students with disabilities. In these debates, inclusion is often posited as a progressive antidote to segregation. As they note, for Deligny, the word *asylum* "does not refer to a particular situation where different subjects become individuals but refers to individuals who live in the presence of each other under equal circumstances."[72] Deligny "dives beneath the asylum as an historical and colonized psychiatric institution, as a site of incarceration to locate its pearl-like essence, uncovering it as a spatial entity, one that exists as a place of refuge."[73]

What sort of asylum would be suitable for a child who had been declared untestable and untreatable by the nation's most prestigious charity hospital? Deligny maintained that it was Janmari's distinctive mode of interacting with his environment that the Monoblet tentative was built to protect and that determined the shape of its daily rhythms. It was therefore a matter of discovering a mode of making or giving asylum that would completely detach itself from the asylum system that was the inheritance of the nineteenth-century psychiatric apparatus. In "A for Asylum," Deligny explicitly writes of the practice of cartographic tracing as a form of asyluming: "If anything intuitive has taken place on this earth or another, it is the maps that we have occasionally traced; it was a matter of making asylum the best we could and we were not yet out of the woods, but rather at the edge."[74] We have been led, then, in pursuit of asylum through the errancy of wander lines, back to the edge of the woods, where Victor of Aveyron first encountered the civilizing gaze of the fields of expertise that would set out (and fail) to diagnose, educate, and treat him.

The Innocent and Us (Nous et l'innocent)—edited together from an interview with Deligny conducted by Copfermann in 1975—contains the following passage:

> One speaks of ritual for these gestures [of Janmari's dancing]. It's an abuse of words, it's an abuse of terms. There is simply a quid pro quo in the fact that we—those who speak—retake the gestures of this order and we give them a ritual dimension because they have a symbolic meaning. But that is not at all to say that, coming from them, these gestures are rituals. It takes on the force of ritual insofar as there is a rite, and the rite is social; it is in tune with the times. It is rites that inherit such innate gestures, and it is not by chance that we find the gestures of Janmari (swinging, dancing) in formalized rituals like the mass. If it resonates so much within us, if it persists even beyond the rite, it's because it has an echo in the innate that is in each of us.[75]

Discussing Janmari's movements that others described as "ritualized gestures," Deligny notes that "I'm much happier to see him dance in front of a sack of flour than if he were to dance in front of me."[76] These passages provide an impetus to rethink—or perhaps abandon entirely—the dramaturgy of subjectivity from the perspective of a renovated performance studies protocol. In confessing that he prefers to observe Janmari dance in front of a sack of flour than to force him to dance for "me" (meaning, by extension, "for" the nonautistic observing other), this passage also suggests a particular vantagepoint from which to rethink the foundational frameworks and presuppositions of performance studies—a departure even from the most radical experiments of the Living Theatre members with whom Deligny and his network briefly happened to coincide with in time and space—in light of the demands, oppositions, and evasions made urgent and apparent by the more recently developing articulations and assertions of neurodivergence as a political, cultural, and aesthetic rubric.

If the inquiries across the various sites and moments within the historical archive traced in this chapter can help us account for emerging discourses of neurodiversity and neurodivergence, then the following chapters pursue these somewhat tattered, errant threads closer toward the anxious present. Indeed, several recent projects within disability community art have returned to the figure of the asylum.[77] These projects that renovate our understanding of asylum find an important poetic antecedent in Deligny's attention to asylum as a place where the individual can find refuge from the demands of being made into a subject, and from "the dominant languages of divergent contemporary professionals and disciplines."[78]

In the next chapter, the question of tracing—as well as wandering and crawling—emerges as a key mode of action for counter-cartographies of neurodivergence; at the same time, the police officer character in Althusser's explanatory "scene" of interpellation—alongside the "roles" inhabited and assumed (always imperfectly, errantly) by the inmates, wardens, doctors, and other denizens of the institution documented in Wiseman's film—will prove to be especially haunting figures in light of contemporary struggles surrounding the way autistic and neurodivergent persons are subjected to (which is also to say are mapped by) the policing powers of surveillance, security, and control.

3

Map, Crawl, Wander, Trace

The art and science of cartography has long been inseparable from the spatial and territorial exercise of official power. Mapping is a key way of rendering a nation-state visible to itself. Cartographic practices—surveying, measuring, calculating, transcribing—are often bound up in the assertion of state power, and the act of producing cartographic representations of local, national, and global topographies can be an authoritative method of claiming and consolidating sovereignty over the territory being represented.

If the major science of cartography depends on the optimal gridding and organizing of space so as to survey it and in so doing bring it under sovereign control, then a radical, alternative, experimental, and indeed *oppositional* model of cartographic thinking and doing can be found across William Pope.L's enormous body of work. A counter-cartographic impulse can be traced across Pope.L's artistic propositions across visual media, performance, and writing. Pope.L's counter-cartographic preoccupations are intensely present in the series of performance pieces that he began to undertake in the early 1990s, in which he crawls along the gutters of busy city streets for hours (sometimes dressed in a Superman costume, sometimes wearing a gray suit and holding a bouquet of yellow flowers). For Pope.L, the landscape is "no longer a static terrain awaiting inscription by our activity" but rather becomes itself an "activity—a field of collective actions and processes."[1] Pope.L's Crawls are viscerally embodied "reflections on the social hierarchies constructed around difference, particularly race, gender, class, disability, and homelessness."[2]

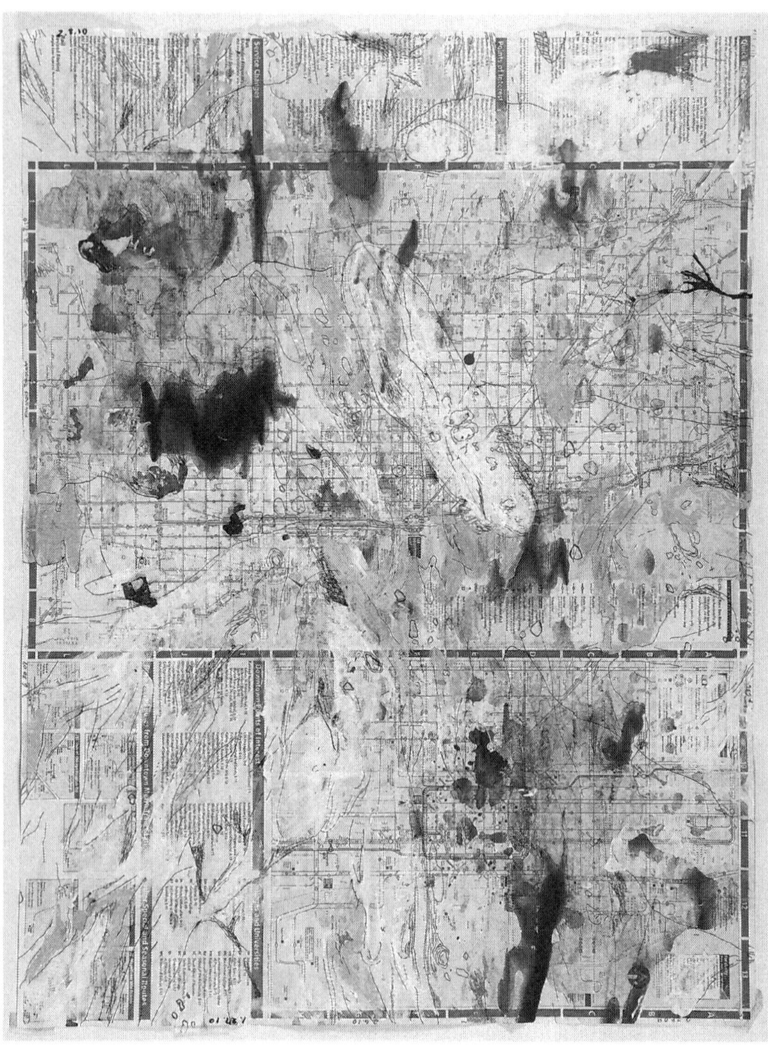

Figure 8. Pope.L, *Failure Drawing #636 Far Above the Ocean* (2009–10). Ink, acrylic, ballpoint pen, oil stick, marker, correction fluid on map. 32 × 24 ¾ in., 81.3 × 62.9 cm. Copyright Pope.L, courtesy of the artist and Mitchell-Innes & Nash, New York.

The Crawls offer an alternative cartography, which involves the *tracing* of space through movement, which takes place precisely at the juncture between the aesthetic and the political. Pope.L's Crawls and his frequent invocation of cartographic imagery converge in the conjunction of racial Blackness with the wandering, indeterminable figure traversing the urban landscape. In "Notes on Crawling Piece," a brief text published in *Art Journal* in 1997, Pope.L reflects on his interest in undertaking the Crawls series, which he describes as "performing social struggle poetically/analytically via the Jeremiad ad agency." He elaborates: "To incite a recursive dynamic between the privileged/subordinate—to test us/our negotiation of the social. To crawl: to SUFFER: provocation to action." Intriguingly, this paragraph ends with Pope.L quoting from his mother: "My Billy, put your money where your mouth is—put your ass where the rest of us live."[3]

Pope.L has revealed in interviews that the initial impetus for the Crawls series emerged from a response to the so-called homelessness crisis that came to the forefront of public debate in many American cities in the 1970s and 1980s—a development that has often been directly, if not without contestation, linked to the successes of the deinstitutionalization movement, which, beginning in the late 1960s, successfully advocated for the closure of the system of large, state-run asylums that had its origins in the nineteenth-century mental hygiene movement. Much of the scholarship on the asylum system and deinstitutionalization has called attention to the ways that asylum medicine, as the predominant form of psychiatric expertise in the United States for nearly a century, was inextricable from the racialized techniques of surveillance and social control that have profoundly shaped the historical emergence of modern taxonomies of mental illness and mental disability, leading to persistent racial and class disparities in the diagnosis and treatment of schizophrenia, autism, and other psychiatric diagnoses.

The Crawls play on the experience of movement through precharted urban streets and territorialities in order to render visceral the matrices of power that both inhibit and adduce the ways that bodies circulate in public space. For Pope.L, the landscape is "no longer a static terrain awaiting inscription by our activity" but rather becomes itself an "activity—a field of collective actions and processes."[4] The Failure Drawings series, begun in 2003, is a set of works on paper that were largely produced on tourist maps that Pope.L collected on his travels across the United States and elsewhere (often making work under the self-proclaimed moniker of the "friendliest black artist in America"). The failure drawings begin with Pope.L's ballpoint pen doodles, notes, and scrawled lines emphasizing, and in some places diverging from, the underlying map's printed lines. Upon returning home from his various trips, Pope.L would continue to cover the surface of these maps with additional layers of marks as well as layers of acrylic paint and correction fluid, among other viscous materials. For instance, *Failure Drawing #636 Far Above the Ocean* (2009–10) consists of layers of ink, acrylic, ballpoint pen, oil stick, marker, and correction fluid that have been applied atop a tourist map of Chicago. The underlying map has been divided into seven distinct rectangular segments by bold red bars. A large rectangle dominates the middle segment of the surface, stretching horizontally across the drawing's entire plane; this large rectangle is vertically positioned a few inches below the drawing's top edge and a little less than halfway from its bottom edge. Above are three smaller rectangular sections formed by the same red bars, filling the space between the large rectangle and the drawing's top edge; below, two tall rectangular sections and one larger one fill out the surface.

These red lines create a grid, designed to present and organize information visually in the clearest possible manner. They are functional and communicative, affirming the map's status as an officially sanctioned visual representation of a specifically delimited territory. Yet the mass of liquids that Pope.L has applied to the paper interrupts the readability of the map underneath, thus destroying its functionality as a visual guide that might to be used to navigate a terrain. The ballpoint segments constitute a haptic interruption, a refusal of the map's functionality as a visual index meant to enable the navigation of the physical world it purports to represent.

In its eruptive play with the viscous materiality on the map's surface, *Failure Drawing #636* is exemplary of Pope.L's career-spanning fixation on the topography of the city street as a site of both social abjection and aesthetic invention. If Pope.L's crawling "cracks open all the kinetic assumptions related to ideological, racial, and gendered mechanisms of urban belonging, circulation, and abjection," then the thickly congealed liquids on the surface of *Failure Drawing #636* take on an aesthetic project that echoes the one that Pope.L himself assumes in his Crawls, which aimed to embody the social abjection of Blackness through a specific manner of bodily comportment (the crawl) and territorial movement (progressing slowly over major urban arteries).[5]

Pope.L's counter-cartographic interventions bring to the surface what might be identified as a critique of or departure from understandings of subjectivity that are structured around what Édouard Glissant describes as Western rationality's demand for *transparency*.[6] The requirement for transparency that is the basis, as Glissant says, for all Western thought finds its most austere and perfect visual expression in the grid, that encapsulation of the Enlightenment dream of rendering the totality of the world completely knowable and accountable by suturing map to territory. But Pope.L's alternative cartographies operate by way of a palpable, deformational suspension of the kind of visual schematization of territory that the gridded surface of a map typically provides. Pope.L's counter-cartographies instead involve layering, ripping, wetting, and drying—a vibrant corporeal surplus that official maps can't capture. If the haptic can be thought of as "the viscera that ruptures the apparent surface of any work," as Rizvana Bradley suggests when writing about Pope.L's art, then the raised, brackish material applied to the flat surface of the ripped-up, discarded, and repurposed map in *Failure Drawing #636* is an example of this visceral rupture, producing a haptic cartography via "the material surplus that remains the condition of possibility for performance."[7]

This chapter is interested in certain kinds of intrusion on the cartographic grid's utility as a functional apparatus for organizing and visualizing the social world, particularly by forms of bodily errancy that have been described variously as wandering or (more often in medical and psychiatric discourse) elopement. The examples considered in this chapter build on the previous chapter's consideration of mapping, turning the focus to the role of maps within the history of psychiatric power as a technology of racial surveillance, security, and control.[8]

While it is imperative to keep sight of the historical and epistemological distinctions separating the racist optics that have contributed to the denial of Black sentience from the visual rhetorics that construe autism and other forms of neurodivergence as an epistemological boundary, it is equally necessary to consider how these separate visual logics function in tandem with one another. Racialized techniques of surveillance and social control have profoundly shaped the historical emergence of modern taxonomies of mental illness and mental disability, leading to persistent racial and class disparities in the diagnosis and treatment of autism and other conditions.[9] This discussion is especially informed by the growing body of scholarship that focuses on how disability and race must be understood not as parallel, comparable, or analogous vectors of difference but as markers of modern taxonomies of identification that have emerged in tandem with one another since at least the beginning of the nineteenth century.[10] The invention of Drapetomania, American physician Samuel Cartwright's 1851 term that rendered slaves' flight from captivity as a form of mental illness, is an early example of the persistent scientific, social, and cultural pathologization of the Black psyche as preternaturally irrational, unruly, criminal, and insane.[11] This psychic and corporeal unruliness has also been important to the development of an aesthetic tradition of "black madness," which La Marr Jurelle Bruce describes as "a form of motion occasioned in treacherous terrain: a wavering, trembling, swelling, zigzagging, drumming, bursting, shattering, or splattering movement that disrupts Reason's supposedly steady order and tidy borders."[12]

Developments in the psychological sciences have both shaped and been shaped by the surveillance and management of hierarchies of difference, often through institutional and indeed carceral modalities of social control. Visual techniques of monitoring and tracking equally determine the way disciplinary institutions, including schools and prisons, alternately medicalize and criminalize mental disability along lines of both race and class. These dynamics have become acutely intensified around childhood and adolescence: since the 1990s, as Julie Passanante Elman notes, "the increasing medicalization of white adolescence paralleled (and, in some ways, facilitated) the increasing criminalization of Black and Latino/a youth in an age of 'school-to-prison pipelines,' in which nonwhite students are disproportionately diagnosed with ADHD, placed in special education programs, suspended, and criminalized."[13] Racial disparities in the diagnosis and treatment of autism and other neurodevelopmental disorders are particularly pronounced. One recent study found that Black and Latino children are diagnosed with autism up to several years later than white children.[14] These disparities persist and in many cases worsen when autistic children enter the public education system. Recent studies have found that Black children are overrepresented in special education classrooms and that they are disproportionately assigned to restrictive educational environments compared to their non-Black counterparts.[15] Behind these profound statistical disparities in access lies a deeper history of shifting ideas of race and class within the genealogical emergence of the modern formations of childhood, psychiatry, and mental health. Disciplinary institutions—including prisons, schools, and psychiatric institutions—have been key sites where shifting scientific concepts of race and disability, criminality, and pathology have played out over the course of the twentieth and into the twenty-first century.

Avonte's Law

Shortly after noon on October 4, 2013, a fourteen-year-old African American eighth-grade student named Avonte Oquendo[16] ran out of the side entrance of Riverview Middle School, in the Long Island City neighborhood of Queens, New York. After being briefly stopped by a security guard after attempting to exit the school's main entrance and instructed to return to his special education classroom, Oquendo can be seen in a security video released by the New York City police department instead running in the direction of the side entrance before vanishing outside.

Oquendo's disappearance prompted an extensive search effort, involving both the police department and the wider New York community, with the latter largely spearheaded by members of his immediate and extended family. In the hope that he may have fled into a nearby subway station, handmade posters with photographs of Avonte's face were soon plastered in stations across the New York City subway system, the largest public transit network of its kind in the world. Over several months in late 2013 and early 2014, daily newspapers including the *New York Post* and the *New York Times* extensively covered the search effort. The police department, the state's department of education, and the Oquendo family provided daily updates on the case and circulated images of Oquendo across print, televised, and online media. For several months, the city seemed captivated by the case. On January 16, 2014, a city search-and-rescue team discovered Oquendo's remains in a forested area near a pier in the College Point section of Queens. Subsequent forensic investigations were unable to determine the precise cause of Oquendo's death.

The city's medical examiner's office concluded that he had most likely fallen from an embankment into the East River and drowned.

Identified by the school system and the police as severely autistic and nonverbal (a description repeated in media accounts of the case), Avonte reportedly had a strong sensory affinity for trains, cars, and water systems. According to reporting on the case by journalist Robert Kolker, he had long loved to run. Drawing on interviews with many of those who knew Avonte, including his mother, Vanessa Fontaine, Kolker reports that Avonte "chafed at confinement, seizing control any way he knew how and seeking out openings to forge out on his own."[17] Even though Fontaine had repeatedly informed the school district of Avonte's propensity to run off, the security systems in place in the school's special education program failed to prevent him from doing so. Avonte's disappearance, and the discovery of his remains several months later, prompted local officials and politicians to call for reviews of educational policies and school security protocols for students with disabilities enrolled in special education programs. One day after Avonte's funeral, which was held at St. Paul's Cathedral and attracted an overflow crowd of hundreds, New York senator Chuck Schumer held a news conference to announce his intention to introduce federal legislation—to be known as Avonte's Law—that would fund a program to provide "voluntary electronic tracking devices" to be worn by autistic students enrolled in public schools, to be administered through the U.S. Department of Justice. In the official congressional record of the U.S. Senate, Schumer's proposed legislation is summarized as follows:

> Avonte's Law Act of 2014—Amends the Omnibus Crime Control and Safe Streets Act of 1968 to authorize the Attorney General to make grants to law enforcement agencies to: (1) reduce the risk of injury and death relating to the wandering characteristics of some individuals with autism and other disabilities, and (2) safeguard the well-being of individuals with disabilities during interactions with law enforcement.
>
> Requires grant awards to be used to: (1) provide education and resources to law enforcement agencies, first responders, schools, clinicians, and the public in order to reduce the risk of wandering by such individuals, help to identify signs of abuse in such individuals, increase their personal safety and survival skills, and facilitate effective communication with individuals

> who have communication-related disabilities; (2) provide training and emergency protocols for school administrators, staff, and families; (3) provide response tools and training for law enforcement and search-and-rescue agencies, including tracking technology; or (4) provide response tools and training to law enforcement agencies in order to recognize and respond to individuals with intellectual and developmental disabilities.[18]

A second piece of legislation, also named Avonte's Law, was approved by the New York City Council in 2015, providing enhanced funding for schools to install automated alarm systems in special education classrooms. Additionally, on March 23, 2018, Kevin and Avonte's Law was passed as a legislative addition to the 2018 fiscal year's omnibus appropriations bill, having been introduced in the House of Representatives in November 2017. According to the text of the bill, "Kevin and Avonte's Law is named in honor of two boys with autism who perished after wandering. Nine-year-old Kevin Curtis Wills wandered from home, slipped into Iowa's Raccoon River and drowned in 2008." Specifically, this additional law

> amends the Violent Crime Control and Law Enforcement Act of 1994 and reauthorizes the Missing Alzheimer's Disease Patient Alert Program. It allows Justice Department grants to be used by law enforcement agencies and nonprofits for programs to:
>
> - Facilitate training and emergency protocols for school personnel
> - Provide first responders with additional information and resources
> - Make locating technology programs available for individuals who may wander from caregivers.[19]

Recent efforts to enhance the policing and electronic tracking of the wandering tendencies ascribed to autistic subjects must be understood in relation to longer histories of surveillance as a technique of power that is inseparable from the historical emergence of both race and disability as categories of social difference. My claim is that such policies—especially insofar as they are predicated on the political infrastructures of what Simone Browne has called "racializing surveillance"—are at best inadequate and at worst harmful to the persistence and flourishing of autistic and other neurologically divergent modes of personhood.[20] Thus, I am hoping here to contribute an anti-racist, anti-ableist, and anti-sanist critique of the surveillance and policing of autistic subjects. To do so, I consider the Oquendo case and Avonte's Law with regard to how visual surveillance operates at the conjunction of racial Blackness and neurological difference and how autistic wandering becomes construed as a dangerously erratic, even pathological category of bodily movement.

The legislative and policy remedies set forth in bills such as Avonte's Law—which seek to provide federal and state funding to law enforcement agencies to track the wandering tendencies ascribed to autism and autistic people by expanding the forensic apparatuses of the criminal justice system—must be understood in relationship to longer histories of surveillance as a technique of power, especially as it operates at the nexus of disability and racial difference. When viewed from this perspective, such policy proposals reflect the persistence of disciplinary, and indeed carceral, logics within the historical formation of power that anthropologist Elizabeth Povinelli has called late liberalism. This is the historical period defined by the ascendency of security, which can be understood as the distinct mode of governmentality shaped by "the twinned formations of neoliberalism and liberal cultural recognition."[21] Avonte's Law offers a particularly vivid example of the way in which appeals to state recognition for the protection of a certain group—in this case, autistic people and other "individuals with communication-related disabilities," to cite the language of U.S. Senate bill S.2386—can be used as the grounds for expanding the surveillance of those same groups. This understanding of surveillance is indebted to Foucault's account of "security as an emergent mode of liberal governance predicated on the equally emergent problematic of the population."[22] Foucault argues that liberal regimes of security are predicated on the historical development, beginning in the nineteenth century, of the statistically derived concept of the population as the primary object of liberal governmentality.[23] Psychiatric power and its techniques of normalization have been central to this process.

Drawing on Foucault's analyses of psychiatric power, Gil Eyal argues that autism "must be understood within an emerging project for the early monitoring and surveillance of childhood."[24] From the inception of modern psychiatry in the nineteenth century through the early decades of the twentieth, childhood mental disorders were grouped together under the broadly applied category of the "feebleminded"—itself a descriptive diagnosis applied to those who were (in the words of the American Association on Mental Deficiency) deemed to be "socially incapable" by medical authorities. Yet as historians of mental health including James Trent have demonstrated, the designation of feeblemindedness was a vague category, the application of which in practice functioned more often as a mechanism of social control.[25] As Eyal writes, "Who were these 'socially incapable' individuals? It is hardly a secret that they were disproportionally likely to come from the lower rungs of society: immigrants, African Americans, and lower-class whites."[26] Eyal's account of the largely overlooked role of race in the genealogy of modern psychiatry is echoed in psychiatrist and historian of medicine Jonathan Metzl's research into the history of schizophrenia. Using the clinical records of the now-defunct Ionia State Hospital for the Criminally Insane in Michigan as the basis for his study, Metzl demonstrates how policy shifts in the institutionalization of the mentally ill transformed schizophrenia from a diagnosis given largely to middle-class white women in the first half of the twentieth century into one that became overwhelmingly assigned to African American men by the 1960s and 1970s. He convincingly argues that this shift can be directly linked to broader national anxieties about racial antagonisms in the wake of the civil rights movement and the growing demands for political enfranchisement made by Black Americans at midcentury. "The civil rights era," Metzl writes, "catalyzed a shift in the structure of buildings, institutions, diagnostic codes, and even in the structure of minds, attitudes, and identities. . . . And prisons emerged where hospitals once stood."[27]

The complexity of this history is particularly important to account for when considering the controversies surrounding the position on the policing of autistic wandering taken by Autism Speaks, a powerful nongovernmental organization that is presently the largest autism advocacy organization in the United States. Since its founding in 2005 with the financial backing of Bob Wright, then chairman of General Electric and the grandfather of an autistic child, Autism Speaks has been the subject of intense debate within the neurodiversity movement and among autistic self-advocates. Organizations including ASAN and the Autism Women's Network (AWN) have forcefully criticized it, focusing on its "rhetorical constitution of autism as enemy through its metaphoric representation of autism as disease, epidemic, and abductor" as well as "the skillful, systematic, pervasive, and global deployment of these and other rhetorical devices through its corporate-style, neoliberal, market approach to cultural and political rhetoric, deploying its rhetorical tactics and strategies more as a powerful corporate lobbying machine than as a traditional disability advocacy organization."[28] Moreover, the Autism Speaks staff, officers, and board of trustees has been made up almost exclusively of neurotypical—that is, nonautistic—people.

For these reasons, many neurodiversity proponents and autistic self-advocates have argued that Autism Speaks operates from the desire for an "autism-free world"—a goal that they identify as being contiguous with the longer history of eugenics and its logics.[29] As blogger and autistic self-advocate Brigianna Spencer writes, "Autism Speaks has accomplished internally what it wishes to accomplish worldwide: zero autistic people."[30] The controversy over Autism Speaks within neurodiversity and self-advocacy communities came to a head in late 2013, when the search for Oquendo was taking place, as the organization prepared to sponsor a "policy and action" summit in Washington, D.C. In response to Autism Speaks' melodramatic rhetoric in describing the event—"this week is the week America will fully wake up to the autism crisis," cofounder Suzanne Wright's essay announcing the summit declares—neurodiversity proponents and self-advocates staged a number of political actions, both online and in person, protesting the summit.[31] John Elder Robison, a writer and autism expert diagnosed with Asperger syndrome, resigned from Autism Speaks' science and treatment board. In his resignation letter addressed to the organization, Robison writes, "Autism Speaks says it's the advocacy group for people with autism and their families. It's not, despite having had many chances to become that voice. Autism Speaks is the only major medical or mental health nonprofit whose legitimacy is constantly challenged by a large percentage of the people affected by the condition they target."[32]

As Robison's letter makes clear, the contemporary politics of autism involve competing and often irreconcilable visions of the very meaning of the condition itself. Through its rhetorical style and political tactics, Autism Speaks represents autism and ASDs as a threat not only to the health of autistic individuals but also to the welfare (financial and emotional) of their families and communities as well as the broader public. Thanks to its considerable financial resources and connections to the private sector, the organization has successfully propagated this view of autism throughout the arenas of social policy, public discourse, and cultural representation. Moreover, the privatized, corporate-style approach taken by Autism Speaks is emblematic of a neoliberal approach to disability more broadly, one that seeks to redirect the obligation to provide resources and care for disabled people away from the social welfare state toward the individual, the family, and the private sphere.

The critiques of Autism Speaks that have emerged from the neurodiversity and autism self-advocacy movements provide an important context for situating the introduction of Avonte's Law within the contemporary politics of neurological difference because it and similar proposals were crafted and introduced with substantial policy guidance and lobbying support from the organization. Its president, Liz Feld, and chief medical research officer, Dr. Paul Wang, each made numerous media appearances in support of the law, and the organization has deployed considerable resources in furthering the law's passage through extensive publicity campaigns.[33] Furthermore, both Autism Speaks' rhetoric asserting the need for the legislation and the language of the law itself subscribe to a neuro-biomedical model of autism and other mental disabilities that simultaneously asserts and fortifies the authority of law enforcement, clinical and educational experts, and families over the lives of autistic individuals.

The legislative proposals that have invoked Oquendo's name would thus seem to conform to a familiar set of procedures within late liberalism, in which the state's recognition of a vulnerable class or population becomes the occasion for reasserting, intensifying, and expanding the elaborate apparatuses of security, surveillance, and control that define contemporary modes of governance, and particularly of the governance of neurodivergence. When such appeals are made on behalf of a group or population that is presumed to be less than fully capable of speaking for or representing its own interests—as has historically been the case for autistic people and others living with communicational and intellectual disabilities—the authority of biomedical and psychiatric expertise attains both a diagnostic and a regulative function. The neurodiversity critiques of Autism Speaks point to how competing models of disability and neurological difference can have material implications for the way disability appears within the spheres of law and social policy.

Racializing Surveillance

If we understand both race and neurodivergence to be categories shaped by the management and regulation of difference, we must account for Oquendo's status as a racialized *and* disabled subject of biopower whose capillary reach has become increasingly "neuromolecular" in scope, saturating not only individual bodies and aggregate populations but also, and increasingly, neurons, nerves, and synapses.[34] In attending to the ever more granular scales at which techniques of securitization, surveillance, and control now operate, we must also be more critically attentive to the different scales at which the limitations and resistances to their reach emerge and take shape. Wandering—understood as a figure or thematics of movement, flight, and escape from constraint—need not be the occasion for further intensifying the infrastructures and techniques of security, surveillance, and control endemic to late liberalism; rather, it can offer an occasion for thinking anew about the historical alignments between racial difference and disability and propose alternative ways of responding to, negotiating, and existing in common with those forms of life that arise at such conjunctions.

In endorsing the view that the well-being of individuals with developmental and/or communicational disabilities will be best served by the use of tracking technologies by the police (in alliance with educational and medical authorities), Avonte's Law also reveals the extent to which the contemporary politics of disability are inextricably bound to the formation of racialized surveillance that is inseparable from modern police power. Consider that the proposal bearing Avonte Oquendo's name was presented to the U.S. Senate as an amendment to the Omnibus Crime Control and Safe Streets Act of 1968, a piece of legislation passed by the Johnson administration that provided billions of dollars of funding to new criminal justice research and training initiatives with a focus on state and local police agencies. The Safe Streets Act was developed in the context of widespread fears that racial unrest would overtake America's urban centers in the late 1960s. The act was formulated on the basis of "a vision of crime and individual acts of violence as the central domestic problem in America" and "called for a rollback of legal efforts to regulate the police in favor of direct fiscal aid for weapons, technology, and personnel."[35] While invoking the security and protection of autistic and other neurodivergent public school students, in other words, Avonte's Law grows out of and extends the police as a modern institution and formation of power that has historically constellated itself around the surveillance of the Black body in motion. Indeed, if the particular modes and techniques of surveillance (forensic GPS tracking devices, etc.) named in the text of Avonte's Law are characteristically associated with late liberal modes of security, the legislation (and the event that prompted it) also must be understood against the backdrop of longer and more far-reaching genealogies involving the visual schematization of the racialized body in motion.

Let us return to the security camera stills described earlier and consider another vantage point from which these images might be read. Surveillance cameras are distinguished by their technological and visual recursivity. As Ann Wagner notes, "the technology of the [video] monitor opens outward, as well as in. Not only does it register a process of surveillance, it itself asks for monitoring."[36] In her description of the simultaneously outward- and inward-facing direction of the surveillance image, Wagner in turn cites a metaphor used by Rosalind Krauss in her 1976 essay "Video: The Aesthetics of Narcissism," a text that became central to the early critical reception of video art where Krauss describes works of video art in which the body appears "as it were centered between two machines"—the camera and the monitor—"that are the opening and closing of a parenthesis."[37]

The video surveillance camera is a technological apparatus that reveals how surveillance functions as a way of "imposing norms" in which, as John Fiske writes, "those who have been othered into the 'abnormal' have [surveillance] focused more intensely upon them."[38] The security camera's recursive technological form reflects a more general structure of surveillance that exerts itself over a broader social field through various techniques of normalization. The surveillance stills render visible an "abnormal" subject, held between parentheses, whose physical safety (it has subsequently been argued) might have been assured with the use of even more extensive apparatuses of technological surveillance that would have been attached to the body itself.

The pixelated blurring that suffuses the figure of Oquendo's body in this surveillance still condenses and makes visible the temporal and spatial dynamism of a body on the move. The pixelated blur was construed as a visible manifestation of autism itself, along with the corresponding social, emotional, and communicational deficits with which the condition is associated. (Recall the rhetorical strategies favored by Autism Speaks, which casts autism as a dangerous abductor of children's minds and bodies.) The proliferation of visual representations of Oquendo's autism was further amplified by the posters that were quickly plastered throughout the New York City subway system as part of the extensive search effort prompted by his disappearance. The posters featured a school portrait in which Oquendo appears, smiling and facing the viewer. The portrait was accompanied by text identifying its subject as "autistic and not able to communicate verbally," and encouraging subway riders to get in touch with the New York City police department with information about his location. For several months, the posters became omnipresent visual emblems reminding subway riders to be on the lookout for the missing student. Yet the inescapable presence of subway search posters had the added consequence of publicly circulating not just the image of an individual autistic person but also a specific representation of autism itself. At the same time, the rapid, errant trajectory evoked by the pixilation of the image's surface reminds us that the policing and violent regulation of Black life takes place at the level of bodily movement. Indeed, adequately attending to the surveillance media generated in the wake of Oquendo's disappearance suggests one way that the surveillance of disability is racialized and reveals that the visualization of Blackness is inseparable from the historical formations of power through which disability emerges as a modern categorization of human difference. Any reading of these security camera images would be insufficient without accounting for the degree to which, as Browne argues, "surveillance reifies the social construct of race."[39]

Scholars in Black studies have called attention to the historical persistence of visual logics that construe the Black body as spectacular, excessive, and "hypervisible" yet simultaneously evacuated of subjective or psychological interiority.[40] This visual coding of Black embodiment,

Saidiya Hartman and others have suggested, has its origins in the scopic regimes of chattel slavery and is structured around a "racist optics in which black flesh is itself identified as the source of opacity, the denial of black humanity, and the effacement of sentience."[41] This "racist optics" in turn shapes the role of visual representation in the dehumanization, and objectification, of the captive slave's body. The very conditions of seeing and perceiving are determined in advance by a "racist schematization of the visible field."[42] Such optical encodings of Blackness have indeed been central to the historical emergence of surveillance as a technology of racial control, shaping the mediating ideological coordinates through which Black bodies are rendered visible.

In her discussion of the role of video surveillance footage in the 1991 Rodney King uprisings in Los Angeles, Judith Butler argues that it was not simply that the prosecutors' subjective interpretation of the surveillance footage that reflected their own racist presumptions. Such schematizations delimit the conditions within which the act of seeing takes place, determining the way visual perception is transmuted into knowledge. "The visual field," as Butler writes, "is not neutral to the question of race; it is itself a racial formation, an episteme, hegemonic and forceful."[43] Pointing toward a central contradiction of the racial "visual field"—one that construes the Black body as at once hypervisible and hollow, emptied of human subjectivity—this dimension of the image's accrued visual schema is compounded by the knowledge that the photograph also captures the pixelated traces of a fleeing *autistic* body. Is it possible to think with these surveillance stills in a way that moves against, or aims beyond, the logics of security that only seek to intensify and extend the choreopolitical reach of surveillance apparatuses, even at the level of the autistic body itself, as proposed by the legislation for tracking devices for autistic students that bears Avonte's name?

Such perspectives are crucial if we wish to understand how, returning to the video surveillance stills, the pixelation of the video images is marshaled as visible evidence of the "wandering characteristics" associated with autism as such—and which was subsequently invoked in accounts of how and why Oquendo eluded the security apparatuses put in place to protect the physical safety of students with disabilities enrolled in New York City public schools. These interlinked histories of racialized surveillance, disability, medico-pedagogical institutions, and policing must inform any critical examination of the anxieties about wandering that have been at the heart of recent political and legislative proposals to enhance the surveillance of autistic students in public schools.

When these images were released and publicly circulated through the media in connection with the search effort, the bodily movement indicated by the distorted pixelation of the security footage was taken as evidence of the wandering tendencies often linked with autism. The visual traces of Oquendo's fleeing form seemed to index an unruly subject, one incapable of controlling the impulse to move. It consequently functioned as a kind of visual correlate to the social, emotional, and communicational difficulties commonly associated with ASD.[44] The observation that surveillance functions as a technique of enforcing social norms can also help us consider how viewing the security footage of Oquendo's running toward his school's exit is shaped by the history of visual representations of autism. In being explicitly identified with Oquendo's autism, the security camera footage and search-poster images are schematized according to a visual episteme that makes it difficult, if not impossible, to view nonverbal autistic persons as fully autonomous, rational subjects.

Though less clearly visible than physical disability, autism has nonetheless been rendered scientifically and culturally intelligible by way of an extensive history of visual scrutiny. The images of autistic subjects that circulate in mainstream media representations and advertising campaigns by charitable organizations such as Autism Speaks have tended to conform to damaging figurations of the condition as a lived and embodied phenomenon. By depicting autistic subjects with vacant stares or engaged in repetitive stimming behaviors[45] that ostensibly isolate them from normal social interaction in a world of their own, the visual tropes that proliferate in cultural representations of autism have shaped how the condition has come to symbolize an epistemological boundary that excludes autistic people from the sphere of autonomous human personhood. The representational and rhetorical construction of autistic people as less than fully rational and autonomous subjects has had dire and often deadly consequences; as autistic literary critic Remi Yergeau writes, "Autistic being is predicated on un-being."[46] Yergeau's accounts reveal how the visual and rhetorical signifiers associated with Oquendo's autism—the pixelated blurring in the surveillance footage and the identification of Oquendo as autistic and nonverbal in the search poster—participate in a representational logic defined by opacity, unknowability, and an attenuated or even wholly absent self.

Wandering Characteristics

Within the clinical literature, the tendency exhibited by many autistic children and adolescents to wander away from or escape the supervision of adult guardians has been termed *elopement*. A study conducted by researchers at the Johns Hopkins Medical School and published in *Pediatrics* in 2012 reported that nearly half of children with ASD were found to have engaged in elopement behavior with a substantial risk of bodily harm, and that the risk of elopement increased with higher degrees of autism severity.[47] This study was cited in the Schumer news conference announcing the senator's intent to introduce the legislation later dubbed Avonte's Law. Like much of the research on autism, definitive explanations accounting for the specific causes of autistic elopement have been much more difficult to identify than the statistical likelihood of such behavior to occur within an increasingly studied population. Most of the medical literature and policy prognostications by mainstream autism advocacy groups have only hazarded a guess at the ostensible cause of this tendency toward elopement. Partly in response to the media scrutiny generated by the Oquendo case, Lori McIlwain, the executive director of the National Autism Association, wrote an editorial essay for the *New York Times* calling for federal funding for electronic tracking devices for autistic students in public schools. Citing the same *Pediatrics* study, McIlwain proposed that elopement might be attributed to the attraction that some autistic individuals feel toward the kind of sensory stimulation provided by highway traffic, trains, or waterways.[48] Other studies, by contrast, have suggested that elopement behavior might represent an attempt to escape overstimulating sensory environments that contain loud noises within confined spaces.

Recent calls to expand and enhance policing technologies and other security measures to prevent autistic elopement derive their legitimacy from forensic science, a professional discipline whose emergence in the late nineteenth century facilitated the incorporation of medical, psychiatric, and criminological expertise into the legal apparatuses of the modern nation-state. Indeed, as the refrain of autistic wandering wends its way through multiple and diffuse sites of articulation—including peer-reviewed pediatrics journals, media campaigns sponsored by parent-led advocacy groups, the editorial pages of the *New York Times,* and an omnibus crime bill presented for congressional debate—it has become increasingly difficult to recognize the multiple and interlocking forms of expertise and surveillance at play. The electronic tracking technology that Avonte's Law and similar proposals would fund has been primarily researched and developed within the subfield of forensic psychiatry, even as clinical research into the effectiveness of such practices remains inadequate. Any sustained consideration of the legal and ethical hazards that would accompany the use of such devices—particularly for persons deemed incapable of communicating consent—has been even more limited.[49] Even as questions about the clinical efficacy of these technologies remain far from settled, calls for their widespread implementation reflect the same mutually reinforcing collusions between biomedical, psychiatric, pedagogical, and state power that saturate the language of Avonte's Law and the political rationality it exemplifies.

Discussions of autistic wandering ultimately concern the profoundly contested definition and meaning of autistic personhood itself. Elopement can be situated along a continuum with other embodied behaviors associated with autism, such as repetitive rocking and stimming. The pathologization of autistic movement indicates the extent to which the unruly kinesthetic symptomologies of autistic embodiment have been interpreted as evidence of a degraded or impaired capacity to exercise rational agency and moral autonomy. This point is addressed directly in a 2011 letter that was sent to the Centers for Disease Control and Prevention's (CDC) National Center for Health Statistics and subsequently published on ASAN's website. Founded in 2006, the Autistic Self Advocacy Network is arguably the most prominent advocacy organization associated with the neurodiversity movement, whose proponents maintain that autism—as well as other forms of neurological difference, including conditions such as schizophrenia and bipolar disorder—should be both recognized and socially accommodated as an integral component of human variation.

The letter responds to a CDC proposal to adopt a "Code for Wandering" in its autism research program, with the aim of promoting "better data collection for and understanding of wandering and to prompt important discussions about safety among healthcare providers, caregivers, and the person with a disability."[50] The letter's signatories, expressing deep misgivings about the effects of such a code, suggest that it "could limit the self-determination rights of adults with disabilities."[51] The letter further contends that the code "makes no distinction between wandering behavior that would qualify for the coding and *a rational and willful effort* by an individual with a disability to remove oneself from a dangerous or uncomfortable situation."[52] Indeed, the letter writers' mention of "rational and willful effort" suggests that the ability to deliberately regulate the movements of one's body has been a primary criterion according to which the political privileges associated with rational personhood, agency, and autonomy are bestowed within the political tradition of liberal humanism.

A perceived diminishment in the capacity to control the movement of one's own body in space is one of the most important justifications used to strip disabled subjects of their autonomy through surveillance, social control, and other restrictive disciplinary measures. In this regard, the surveillance of autistic wandering might be understood as a matter of "choreopolicing," as proposed by dance theorist André Lepecki, who draws on two influential philosophical accounts of policing to describe the political mobilization of bodies by police power: Louis Althusser's account of the cop's hailing the individual on the street as an allegorical scene for how ideology conscripts us into subjectivity, and a contrasting account of the police more recently formulated by Jacques Rancière. For the latter, the policeman is not so much the embodiment of the ideological apparatus of the state. Instead, for Rancière, "the police" are the force that regulates, manages, and propels the kinetic movement and circulation of bodies in public spaces. The police are the ones who say, "Move along, there is nothing to see here!"[53] Based on Rancière's account, Lepecki offers the following definition of police power: "The police is that which is pregiven in the circulatory organization of the polis as what predetermines pathways, establishes routes for circulation, and fits both into one single mode of being. In that sense it does not hail. Instead, it choreographs."[54]

Situating anxieties about autistic wandering in a perspective that is attentive to the choreopolicing of bodily movement suggests a new way of considering how police and policing have increasingly come to the forefront of policy discussions concerning the safety of autistic and other neurodivergent individuals and groups. Autism Unites, a national autism organization run largely by the parents of autistic children that advocates "community integration" practices, hosts events with local police departments under the title "Be Safe" to "teach individuals with ASD to interact safely with the police in situations ranging from an everyday encounter to an arrest."[55] In this regard, we can consider the proposals to fund forensic GPS tracking devices in relation to such choreopolitical perspectives on the "policing of the synapse" as an ever more molecular attention to the workings of the brain within specific populations and territories has become more integrated into the techniques of police surveillance and the technologies developed to further its reach.[56]

Autistic wandering would seem to consist of the kind of unruly bodily movement that violates liberal conceptions of practical reason (a faculty that Kant defines according to a presupposition of "the will's independence of coercion through sensuous impulses"[57]). The sensuous impulses of autistic wandering pose a particular challenge to late liberalism's regimes of movement, which, as political theorist Hagar Kotef argues, determine "the means through which movement is produced as freedom or as threat."[58] As Black performance and cultural theory have illuminated, the figure of the fugitive who "evades the regularized and regulated paths of circulation—of goods, of persons, of information" occupies a rogue position within the rigidly ordered regimes of choreopolitical surveillance.[59] Indeed, wandering itself, as Sarah Jane Cervenak argues, has been a significant philosophical modality in response to the violent racial exclusions of Enlightenment rationality, which has persistently denigrated and pathologized Blackness by seeking to render it into a manageable object of scientific knowledge. Cervenak defines wandering as "errant, nonenunciative, unreadable movement" and suggests that such forms of movement are crucial strategies by which Black subjects have negotiated and resisted the forms of objectification and regulation to which they have been subjected.[60] Discussions of Blackness as fugitive, wandering movement suggest a gestalt shift in the terms through which recent responses to autistic wandering can be analyzed—a change in perspective and scale that would position the specific anxieties about autistic elopement that have surfaced in response to Oquendo's disappearance against, and in connection to, much further-reaching and historically encompassing legacies of Black pathologization. Indeed, these perspectives reveal that the very concepts of fugitivity and wandering are inseparable from the racialized schematizations endemic to liberal regimes of security.[61] From this perspective, it should perhaps not be surprising that the surveillance of subjects who have been identified with the tendency to stray from predetermined pathways and established routes for circulation has been increasingly entrusted to the domains of policing and police power.

Neither Avonte Oquendo's love of running nor his chafing against being constrained or confined can be unambiguously characterized in any easily definable sense. If Avonte's wandering has been made to stand in for the interests channeled through the legislation that bears his name, the question is not how these movements and trajectories are translated or interpreted as a cartography that would tell us something—into, that is, a hidden code or scrambled message. Rather, it is how a mode of witnessing, attending, being with, or watching might be cultivated that does not demand that autistic wanderings be made to mean something or speak something, but instead that they are respected and recognized as a mode of doing and acting.

These questions speak to the urgency of developing alternative ways of responding to the forms of errant movement evoked by terms such as *wandering* and *elopement*—ways that are organized instead around the possibility of embracing (rather than policing or pathologizing) the distinctive sensory dimensions of autistic embodiment or what could be called neurodivergent lifeworlds. Asking after such a potentiality is not, of course, akin to the urgent projects of developing alternative concrete practices that could help prevent deaths like Oquendo's from occurring again. But it does point us toward the urgency of developing alternative ways of accounting for—and responding to—those forms of bodily movement deemed errant, dangerous, or pathological, and it offers glimpses of alternative ways of sensing a "fugitive law of movement"—perhaps a very different Avonte's Law—that would open new cartographic trajectories at the conjunction of Black life and neurodivergence.[62] Rather than being mapped pathologically, perhaps such forms of movement and sensation might instead be considered according to Fred Moten's account of the "fugitive law of movement" that "makes black social life ungovernable" because it is that which constantly escapes and exceeds any "externally imposed social logic."[63] This law of movement poses a "para-ontological disruption of the supposed connection between explanation and resistance" that underlies the historical-racial schematizations that have produced a visual field riven with anxieties about ungovernable, errant forms of bodily movement.[64] It should not come as a surprise that the official response to minoritarian fugitivity has been to call for more surveillance.[65] Yet wandering need not be the occasion for the further intensification of the apparatuses of security. Can we conceive of a practice, or a politics, of neurodivergent and racialized embodiment that would also move errantly, fugitively away from such logics?

Keeping an Eye Out: Haptic Counter-cartographies

Until recently, the voices of autistic people themselves have been notably absent from most of the political, clinical, and cultural conversation about autistic wandering. The growing body of published writing about autism authored by autistic people as well as the continuously proliferating blogs, message boards, and discussion forums that make up the online neurodiversity community offer a rich archive of first-person insights into this important aspect of autistic embodiment and experience. One such account can be found in *The Reason I Jump,* a book by Naoki Higashida, a thirteen-year-old Japanese nonverbal autistic teenager who uses a facilitated communication (FC) system developed in tandem with his mother and a special education teacher. The book was translated into English in 2013 by British novelist David Mitchell and Japanese poet KA Yoshida. The book is structured as a series of fifty-eight questions about various aspects of Higashida's experiences of life with autism. One of the questions directly concerns elopement:

> Q50: Why do you wander off from home?
>
> A: Once, when I was a little kid at kindergarten, I wandered off from home and had to be picked up by the police. Back then, in fact, I used to leave home quite regularly and, as I look back from this distance, I can think of several reasons why I did it. It wasn't because I wanted to go out for a specific purpose, like wanting fresh air. It was because—this is hard to put into words—my body moved because it was lured outside by something there.
>
> As I was walking farther from home, I didn't feel any fear or anxiety. It came down to this: if I didn't go outside, then I would

> cease to exist. Why? I can't say, but I *had* to keep walking, on and on and on. Turning back was not permitted, because roads never come to an end. Roads speak to us people with autism, and invite us outward. There's not much logic in any of this, I know. Until someone brings us back home, we don't know what we've done, and then we're as shocked as anyone.
>
> I stopped wandering off from home on the day I very nearly got mowed down by a car, because the fear of it made a deep impact on my memory. So when something enough happens, I think we can rein in this habit of wandering off. Meanwhile, please keep an eye out for us.[66]

Among a number of striking elements in Higashida's account is the notable assertion that his impulse to wander farther and farther from home is directly tied to his existential persistence: "if I didn't go outside, then I would cease to exist." Higashida offers an account of autistic being rooted in his felt need to move outward toward the external environment. "Lured outside by something there," Higashida's sense of his body being pulled outside and along endless roadways challenges the limits of both his descriptive abilities ("this is hard to put into words") and what he recognizes to be the rational terms of intelligibility ("there's not much logic to any of this, I know"). The passage ends with Higashida's reassurance that once confronted by the potential dangers of elopement, autistic people can "rein in this habit of wandering off" if they are suitably instructed to avoid the dangers that they might face if their wandering habits continued unchecked.

Higashida's insightful and compassionate assertion that autistic people need the careful guardianship of those who are nonautistic to be aware of their wandering proclivities finds a pernicious political echo within recent policy and legislative efforts to expand the technological surveillance of neurologically disabled students through the "voluntary" use of GPS tracking devices for students enrolled in public schools. In place of Higashida's intensely personal request to his nonautistic readers to "please keep an eye out for us," such policies seek to expand the panoptic eye of surveillance through the ever-proliferating apparatuses of security that have come to characterize late liberal modes of governance. I want to invite us to think more carefully about the diverging ways of seeing that are involved in Higashida's request on the one hand, and the surveillance footage of Oquendo's fleeing form, on the other. How can we understand the gap between these two scopic regimes?

To ask this question, importantly, is not to ask how to translate or "interpret" these forms of errant movement into a counter-discourse—into, that is, a scrambled code or message addressed to a (neurotypical) "us,"—but rather how modes of witnessing, attending, being with, or watching might be cultivated that do not demand that Avonte Oquendo's "wanderings" be made to mean something or say something, but rather that they be respected as an aspect or characteristic of the singularity and distinctivenesss of his mode of being. Heeding this call does not discount the importance or even the necessity of pursuing practical, strategic tactics that can be applied in the here and now. But it remains aware that these are bound to be provisional and contingent, and liable to be absorbed and reintegrated into the logics and procedures that produced the need for them to begin with. The ways in which legislative solutions set forth in bills such as Avonte's Law, which seek to provide federal and state funding to law enforcement agencies to track the wandering tendencies ascribed to autism and autistics by expanding the forensic apparatuses of the criminal justice system, must be understood in relationship to longer histories of surveillance as a technique of power, especially as it operates at the nexus of disability and racial difference.

Errant Cognitive Mapping

Maps and cartographic diagrams are not simply visual representations of the ways space is organized within an existing social order, but forceful *agents* that "grid life according to the force-patterns [they impose] on social bodies."[67] Modern techniques of mapping reveal "the ways that human experience is spatialized according to strategic operations" of disciplinary power.[68] Between the ligne d'erre that is traced through a "becoming visible of form"[69] and the "wandering characteristics" glimpsed as spectral pixelation on a security camera still and tracked by police surveillance via GPS devices, we have found ourselves at the conjunction of the counter-cartographic and the choreopolitical.

Borrowing and perhaps deforming a concept from Fredric Jameson, might we describe such practices as an *errant cognitive mapping?* Cognitve mapping is a concept first proposed by British geographer Kevin Lynch to describe the practical strategies individual city dwellers employ to navigate and make sense of urban environments that are increasingly difficult to conceptualize in their spatial totality.[70] For Jameson, cognitive mapping provided a metaphor for tracking how specific aesthetic works are shaped by the local, provisional, and *practical* strategies that individual subjects develop in order to negotiate "the gap between phenomenological perception and a reality that transcends all individual thinking or experience."[71] As such, Jameson's cognitive mapping is an aesthetic procedure that arises at the nexus between the realm of individual experience and the abstract reality of a social structure that is unknowable in its full totality. For Jameson, as Colin McCabe writes, cognitive mapping is "the missing psychology of the political unconscious," which is to say it lends a psychological dimension to broader historical and structural considerations and is situated where the psychic meets the social.[72]

In turn, cognitive mapping and other minor or counter-cartographic practices have been increasingly described in performative terms by critical geography scholars. Geographer Joe Gerlach maintains that "all cartographic articulations are caught up in some form of theatrics, a staging of propositions, claims and anticipations."[73] Attuning us to what he calls the vital role that "vernacular mapping" has played in a range of social and political struggles, Gerlach maintains that understanding the performative dimensions of mapmaking is crucial to "wresting maps away from accounts of their neutral or mirroring propensities." For Gerlach, "vernacular mappings involve bodily gestures, movements, motions, disruptions and liminal space-times which orientate and disorientate each other." But though these movements, gestures, and disruptions "can be sketched and diagrammed," they can never be "captured fully." What remain unmappable are "performances that exceed representation and refuse compartmentalization into subject-object relations."[74] Autistic author Donna Williams, in her book *Autism and Sensing,* offers a provocative account of her own cartographic approach to navigating the sensorium in a passage that recalls Jameson's emphasis on the practical and embodied dimensions of cognitive mapping: "I developed physically-based mapping, which involved knowing things not through their visual shape but through their shape experienced through my own physical movement. So, for example, if I felt a glass with my hands or gripped it in my teeth, my concept of that glass had nothing to do with the word 'glass' or with how it looked or what it was used for, it had to do with the pattern of movement involved in feeling its form."[75] Indeed, Williams's description of mapping as a process of physical movement, patterning, and feeling of form is additionally illuminating for the discussions of autistic wandering and elopement that have been considered in this chapter.

It is equally suggestive for returning to Pope.L's "failure drawings" and Crawls, now with a renewed attention to the counter-cartographic impulse they express: one that is more attuned to the lower frequencies of acting and being that take place at the margins of the human community than it is to a disruptive program of urban revolutionary action. Pope.L explains, "My earliest idea for crawls, from the very beginning, involved groups but alas alack I was the only crawler available at that time."[76] Though he was able to eventually arrange for a number of group Crawls as the project grew and evolved, Pope.L insists that the experience of the group Crawl fundamentally differs from the solo crawl: "Even when I do a group crawl, I do not feel the choc-a-block of feelings I have when doing solo crawls. Maybe cause group crawls have a definite finish line. Solo crawls usually had no clearly defined stopping point."[77] In a solo Crawl, Pope.L observes, "ideas like goal or direction or motivation or motility or even being escape me like the air of out of a potato chip bag."[78] He continues:

> The hardest aspect of solo crawling to describe and, in a way, the most interesting aspect is what happens to me inside. I believe some of the feelings and mental states I experience have to do with merely engaging in a marathon activity. When I say "merely" I do not mean un-important. One of the most difficult aspects of prolonged and willed discomfort is mental perambulation – the creamy nougat center of being, as it were – very messy. All sorts of nonsense gets a foot in there, in the noggin. Maybe it's a lack of oxygen, maybe the heat or cold, the carbon monoxide from cars, the pain, the exhaustion, the fear that you might never walk again, all the old fears and a few new ones.[79]

The following chapter continues to pursue this trajectory, expanding further on the haptic, performatively material surplus that renovates the sensorium of the streets and byways of the premapped, premade, gridded world—a haptic, unmappable surplus evoked by the aimless yet richly attuned counter-cartographies elaborated by Higashida, Williams, and Pope.L—by turning to consider how questions of neurodivergent voice and voicings have become the grounds for deep political and aesthetic contestation.

4

The Missing Voice

> It seems indeed that if, in autistic beings, the voice is lacking, it is because the voice has missed them as beings—or that these beings have missed their voices, as we would say of a tennis player who wasn't in the right position to receive and return the ball.
>
> —Fernand Deligny, "The Missing Voice"

An anthology of writings by autistic people published in 2012 by members of ASAN entitled *Loud Hands: Autistic People, Speaking* reflects the seemingly contradictory position occupied by the autistic "speaking subject," in both its title and in the essays it contains.[1] The phrase "loud hands" refers to how behavioral specialists often instruct autistic children to practice "quiet hands," to encourage them to resist the desire to stim.

What might be alternative ways of addressing voice as a key point of contention within the history of autism and neurological difference, particularly concerning the assessment of an individual's capacity for linguistic expression through speech? With the emergence of autistic self-advocacy and the advent of neurodiversity discourses in the 1990s, this point has been especially contested in the ongoing debates over the diagnostic distinction between LFA and HFA, which is largely (though by no means exclusively) made on the basis of an individual's perceived or assessed capacity for verbal communication. Many autistic self-advocates and neurodiversity proponents reject the validity of such distinctions; in response, some critics of neurodiversity—many of them family members and caretakers of individuals labeled as low functioning—have argued that rejecting such distinctions glosses over and marginalizes the needs and experiences of low-functioning autistic people.

Rather than attempting to resolve this debate, I examine works that point toward ways of reframing its terms. I focus on how these works navigate the relation between *voice* and *touch.* As I will suggest, these works proceed by way of a patient interrogation of the aesthetic and political consequences that might follow once the "voice"—understood as that "phonic substance" that both supports and exceeds the verbal utterance[2]—is (re)routed and (re)circuited through *tactility*—a sensory mode that also involves proximate vocabularies of *texture, pressure,* and *haptics.* In different but complementary ways, the works I discuss in this chapter draw attention to the gaps, elisions, and misrecognitions that are inevitably produced when the capacity for verbal language is no longer considered the primary criterion for being granted the status of full, autonomous personhood. Indeed, the use of voice and touch found in these works unsettles efforts to distinguish between high and low functioning levels within the broader discursive field of autism research and treatment and reveals such efforts to be a symptomatic extension of the broader processes and techniques of normalization within which autism and neurological difference have attained coherence over the past half century. Prompted by these aesthetic cross-hatchings, the chapter also explores how recent efforts to consider autism in relationship to gender and sexuality have been marked by preoccupations and anxieties having to do with touch, tactility, and bodily pressure. What embodied and performative strategies might challenge and unsettle neurotypical understandings of the alignments between body and voice, language and gesture, sensation and identity?

The aesthetic strategies discussed here can be situated in a longer history concerning how works of theater and performance can reflect on—and perhaps intervene in—their own social and historical conditions. Mel Baggs's 2007 YouTube video *In My Language* and Wu Tsang's 2008 video art piece *The Shape of the Right Statement* work against normative conceptions of language through specific aesthetic and performative strategies, seeking to reroute and refigure how (bodily) *sensation* is linked to contemporary articulations of (collective, social, and political) *identity.*[3] This is especially evident in the extent to which Baggs, Tsang, and Berger uncover unexpected performative and epistemological resonances between FC technologies used by individuals with communication-based impairments and the queer performance techniques of drag and lip-synching.[4]

Queer and disabled modes of subjectivity and taxonomies of personhood are each positioned within broader histories of normalization. Yet these works also point toward wayward trajectories within these broader histories, unsettling any straightforward understanding of the alignment between bodily sensation, political identification, and verbal expression.[5]

Jonathan Berger's *An Introduction to Nameless Love,* like the other examples considered in this chapter, was created in direct response to and in engagement with the historical emergence of the concept of neurodiversity. Previous chapters in this study have focused on events and practices situated, for the most part, historically before the advent of neurodiversity so named; they looked back on earlier moments in light of later developments. I use the term *neurodiversity* both to designate the specific social movements organized around the concept of autistic self-advocacy that began to take shape in the 1990s and to more generally denote the range of political claims and theoretical consequences that continue to be generated in the wake of these movements. This chapter endeavors to bring the considerations of the voice within both fields to bear on the question of how performance enables autistic and neurodivergent modes of expression, resistance, and subversive formations of neurodivergent lifeworlds.

When approaching *An Introduction to Nameless Love,* the viewer at first encounters an almost overwhelming sequence of large, semitranslucent rectangular panels that appear suspended throughout the large gallery space in a range of configurations. Some simply hang vertically, displayed like monochromatic works of stained glass; others are positioned side by side at diagonal angles with doorway-like spaces between them, allowing visitors to pass through them, or slanted upward and orthogonally paired, suggesting the pages of an enormous open book. The panels, which seem to oscillate between transparency and opacity as the viewer moves through the space in which they are installed, are themselves made up of lines of text—sentences and words consisting of individual letters that are forged from carved tin and soldered into readable order via the large frames that suspend the panels in space.

The installation has taken on quite divergent forms to suit the spatial contours of the various institutional spaces where it has appeared: first at the Carpenter Center for the Visual Arts at Harvard University, then at Participant Inc., an independent gallery on the Lower East Side of

Figure 9. Jonathan Berger, *Untitled* (Emily Anderson and Mark Utter, with Erica Heilman), 2019, tin, nickel, charcoal; dimensions variable; in *An Introduction to Nameless Love,* installation view at Participant Inc., New York, 2020. Co-commissioned and copresented by The Carpenter Center for the Visual Arts, Cambridge, Mass., and Participant Inc., New York. Copyright Jonathan Berger. Courtesy of the artist, The Carpenter Center for the Visual Arts, Participant Inc., Luhring Augustine, New York, and VEDA, Florence. Photo by Mark Waldhauser.

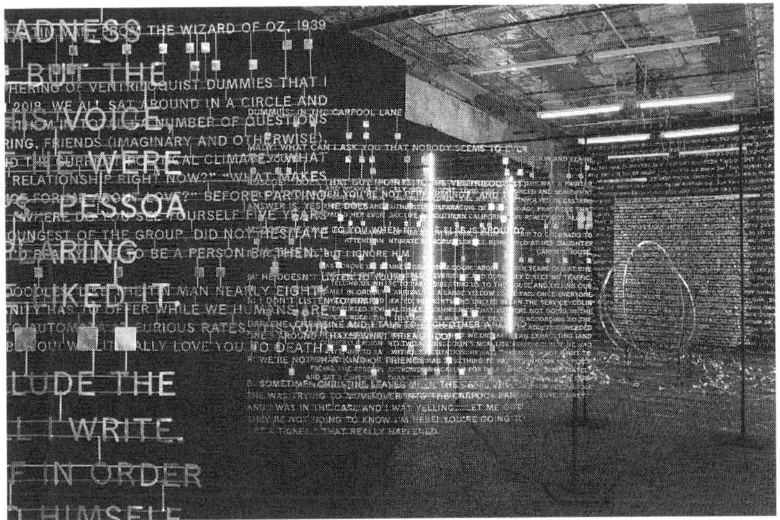

Figure 10. Jonathan Berger, *An Introduction to Nameless Love,* 2019, tin, nickel, charcoal; dimensions variable; installation view at Participant Inc., New York, 2020. Co-commissioned and copresented by The Carpenter Center for the Visual Arts, Cambridge, Mass., and Participant Inc., New York. Copyright Jonathan Berger. Courtesy of the artist, The Carpenter Center for the Visual Arts, Participant Inc., Luhring Augustine, New York, and VEDA, Florence. Photo by Mark Waldhauser.

Manhattan, and subsequently at the Whitney Museum as part of the 2022 Whitney Biennial, among others. But in all these iterations, the effect of moving through the installation is strikingly multisensory. The sheer size of the panels, the subtly dramatic lighting that illuminates them, and the way that the deliberate placement of the suspensions bisect and mold the space all combine to produce a feeling of hushed reverence that makes the experience of walking through the room akin to entering sacred space. This effect is compounded by the unusual floor treatment that undergirds the installation's more immediately apparent vertical elements: a grid of irregularly shaped, inch-long square charcoal briquettes that first become apparent through a surprising shift in the textured feeling of the floor beneath the visitor's feet when entering the installation. This charcoal landscape has a subtle but unmistakable transformative effect on what audiologists would call the "room tone" of the gallery in which the work is installed, as distinct from the spaces that surround it. Upon spending more time moving through the work, this distinctive sonic tonality of quietness is complemented by the subtle but unmistakable smell—and, indeed, if one lingers long enough, a hint of the "taste"—of the materials that have gone into the work's construction and manufacture. One thus senses, in multiple ways, the charcoal, which subtly degrades and loosens over time through the accumulated pressure of the viewers' footsteps, in combination with the metallic residue of the tin letters: "Comprised of some 33,000 one-inch tin letters, meticulously fashioned by Berger and a team of associates, each letter was soldered by hand to nickel wire and affixed in various configurations," as the curatorial statement accompanying the installation explains. "Imbued with a reverence for their subject, evidenced in the detail, effort, and labor of the human hand, the sculptures create unique embodiments of the stories they tell."[6]

The words that are spelled out in tin on the panels are drawn from a series of texts and dialogues relating unusual or distinctive relationships that exist beyond the parameters of conventional romance. One set of panels contains words exchanged between the married couple Charles and Ray Eames, the well-known midcentury furniture designers and architects; another includes an interview with turtle conservationist Richard Ogust describing his relationship with the shelled reptiles he has spent his life studying; still other panels include the words of Brother Arnold Hadd, described as one of the last remaining Shakers in America, and Maria A. Prado, a former resident of the New York City underground homeless community known as the Tunnel.[7]

The installation panels contain text of dialogues and writings by autistic writer and philosopher Mark Utter and Emily Anderson, who worked with Utter for several years as his facilitative communication aide. Utter lived under the diagnosis and assumption of nonverbal autism until he was in his early thirties, when he learned a technique of supported typing that enabled him to communicate using text-to-speech software, which he uses with the support of a human facilitator. The role of this aide, who assists him by gently applying pressure to his arm, proprioceptively orienting himself toward the use of the keyboard, is absolutely crucial to Utter's ability to gain a voice but strictly supportive in the bodily sense of a human presence.

Berger understands the core of his artistic practice as chronicling forms of what he categorizes as "love" in the lives of others. The work's title,

Nameless Love, drawn from an interview with poet Allan Ginsberg that appeared in *Gay News Network* in 1975, points us toward what cannot be named—or perhaps, indeed, voiced—by the texts that appear on the transparent flat solidities that the viewers move through. The artist describes the installation as "an examination of the profound intensity and depth of meaning most often associated with 'true love,' but found instead through bonds based in work, friendship, religion, service, mentorship, community, and family—as well as between people and themselves, places, objects, and animals. Even as they are persistently unacknowledged by contemporary society at large, these instances [of] 'nameless love' nonetheless enable people to live wholly fulfilling lives steeped in tenderness, ardor, empathy, care, vulnerability, salvation, redemption, and pleasure."[8]

The panels in Berger's installation, as critic Cate McQuaid notes, "are not easy to read; they perch on a narrow perceptual precipice between reading and looking, between text and object. Light and shadow play over their hammered surfaces, obscuring words. To read a whole sentence, you have to move. You have to concentrate."[9] The effort that it takes the viewer to discern the words and sentences on the panels evokes, without replicating, the painstaking slowness of the process by which Utter spells out, letter by letter—and with Anderson's facilitation—the words that we, the viewers, now struggle to read. With this effect, we enter into a different temporality with respect to language and communication, so often (at least for the neurotypical) experienced as frictionless and transparent. But we are also compelled into a disconcerting and almost alienating *spatialization* of language—and indeed of the material impediments that get in the way of the process by which letters come to form words and sentences that somehow bear the meaning from a speaker to a listener, or a writer to a reader. It is here that Berger's installation stages—and I am tempted to say *theatricalizes*—the dilemma of the voice in shaping the possibilities and limitations of neurodivergent lifeworlds—*voice* here understood as connected to a phonic substance that both supports and exceeds its function as the material/sonic carrier of meaning within speech.

But in *An Introduction to Nameless Love,* the time and substance of voice are not absent, even if the experience of viewing the work itself is marked by a certain reverential silence; rather, I am interested in how this putatively absent or missing voice—which, as Fernand Deligny has noted, is so often imputed to so-called nonverbal autistic subjects, incapable of speaking on their own behalf—is in effect re-presented, or perhaps experientially retemporalized and spatialized, by the process of moving through the room. The process of viewing this installation takes time. In its materialization as a work of installation art, *An Introduction to Nameless Love* effectively produces a sense of voice that materializes as a spatialization of an otherwise temporal, sonic, textual, and phonic phenomenon. Voice itself is made into a room that the viewer walks through. Indeed, the installation format that Berger created seems to directly allude to Utter's observations, quoted in the text reproduced in tin letters on an installation panel, about his unique way of experiencing the temporal relationship of language and information:

> Q: Did your experience of the passage of time change with language?
>
> A: Oh, I love time. I can condense it or expand it somewhat. I can move back in time because of the way my mind holds information.[10]

Berger's installation is in this sense a mediation of a mediation. A sort of deferred theatricalization is also at work in *Nameless Love,* in the sense that most texts reproduced on wall-sized panels of tin letters are dialogic, or at least allude to a back-and-forth. In the case of the texts of Utter and Anderson, one of the panels is literally in the form of a theatrical script—which Utter describes as a "tragedy." In the installation's excerpt, which Utter entitled "Doll's House Movements: Out into the World," we read of Mark's wish to hold onto Emily even as their relationship comes into conflict with Emily's own needs, once she asserts the need to leave her role as his facilitator:

> SCENE I
>
> M: I LONG TO MAKE THIS WAY OF BEING LAST FOREVER.
>
> E: THIS IS NOT POSSIBLE. I NEED TO NOT BE A PERSON HELD FOR SO LONG IN THIS ROLE OF COMMUNICATION SUPPORT.
>
> M: WILL YOU SOMETIMES SUPPORT MY THOUGHTS COMING OUT?
>
> E: ON THE TABLE IS THE BOOK I HAVE ASSISTED YOU IN CREATING. IN IT ARE LOTS OF THINGS I HAVE LEARNED ABOUT YOU AND YOUR LARGER WAY OF LOOKING AT THE WORLD. THIS IS GOING TO ASSIST YOU AMAZINGLY.

M: HALLELUJAH. I KNOW IT EASILY WILL FILL THE SPACE YOU ARE LEAVING. ARGH. THIS IS PAINFUL. DO NOT GO.

E: I WILL ALWAYS THINK OF YOU AND OUR WORK TOGETHER AND WHAT AN IMPACT WE HAVE HAD ON EACH OTHER'S LIVES.

M: MAY I EMAIL YOU?

E: YES. IT WILL BE SUCH A PLEASURE TO HEAR FROM YOU.

This exchange, so dense with tenderness, ambivalence, and desperation, dramatizes precisely the dilemma of the nameless but imminently concrete and material contours of forms of relationality in which the status of voice and voicelessness is produced and contested. Here I would also like to note that Utter himself was delighted by Berger's installation, of which he wrote on his blog: "Jonathan Berger's Introduction to Nameless Love is an amazing feat. For a guy like me who slowly gets letters out, it is a wondrous celebration of quite equally impressive production. Thousands of tin letters make up this show. Emily and I have our long-time working relationship on display in the form of edited interviews and a dramatic piece of writing. It shares a room with two other explorations of life through words."[11]

What novel ways of conceptualizing the aesthetic and political consequences might follow once the voice—understood as a phonic substance that both supports and exceeds the verbal utterance—is (re)routed and (re)circuited through tactility? Voice here becomes haptic, but also a switch point for other sensorial relays: between touch and sight, but also smell, sound, and taste. In particular, by attending to the formal aesthetic strategies through which works such as Berger's installation mediate the relation between *voice* and *touch,* we can glimpse modes of personhood and sensorial attunement that are often unrecognized but that are nonetheless vital to the persistence, survival, and flourishing of neurodivergent lifeworlds.

The problem of the autistic subject's voice has been a perennial concern within the scientific and cultural history of autism since the days of Leo Kanner in the decades surrounding World War II. The clinical literature has evinced a nearly obsessive level of interest in the patterns, tones, and pitch vocalized by autistic children. Much early psychiatric research on autism focused on what researchers termed *echolalia,* in which autistic children were identified as being especially prone to mimicking the speech sounds of others in a manner that Kanner and others characterized as "rote and literal."[12] The "problem" of echolalia is considered one of the most telling symptoms of the communicational, behavioral, and social "deficits" that continue to make up the disorder's diagnostic criteria. Echolalia and other vocal attributes associated with autism, in other words, have been taken as evidence of autistic subjects' obsessive and perseverative behavioral tendencies, difficulties in communicating verbally, and ultimately failure to (in the words of Kanner) "relate themselves in the ordinary way to people and situations."[13] While there have been significant scientific and therapeutic advances in the medical research and psychiatric treatment paradigms used to address the pathologized speech patterns and vocal behaviors of persons diagnosed with autism in the ensuing decades, echolalic speech continues to be one of the primary diagnostic hallmarks of autism and associated ASDs.

Venturing beyond the clinical precincts of the psychiatric literature and scientific research, it is equally clear that processes involving voicing and verbal speech have been major points of contention in the wider cultural terrain within which the politics of autism, mental disability, and neurological difference have taken shape. Indeed, the assertion of voice in its more abstract or metaphorical dimensions—which is to say the capacity of articulating one's subjective experiences, needs, and desires in ways that can gain recognition and accommodation within a broader social world—has been at the heart of the ethical and political claims of neurodiversity discourse and rhetoric. Neurodiversity has taken as its principal aim the project of making space for the "voices" of autistic people and others stigmatized as neurologically atypical (even though the form that such appeals have taken is language and speech based).

Shaping the Statement

In 2007, Mel Baggs uploaded an eight-minute video to YouTube entitled *In My Language.* The video opens with a shot of Baggs's upper body in silhouette against a window and shows her repetitively flapping her hands. The video soon cuts to a shot of Baggs scraping a basin with a wooden tool, then scratching a plastic corrugated surface with her fingertips, and next batting a piece of string with her hands. Further shots follow; we see Baggs rubbing her face with the pages of a magazine and running her hand over a metal grate, and finally a close-up of her hand flapping gently against a window. The soundtrack to these images is Baggs's voice, emitting a soft but sustained hum. At about the four-minute mark, the screen goes black, and the single word "Translation" appears center screen. We next fade up on a close-up of Baggs's fingers flipping gently beneath a stream of water flowing from a bathroom sink faucet. A computerized (female) voice begins to speak. (Baggs uses a text-to-speech voice-generating software program to speak—a process that falls within the category of FC.) In Baggs's video, the computer-spoken text is accompanied by subtitles:

> The previous part of this video was in my native language. Many people have assumed that when I talk about this being my language that means that each part of the video must have a particular symbolic message within it designed for the human mind to interpret. But my language is not about designing words or even visual symbols for people to interpret. It is about being in a constant conversation with every aspect of my environment. Reacting physically to all parts of my surroundings.[14]

Baggs writes in the description accompanying the video on YouTube that it is "a statement about what gets considered thought, intelligence, personhood, language, and communication, and what does not."[15] In this way, Baggs insists that the capacity for complex symbolization—a capacity autistic minds are frequently presumed to lack—should not be taken as equivalent to language and communication as such. Baggs reconfigures language through the body's sensory interaction with its environment and the environment's interaction with the body.

Soon after it was posted online, Baggs's video began to circulate among members of various online autism self-advocacy communities, in which she is an active participant, and the video's popularity soon began to rise, quickly surpassing half a million views. It caught the attention of CNN and *Wired* magazine, both of which featured stories on Baggs, describing her video work as putting "a new face on autism"[16] and providing a glimpse "behind the veil" of autistic experience. Baggs, who was living in public housing for people with disabilities in Vermont, vehemently objected to interpretations that frame her video and online writing in such terms. "I've said a million times I'm not trapped in my own world," she told *Wired*. "Yet what do most of these news stories lead with? Saying exactly that."[17]

Despite Baggs's objections to the misreadings to which it has been subjected, *In My Language* has gone on to become one of the best-known and frequently viewed statements associated with neurodiversity and autistic self-advocacy. The video has also attracted a significant amount of critical and scholarly attention. Anthropologist Paul Antze, for example, discusses Baggs's video in relationship to the broader ethical dimensions of autistic and disability self-advocacy. He argues that Baggs's video reflects an unresolved tension within the political rhetoric of neurodiversity between an appeal to the tenets of liberal universalism and a more radical critique of the liberal sensorium in which medicalized and pathologizing accounts of autism, mental disability, and neurological difference have been produced and disciplined.[18] Media theorist Mark Coté, for his part, suggests that Baggs's video is indicative of the new sensory affordances made possible through widespread access to digital technology and the internet, suggesting that *In My Language* reflects a newly democratized landscape of media production in which "the human and

Figure 11. Still from Mel Baggs's *In My Language.* The fingers of Baggs's left hand are shown wiggling beneath a stream of water flowing from an unseen faucet into the basin of a sink, above a caption that reads, "The water doesn't symbolize anything." YouTube video, 2007.

technics are in transductive relation." Indeed, Coté suggests that Baggs's video shows how digital videos like these "stake out a new mediated realm of the senses."[19] For both of these authors, Baggs's emphasis on the particularity of her experience of language serves as the occasion for broader reflections on ethics, politics, technology, and the senses.

Erin Manning discusses Baggs's video in her philosophical reflections on perception and individuation. For Manning, *In My Language*—and most pointedly the rhetorical strategies at play within the video's spoken text—offers insight into phenomenological dimensions of autism. Referring to Baggs's video, Manning writes that for autistic people, "it's not that communication doesn't happen, it's that communication is everywhere amplified by the more-than of its apparent content."[20] In Manning's reading, the "language" of Baggs's autism operates according to a nonrepresentational syntax that collapses distinctions between referent, concept, and expression through the felt force of an encounter, creating what she describes as "a symphony of complex inframodal relations between

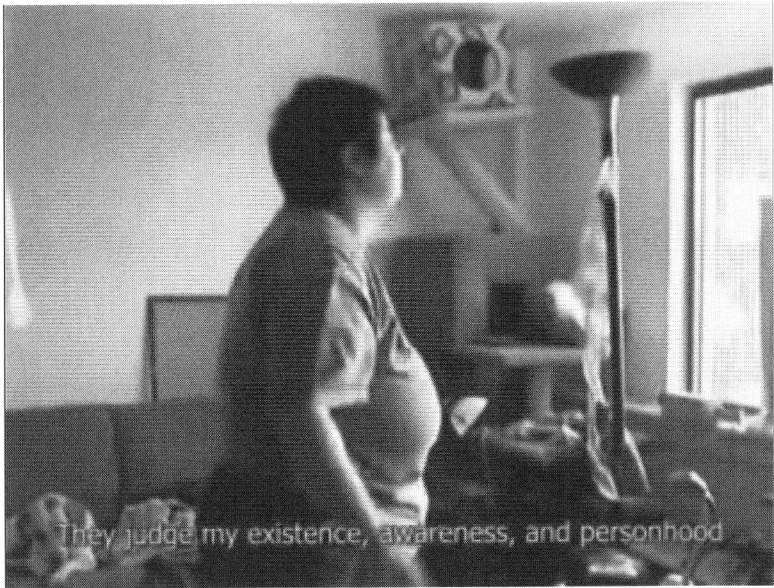

Figure 12. Still from Mel Baggs's *In My Language.* Baggs is shown in profile standing in the middle of a living room, facing a window, while a caption at the bottom of the screen reads, "They judge my existence, awareness, and personhood." YouTube video, 2007.

objects, gesture, and sound."[21] Still, Manning seems to imply that autistic people are (perhaps uniquely) capable of encountering the world "as it really is," in all of its sensory plenitude. Such quasi-romantic and almost mystical discussions of autistic perception risk glossing over, or even ignoring, the lived experiences and material struggles of autistic people, and precisely in ways that mirror the political logics that Baggs's video itself warns against.[22] This is not to suggest that philosophical or aesthetic approaches should not be applicable to discussions of autism and the cultural production of autistic people. Rather, it is meant to indicate the importance of emphasizing the theoretical and conceptual operations that are already at work within the quotidian modes of experience represented within Baggs's video.

The Shape of the Right Statement, a five-minute work of HD digital video art created in 2008 by Los Angeles–based artist and filmmaker Wu Tsang, responds to *In My Language* in ways that are decidedly different from most critical and scholarly assessments of Baggs's work. Tsang's piece consists of a single, static shot of the artist directly facing the viewer, seated in front of a shimmering, silvery backdrop. Tsang wears a collarbone-exposing black top, thin gold chain necklace, and elastic beige wig cap. With a fixed and unblinking gaze, she recites excerpts from the text voiced in the second half of Baggs's original video. Despite its apparent formal simplicity and visual directness, Tsang's video is distinguished by the virtuosic achievement of the artist's vocal performance, which mimics the sonic valances of Baggs's speech-generating software with remarkable, even uncanny, precision. As the work progresses, the artist's concentration and her effortful exertions to evoke the sonic qualities of the computerized speech heard in Baggs's earlier video become gradually more discernible in her face, as tears begin to pool in the corners of her eyes and eventually stream down her cheeks.

The Shape of the Right Statement was filmed at the Silver Platter, a local dive bar in Los Angeles's MacArthur Park neighborhood that for many years served a predominantly Latino/a, lower- and working-class gay and transgender clientele, a large number of whom were also undocumented immigrants. For several years in the early to mid-2000s, the Silver Platter was the location of Wildness, a weekly queer party run by Tsang and several friends and collaborators from the Los Angeles performance art and nightlife communities. During this time, the Silver Platter provided

Figure 13. Installation view of Wu Tsang, *The Shape of the Right Statement* (2008). HD video. Courtesy of NoguerasBlanchard Barcelona/Madrid. Photo by Roberto Ruiz.

Tsang with a space to create works of art and performance within a local context that was both generative of and fraught with political tensions related to the potentials and limitations of forging alliances and communities across several lines of social difference.[23] The numerous works of video, visual art, and performance that Tsang and her collaborators produced there reflect the bare-bones glamour that made the bar into a fragile site for exploring the possibilities of social coalition and collective creation. Unabashedly engaging the politics of marginalization, these works grapple with overlapping—but unevenly distributed and experienced—positions of social exclusion.

The Shape of the Right Statement was Tsang's first attempt to make artwork using a performance technique that the artist has come to call "full body quotation," in which performers speak and embody previously existing texts or recorded documents. Tsang describes the technique as follows:

> Full body quotation is a performance technique I've been working on, but the name could change as it evolves. The performer has a hidden audio

> source and she re-speaks voices mimetically—not just the text but tone, breath, accent, idiom, etc. The idea is to question authenticity and intention of the speaker, and understand content differently, out of its original context. For the two films in the Triennial, I was working with really different source material, and at very different times. The earlier film "SRS" *[Shape of a Right Statement]* is quoting [Mel] Baggs an autism rights activist, who at the time I was very interested in cross-identification between autism rights and trans/gay rights as being struggles to de-pathologize so-called "conditions" of being autistic, etc. This new film "FHWPALT3" *[For How We Perceived a Life (Take 3)]* is quoting various sources from research and field work about the making of Jennie Livingston's 1990 documentary, "Paris is Burning." In both instances, I chose material where the performers all had complicated relationships to the sources. The full body quotation technique is a way to perform our ambivalences.[24]

Here, Tsang allows us to read a performance technique that involves specific and precisely defined *bodily* practices—involving speech, but also "breath, accent, idiom, etc."—in relation to the explicitly *political* projects it is intended to advance. Tsang's full body quotation might thus be understood as a formal aesthetic strategy that uses the performing body, and voice, to index relational dynamics such as identification, empathy, and coalitional alliance—and especially to register the hazards (what the artist calls "ambivalences") that surround and support such relational structures. The very nomenclature of Tsang's technique—full body quotation—highlights the corporeal dimensions of the rhetorical citationality exhibited in *The Shape of the Right Statement.* Tsang's technique directly and explicitly reveals the political ramifications of the link between body and voice. Furthermore, Tsang associates this vocal and bodily technique with the struggle against pathologization that is shared by people with autism on the one hand, and transgender and queer subjects on the other. In *The Shape of the Right Statement,* the shared struggle for depathologization is linked to the physical exertions of the performing body by way of a virtuosic feat of vocal mimicry.

When viewed together, *In My Language* and *The Shape of the Right Statement* suggest that recent political movements organized around depathologizing understandings of autism, mental disability, and neurological difference (on the one hand) and those having to do with nonnormative forms of gender and sexuality (on the other) should not be conceived as simply parallel or analogous projects. Indeed, these works demonstrate how the politics of neurological difference and those of sexual and gender difference—especially the historical (and ongoing) relation of each of these mobilizations to struggles for depathologization—are more tightly enmeshed than might be immediately apparent. Moreover, these video works help illuminate why this is so by drawing out a set of interconnected relations between voice and touch, language and the body, and (political) identity and (corporeal) sensation. In the section that follows, I consider in greater detail how and why the voice—understood as that which provides the phonic substance of speech and therefore is situated at the place where language meets the body, even as it exceeds the terms of this relation—has been a key topic of contestation within clinical and cultural representations of autism and adjacent forms of neurological difference involving the impairment of communicative functions.

Seeing, Touching, Voicing

As the text of *In My Language* indicates, the autistic subject's vexed relation to language draws attention to what might be called the existential, even ontological trouble that autism and other disabilities affecting rhetorical capacities might be said to represent. Indeed, Baggs and other neurodiversity self-advocates have developed alternative accounts of the place of voice, speech, and language within the political and philosophical consolidation of the human as an autonomous, self-reflective, sovereign subject. (In so doing, they also echo Fernand Deligny's critique of Althusser's account of subjectivity as being formed by the vocal hail of ideology, and the former's subsequent attention for finding the autistic subject's "missing" voice in his experimental cinematic and cartographic projects.) The bifurcated structure of *In My Language* reflects the paradoxical political mandate that the essentially nonverbal aspects of autism and other forms of neurological difference must be rendered into verbal terms to become capable of receiving broader political recognition and accommodation.

The aesthetic procedures found in the video works by Baggs and Tsang reflect the political ramifications of debates surrounding the status of autistic function, particularly in how these videos elaborate an alternative relation between vocal and tactile sensory registers. *In My Language* begins with a sound, a soft, almost gentle hum, not quite a song or melody but instead a kind of intoned refrain oscillating between several low pitches. The voice is identifiably feminine and is largely responsible for lending the video a haunting, almost mournful sonic atmosphere. Along with the sounds made by Baggs's manipulation of objects—scraping, hitting, stroking—this humming generates the entirety of the sound world of the video's first half and shapes the sequence of images it accompanies according to an audibly continuous, if not quite musical, organizing structure. Baggs's humming departs from the typical function of the voice as the phonic-material support for verbal expression—as, that is to say, the supplemental, bodily substratum of speech (and hence of communication and its attendant facilitation of intersubjective exchange, recognition, and sociality). Instead, Baggs's humming reveals the human voice to be another means by which the body physically engages, negotiates, and interacts with the materiality of the world. The hum of Baggs's voice seems to function as a palpable anchor or barrier, delimiting the boundary between (human) self and (object) world. Complementing the images of Baggs's deliberate, rhythmic, and repetitive bodily movements, the humming becomes an almost pliable sonic surface—a ground (but also a ceiling and a wall) on or against which Baggs marks out a certain territory of action and negotiates the terrain between herself and the quotidian world of domestic objects that surrounds her.

In the latter "Translation" half of the video, Baggs's nonverbal humming is replaced by a computerized voice generated by DynaVox, the speech-generating software that Baggs uses to communicate verbally. While the incidental sounds produced as Baggs interacts with the objects of her environment persist (we hear, for instance, water trickle as it runs over her fingers and into the sink), the video's mode of address shifts dramatically with the introduction of the sound of the spoken text. In contrast to the first half of the video's distinctly amorphous visual and sonic composition, the directness and forthrightness of Baggs's words lend the latter half of the video the quality of a manifesto. Yet the semantic content that this voice communicates to its viewer-listeners reaches us at a remove from its putative origin, having been first manually typed as written text into a text-to-speech computer program and subsequently voiced by way of the computer's technological apparatuses that facilitate the production of sounds that are recognizable and decipherable as words and sentences.

Tsang's full body quotation, discussed earlier, has at least two significant referents woven through her decision to bring Baggs's video into the context of a queer club space. The first is lip-synching, a performance technique associated with virtuosic drag performance. The second is the assistive technology that Baggs uses in her video to generate speech. In each case, the act of speaking—and the self-presence that is assumed to undergird it—is fractured and displaced, attaining a more complex and lasting *temporal* dimension. This gap between enunciation and enunciator is responsible for a specific kind of frisson in which the unseen source of a given sound produces an anxiety in the viewer/auditor. In Tsang's piece, this gap is closed and resolved in the self-presence of the sound and image of the artist, who is seen and heard declaiming Baggs's text. Yet this gap is also held open by the parameters of the full body quotation, in that Tsang's vocal performance mimics the artificial pacing and tonality of Baggs's speech-generating software.

The disruption of the vocal circuit between psychic interiority and expression that *In My Language* stages finds a kind of recursive—or, perhaps more accurately, chiasmic—doubling in Tsang's *The Shape of the Right Statement*. If Baggs's FC voice has been designed to mimic, as closely as possible, the recognizable tonalities of human speech, Tsang's performance strives to mimic the artificial sonorities of computerized speech. In Baggs's video, we are presented with a voice through the mediated technology of the text-to-speech software that she uses to communicate with others. In Tsang's video, the artist attempts to mimic the sonic valences of Baggs's technologically mediated voice through a virtuosic vocal performance—a technique that has in turn become the basis for Tsang's elaboration in subsequent artistic projects that also involve strategic re-voicings of previously recorded material. In each case, the alliance between human voice and verbal expression is precisely disrupted to polemically expand the purview of what kinds of expressive behavior can be considered language, communication, and even thought as such.

In place of the variously telescoping and circuiting layers of mediation that the two videos construct to further widen the gap between the body of the speaking autistic subject and the content communicated by the speech, *In My Language* and *The Shape of the Right Statement* propose different modes of organizing and arranging sensory experience. More specifically, the videos are each acutely attuned to the role of tactility—and more particularly haptic sensory modes—in the (performative) production of linguistic, communicational, and expressive content. Yet for Baggs and Tsang, the haptic is not simply an especially prominent or aesthetically privileged sensory mode. It also functions as a structuring, formal element in these videos' performative interventions.

The haptic offers a mode of describing visual media that would depart from prevailing epistemological traditions in which other sensory modes are subordinated to the priority of the ocular. *Haptics* has been defined as "that subsystem of nonlanguage communication which conveys meaning through physical contact."[25] If this definition hews remarkably closely to the narration offered in Baggs's video, I also mean to evoke a description of the term offered by Gilles Deleuze in his study of painter Francis Bacon: "We will speak of the *haptic* whenever there is no longer a strict subordination in either direction"—that is, toward the eye (optical) or hand (tactile)—"but when sight discovers in itself a specific function of touch that is uniquely its own, distinct from its optical function."[26] The concept of the haptic upends the ocularcentrism of modern regimes of visuality, orienting us instead to instances in which touch and tactility overtake the sensorial "purity" of vision. Extending from Deleuze, we might say that the haptic returns the body to the act of seeing, undoing the Cartesian equation of sight with (disembodied) cognition.[27] Laura U. Marks offers a powerful account of "haptic cinema" in her book *The Skin of the Film: Intercultural Cinema, Embodiment, and the Senses.* Marks notes how certain formal properties of the cinematic image, such as "changes in focus, graininess (achieved differently in each medium), and effects of under- and over-exposure," can all effectively "discourage the viewer from distinguishing objects and encourage a relationship to the screen as a whole."[28] The haptic has been an important aesthetic strategy within feminist filmmaking because it subverts and disrupts dominant cinematic protocols that have metonymically linked the disembodied purity of ocular vision with the equally disembodied values of scientific knowledge and rationality. Extending from Marks, I propose haptic strategies and approaches to be equally central to the account of disability aesthetics I am seeking to explicate in this study. As such, I suggest that *In My Language* and *The Shape of the Right Statement* each positions itself against dominant epistemological and sensory logics that analogize the purity of ocular vision with the transparency of language, developing instead an aesthetic and performative association between haptic vision and autistic language.

In the case of *In My Language,* this haptic dimension is achieved in part through the formal composition of individual shots, as in the striking sequences filmed through the center of a bouncing plastic Slinky. In one of these shots, the Slinky creates a yellow and orange spiral through which Baggs's bare feet and the tip of her finger are visible on the floor. In this shot, the entire screen fills with the spiraling, kinetic dynamism of the bouncing orange rings, the rhythmic movement of which dominates the whole surface of the image and produces a palpable sense of repetitive rocking or swaying. (This sequence recalls the visual vocabulary of Alfred Hitchcock's film *Vertigo,* in which brightly colored circular spirals mimic the circling camera movements that are meant to both signal the protagonist's dizzying spells of vertigo and haptically induce a comparable proprioceptive experience in the viewer's body.)

The video also contains several powerfully visceral images of sensory "smearing"—as in the shot where Baggs is shown with her face grazing over the pages of an open book held up to her face, smelling and touching the pages as they graze by her nose in a single, multi- (or perhaps cross-)sensory motion. I would additionally describe Baggs's deliberate, almost rhythmic use of editing and montage as haptic: Baggs enlists the percussive quality of the jump cut to produce a visual/haptic effect that seems to evoke the rhythmically repetitive qualities associated with autistic stereotypical behavior, such as stimming and vocal echolalia.

The haptic qualities of Tsang's work function differently, evoking by other means the tactile preoccupations of its antecedent. In contrast to the elaborate, kinetically patterned visual style of Baggs's video, *The Shape of the Right Statement* is formally austere and presentational. Its single-take, static midrange shot captures the artist facing the camera, gazing steadily outward at the unseen viewers she addresses. I want to focus in particular on the several tears that begin to well at the corners of Tsang's eyes partway through the video before spilling over and rolling down her cheeks near the work's close. I would suggest that there are several ways to understand Tsang's tears. The first would be to read them as an unconscious, somatic response to the bodily strain involved in the performance—as issuing, that is, from the artist's tear ducts simply because her eyes have been held open for too long without blinking. In this case, the tears are not correlated with an interior psychic state ascribed to the speaker. However, a second interpretation of the tears would be to view them as a symptomatic indication of Tsang's emotional response to, and investment in, the semantic content of Baggs's text that she recites. In this account, the tears are read as visual indications of the artist's subjectively interior emotional state.[29] Yet it is possible for the viewer to hold both of these understandings of the tear simultaneously—and this ambiguity only heightens the interpretive and aesthetic complexity of the work. In each case, the tear communicates (via the haptic "subsystem of nonlanguage") in a way that exceeds the semantic content of the spoken text.

Voice and Gestus

In linking this queer tradition of citation to autism and linguistic disability more broadly, Tsang queers and crips the voice itself. Each of these videos reroutes the voice into touch, texture, and haptics. Tsang's discussion of full body quotation can be situated within a longer theatrical tradition of thinking about the body, performance, and politics—a theatrical tradition that, moreover, hinges around disability and specifically disabilities of speech, voice, and language in ways that have not often been fully accounted for or acknowledged. Here I am referring to the ensemble of theatrical thinking that has come to be associated with the concepts of the gestus and the gestic. These concepts were most influentially formulated by Bertolt Brecht, who uses the terms throughout his writing, aiming toward a theater of "nonmimetic realism," although in notoriously ambiguous ways. More broad and expansive than the gestures, movements, and expressions that an actor develops to flesh out a role, gestus and the gestic have come to index theatrical techniques of distancing and estrangement that are designed "to denaturalize and defamiliarize what ideology makes seem normal, acceptable, inescapable"—as feminist theater scholar Elin Diamond writes in an influential essay from 1988 calling for a "gestic feminist criticism."[30] This aspect of denaturalizing and defamiliarizing the normal makes the gestus particularly significant to consider in relation to disability.

Consider the gestus with regard to Brecht's play *Mother Courage and Her Children,* first staged in 1941, specifically Mother Courage's notably "voiceless" daughter, Kattrin, referred to by other characters in the play variously as a "mute" or as a "dumb animal." Kattrin has been described as "the most complex and engaging character in all of Brechtian drama"[31] because her role in the narrative is so thoroughly structured by the ironies, estrangements, and dialectical contradictions associated with the play's author. In the play's climactic and justly famous eleventh scene, Kattrin climbs onto the roof of a house just outside the town of Halle, beating a drum to awaken its residents and warn them of the impending invasion by enemy soldiers. As the peasant couple whose house she and her mother are staying in plead with her to stop, Kattrin is shot and killed by soldiers from the invading army. In the scene, despite her voicelessness, Kattrin seizes some vestige of expressive agency even as she performs a defiant act of self-sacrifice.

Earlier in the play, we learn the source of Kattrin's muteness: in the final line of scene 6, Mother Courage reveals that Kattrin "is only dumb from the war, soldiers stuffed something in her mouth when she was little."[32] The unseen act of violence that caused Kattrin's voicelessness, with the added suggestion of sexual violation hinted at by the ambiguity of the "something" stuffed in her mouth, "makes concretely manifest an underlying history of literally unspeakable, traumatic violence" of war, and by extension the ruthlessness of capitalist exploitation that Brecht's portrayal of the Thirty Years' War aims to make clear through the story of Courage.[33] Viewed in this light, Kattrin's missing voice functions as what disability theorists David Mitchell and Sharon Snyder have termed a "narrative prosthesis," an "opportunistic metaphorical device" that relies on the symbolic "potency of disability" to achieve certain narrative and thematic ends.[34] The climactic drumming scene signals to the audience the ironic consequences of how, throughout the play, the other characters' "collective failure to recognize Kattrin as a speaking subject" indexes a wider inability to confront the dehumanizing horrors of the war around them.[35] It is thus clear that Kattrin's "disability"—which excludes her from being afforded the status of full human personhood by the play's other characters, reducing her to the status of "creaturely life"—is a direct consequence of her position within a specific social and historical milieu.

Yet the consequences of Kattrin's status as disabled go beyond the drama's narrative construction, for Kattrin's voicelessness seems also to function as the source of what literary critic Ato Quayson calls "aesthetic nervousness"—a formal disruption or short-circuiting that the presence of disability can provoke within the operating procedures of aesthetic realism and its mimetic stability and coherence. Quayson suggests that aesthetic nervousness sparked by representations of disability can also function to "make visible"—intentionally or not—"the aesthetic field's relationship to the social situation of persons with disability in the real world."[36]

Note here the striking parallels with what Brecht (and subsequent theater artists and critics) have identified as the radical political potential of gestic theater: the gestus is defined by its exceeding the boundaries of the theatrical narrative by emphasizing and highlighting the materiality of the bodies that are performing it (and indeed watching it unfold). Kattrin's status as a voiceless character in the play's narrative "demands" that the actor who plays her stand "at all times—in dialectical relation to [the character's] own attitudes and actions."[37] As theater scholar Kim Solga observes, "on a metatheatrical level," Kattrin "visibly ([and] audibly) lacks the primary tool of stage realism: the voice as a source of identity, the word as guarantor of the real."[38] Indeed, it is for this reason that Kattrin is the ultimate exemplar of gestic characterization. To again cite Diamond: "Because the gestus is effected by a historical subject/actor[,] what the spectator sees is not a mere miming of a social relationship, but a *reading* of it, an interpretation by a historical subject who supplements (rather than disappears into) the production of meaning."[39]

In the bourgeois realist drama that Brecht sought to disrupt, the actor speaks as if her voice were the source of the character's identity. If the voice is indeed the "primary tool of stage realism," there is already a displacement at work in the theatrical scenario—as J. L. Austin recognizes in his denigration of theatrical utterances as peculiarly "hollow or void"[40] and therefore excluded from the category of the happy performative. But the gestic performer uses her own performing body to signal its status as an historical site of social contestation and potential transformation. This is why the gestic offered a powerful framework for feminist critics writing in the 1980s and 1990s, such as Diamond, who were drawn to the gestus as a way of thinking about how theater and performance unsettled the norms of gender through practices of parody, estrangement, and denaturalization.

Tsang's full body quotation can thus be understood as a specifically queer mode of gestic performance that chafes against histories of pathologization through the materiality of the voice. The voice, as we know, has been a central issue within a specifically queer performance lineage. Tsang's piece points to unexpected resonances between text-to-speech technologies and other forms of FC used by individuals with verbal impairments and the decidedly queer performance traditions of citation. I am thinking here not only of Judith Butler's assertion in her 1993 essay "Critically Queer" that "if a performative [speech act] provisionally succeeds . . . [it is] only because . . . [it] *accumulates the force of authority through the repetition or citation of a prior, authoritative set of practices,*"[41] but also of queer performance traditions of drag and lip-synching. These are associated with the denaturalizing tendencies of camp. The gently glittering silver curtain that serves as the backdrop to Tsang's otherwise visually austere framing reflects, literally, on the glint of red stage lights of the alternative queer and trans performance space's social context and the sociality in which it was made. Indeed, it is notable that Tsang has subsequently used "full body quotation" in works of movement-based performance involving citations from *Paris Is Burning,* Jennie Livingston's iconic 1991 documentary about the Black and Brown queer denizens of Harlem's ballroom/vogue scene during the first decade of the AIDS epidemic.

Yet Tsang's performance offers a reading of the voice's materiality and its relationship to the speaking body. This relationship, I would suggest, is structured ideologically, namely by the ideologies of the ableist and neurotypical demands that Baggs sets out to critique. In this way, Tsang foregrounds the embodied work of her own performance in ways that are viscerally affecting, especially the tears that stream down the artist's cheek by the end of the piece, wet and glistening in shimmery counterpoint to the silver curtain behind Tsang's head. Are we to read the tears as an indication of the artist's emotional response to the text she is reciting, or rather as a purely physical result of the effortful labor that the performance of vocal mimicry demands?

The haptic dimensions of these works can be viewed in resonance with a critical gestic interest in how the material traces of embodied performance can disrupt mimetic realism and the ideological ends to which it is put. Significantly, I think these same *haptic* qualities also point to further conjunctions between disability, sexuality, and gender as targets of normalization.

It is important to acknowledge that Tsang and Baggs are working in genres that differ, in significant ways, from the narrative dramatic forms that shaped Brecht's original understanding of the gestic. Instead, with their imaginative conjuring calls for, and enactments of, a world that might be arranged otherwise, perhaps the most pertinent genre tradition that these works engage is that of the avant-garde manifesto. The manifesto is defined by a certain "investment in efficacious performativity" that aims to instrumentalize its language to achieve specific effects in the world it calls for. This is also why "theatricality," as Martin Puchner notes, "is something of a specter haunting the manifesto, the threat that its speech acts might turn out to be nothing but stage acts."[42] Baggs seems to invoke this specter of theatricality, or at least of the long historical legacy of prurient stagings of the disabled body, when she insists that *In My Language* "has not been intended as a voyeuristic freak show where you get to look at the bizarre workings of the autistic mind. It is meant as a strong statement on the existence and value of many different kinds of thinking and interaction."

What I have been describing as the haptic elements in Baggs's and Tsang's videos thus could be said to arise specifically within the interstices between movement and expression. Indeed, Baggs's assertion that "my language is not about designing words or even visual symbols for people to interpret" can be read as a refusal of the "representative structure" through which "expressive communication" is adjudicated. Showing herself "in a constant conversation with every aspect of my environment," Baggs insists that her tactile interaction with her surroundings is just as expressively communicative as neurotypical spoken language.

Baggs's use of text-to-speech software to voice the words heard in the video's second half also invokes the practice of facilitated communication, a mode of producing speech that challenges notions of individual autonomy and the representative structure of expressive communication through what Cynthia Lewiecki-Wilson has called the "performative rhetoric of the body."[43] Lisa Cartwright's work on the ethics of intersubjective communication has shown how language and touch have overlapped within the history of autism. In her study of the controversies that emerged in the early 1990s surrounding the use of FC with autistic and other children with language impairments, Cartwright notes that debates centered around the question of physical touch between facilitators and their clients; it "opened up the larger question about the relationship between affect and expressive representation."[44]

Once the fantasy of speech as an autonomous exercise of subjective expression was shattered by those previously considered voiceless emerging into sociality, the very embodied/physical and tactile practices of these methods were placed under suspicion. From its inception, the method was controversial, with many researchers doubting the veracity of the content it generated. As Cartwright notes, "Both sides' ways of understanding the human subject and its constitution through speech . . . precluded a more complex understanding of human voice and agency as always coproduced, with the splitting of the subject always enacted in relationship to and in dependency upon others."[45] The use of FC among people with disabilities points toward an account of expressive communication that is collaborative and relational, enmeshed as it is in a social world where human agency and voice are "coproduced." Tsang's video, in turn, makes canny reference to Baggs's use of FC through the technique of full body quotation, which is in part a riff on the queer performance practices of drag and lip-synching. Recalling the denaturalizing tendencies of camp, Tsang's technique is designed "to question authenticity and intention of the speaker, and understand content differently, out of its original context."[46] It is a way of performing ambivalence that further layers and interweaves separate but intersecting histories, traditions, and strategies of vocal expression.

The thematics of touch, pressure, and texture, in turn, have been key to how autism has been articulated with regard to questions of gender and sexual difference and ongoing debates concerning the sexuality of autism. In one of the few critical essays addressing sexuality and autism, Groner surveys a range of autobiographical literature authored by autistic people addressing their experience of sexuality. She notes, "One of the seemingly universal sensations that many people with ASD tolerate, and even crave, is intense pressure."[47] Recall an account by autistic writer Lucy Blackman, who describes her experience of her facilitator's hand as a rich site of both attention and information: "The steady touch on my own hand and forearm somehow made me bring it into focus, and at the same time feeling the point of contact gave me an accurate measurement as to the distance between my fingertip and my sensation of that touch."[48] Blackman's description also evokes a passage from the work of Temple Grandin, perhaps the most widely recognized and influential autistic writer. In her 1998 memoir *Thinking in Pictures*, Grandin famously describes how as a high school student at a Vermont boarding school in the 1950s, she constructed a "squeeze machine" in which she could place her body to generate "the tactile equivalent of a complex emotion." By controlling the machine's degree of pressure on her body, Grandin reports that it "has helped me to understand complexity of [human] feelings."[49] In turn, Grandin's use of the squeeze machine as what might be called an *affective prosthesis* led to her subsequent work developing widely used animal husbandry techniques, which rely on similar machines to mediate the bodily pressure experienced by animals in industrial slaughterhouses. Throughout her work, Grandin frequently attributes her unique empathic relations with livestock animals to the intensely tactile aspects of her experience of autism, especially referring to the squeeze machine's "language of pressure." Grandin writes that using her squeeze machine "enabled me to learn to be gentle, to have empathy, to know that gentleness is not synonymous with weakness. I was learning how to feel."[50] These examples from the writing of Blackman and Grandin already indicate how Baggs's concern with touch and texture in *In My Language* can be placed within a larger conversation among autistic people about the relation between sensory experience and the capacity to experience and communicate emotion in ways that might be understood by a broader (neurotypical) world.

Here, we might also find the terms to situate Baggs's video as a work of queer performance. Groner makes a case for autistic sexuality as a queer formation, arguing that it is "illegible to heteronormativity."[51] Previous discussions of Baggs's video have overlooked the fact that Baggs identifies as a lesbian, in more recent remarks writing, "I don't experience myself as having a gender identity, I call it being genderless."[52] Yet beyond Baggs's recourse to legible (or "illegible") markers of sexual and gender identity, the *haptic* account of language and communication set forth in the video indicates a queer relation to both neurotypical and heteronormative matrices of intelligibility, navigating an errant pathway through the thicket of language, sensation, and identity. Baggs, Tsang, and Utter each in different ways investigates how the *shaping* of a statement can be as determined by the feel of an object as content expressed by a single voice.

Coda

Shy Undergrounds

But can we say that the spider's project is to weave its web? I don't think so. We might as well say that the web's project is to be woven.

—Fernand Deligny, *The Arachnean*

It is said that we are non-communicative, yet our message has been making international news. Most labor struggles would envy the amount of attention our strike is drawing. And our silence and reclusiveness means that our message cannot be misused or instrumentalized.
We cannot be stopped.

—A Message from the Hikikomori Delegation to the Global Shy Underground, in Hamja Ahsan, *Shy Radicals*

To *destitute* is not primarily to attack the institution, but to attack the need we have of it.

—The Invisible Committee, *Now*

The Web's Project Is to Be Woven

On April 11, 2020, Mel Baggs died at the home of Laura Tisoncik in Burlington, Vermont. Baggs had come to live with Tisoncik, an autism activist and advocate, after a cascading series of experiences with institutional and home health care aid workers. In a 2014 entry on Baggs's blog, Ballastexistenz, a video and a series of photos document Baggs's intense interest in crochet. To accompany these images, she offers a series of reflections on her recent preoccupations with crochet and weaving:

> Crocheting is my new perseveration. You can call what I was doing in this video stimming, dancing, or whatever you want, but it's how my body moved naturally and it felt great. Crocheting is pretty much all I do these days. It's nice to have something I can do with my hands that doesn't require language or strenuous activity. I could never crochet or knit, growing up. It was visually too confusing to find where the stitches were. I had some of that problem when I was trying to learn this time, but apparently my visual processing is finally mature enough that I can distinguish what a stitch looks like. Once I figured that out, the rest became easy, and I took off really fast.
>
> As an autistic person, and my particular type of autistic person, I need things to do that aren't words, aren't abstract, and aren't surfing the net. I've been looking for something like this a long time. I was trying to get into sewing, when I found my old childhood crochet hooks in my sewing box. I never did get into sewing, because I took off so fast with crochet I haven't looked back. It's my only real interest at this point, and I bore people by trying to talk about it. But I love it. I always have at least three projects going at once that I switch off between depending on how I'm feeling.[1]

Baggs's writing, photographs, and video reveal how crocheting became strategy for inhabiting the world "as an autistic person," one that is particularly effective and absorbing because it is a type of activity done with one's hands that is "not abstract." The photographs posted alongside this blog entry show Baggs interacting with beautifully complex and elaborate textile creations. The inventive and playful manipulation of thread and yarn on view in the video and photographs suggests a nonabstract and absorptive mode of engagement, a form of communication that particularly chimes with Eve Kosofsky Sedgwick's writings on texture. In her later writing, the association between texture and bodily fallibility take on an increasingly autobiographical cast, as Sedgwick reveals how her own diagnosis with metastatic breast cancer shaped the development of her textile art practice, her growing fascination with the nondualistic tenets of Tibetan Buddhism, and her increasing interest in exploring what she calls "the middle ranges of agency"—a phrase that recurs repeatedly in her writing.

"To touch is always already to reach out, to fondle, to heft, to tap or enfold," Sedgwick writes, "and always also to understand other people or natural forces as having effectually done so before oneself, if only in the making of the textured object."[2] Sedgwick's preoccupations with texture, reflected in both her theoretical writing and her growing devotion to a textile art practice, became central aspects of her attempt to navigate a number of problems having to do with the exchange between language (written and spoken) and materiality. In "Making Things, Practicing Emptiness," Sedgwick describes her work in textile art as having a "quite strenuous resistance to being translated into verbal propositions."[3] Later in the essay, she asserts that "unlike making things, speech and writing and conceptual thought impose no material obstacles to a fantasy of instant, limitless efficacy."[4]

Sedgwick's essay "Affect Theory, Theory of Mind," touches on contemporary debates about autism and neurodiversity. She offers a largely critical assessment of the recent vogue within academic literary studies for adapting insights from cognitive psychology and adjacent fields of scientific research in order to study the aesthetic and social functions of literature. In its final pages, the essay takes a surprising turn. She refers to a collectively authored paper by autistic self-advocates responding to the prevalence of Theory of Mind–based models for categorizing autism, situating its claims in the context of the "loosely organized international movement" of neurodiversity. For Sedgwick—who evinces a deep interest in the affective-cognitive systems developed by midcentury psychologist Silvan Tomkins—this meant that neurodiversity could be viewed as both "a rights movement for people disenfranchised by a certain range of particular mental diagnoses" *and* as "the source of a kind of analysis whose limits of applicability would be very hard to circumscribe."[5] In the case of Theory of Mind, the perspectives of autistic self-advocates serve as a corrective to the dominant assumptions of cognitive science and the modes of psychiatric expertise that draw on its findings to justify the management of human difference. Sedgwick quotes from an article entitled "Theory of Mind: From an Autistic Perspective" to show the implicit limitations of defining autism as a lack of Theory of Mind. One of the article's contributors whom Sedgwick quotes, Jared Blackburn, offers an explanation for "why Autistic people often seem to lack 'Theory of Mind' to normal people" by drawing from his personal experience: "I think my view of other people was/is unusually flexible because I lack a specific 'people' way of thinking (separate from objects), so I do not 'see' myself in others. Instead, it's all processing abstract concepts and systems—much like computer programs or physical forces. However, I have been quite aware for a long time that others had (different) knowledge and motives."[6]

At the essay's conclusion, Sedgwick offers a series of closing reflections in the form of a numbered list, concerning how an affect theory informed by neurodiverse perspectives, such as the ones offered by Blackburn and his coauthors, might reshape critical approaches for thinking about Theory of Mind:

1. Don't work toward, or depend upon the model of, a single, normative outcome—with differences from that outcome analyzed in terms of deficiency or at best detour.
2. Instead, find ways of discerning and describing a variety of outcomes, qualitatively and phenomenologically distinct; not understood in terms of a preimagined evolutionary teleology, but instead in terms of a diversity of potentials.[7]

The fourth point reads as follows:

4. Such qualitative differences may or may not be rooted in detectable, hard-wired, and/or immutable biological difference. Conceptually it doesn't matter much—especially as thresholds of detectability are constantly changing. So too, importantly, are understandings of neural plasticity—with regard to genetics, prenatal environments, and the overall lifespan, and equally with regard to the temporary, nonce, and provisional.[8]

Sedgwick's discussion of autism in the context of affect theory suggests that neurodiversity could be considered both a rights-based social movement and a kind of hermeneutic provocation with potentially limitless applicability. This line of reasoning follows a parallel path to the one that Sedgwick traces in her previous work in queer theory—most pointedly, in her account of the tensions between "universalizing" and "minoritizing" accounts of sexual identity that were produced by what she terms the "crisis" within definitions of sexuality that accompanied the modern emergence of the hetero/homo divide.[9] For Sedgwick, the relation between universalizing and minoritizing perspectives was not antagonistic but instead convivial. This relation takes on a both/and quality that simultaneously retains an awareness of the durability of identity and the particularity of difference even as it seeks avenues of generalization, diffusion, and dispersal. In turn, this move suggests a queer hermeneutics on a potentially boundless range of situations and contexts, even those that would seem to be absent recognizably minoritarian sexual identities.

Sedgwick's list is highly suggestive for thinking about the politics and aesthetics of neurological difference. Her searching pursuit of nondualistic accounts of personhood and relationality—of acting, doing, being, and making *with* or *alongside*—is suggestive for the possibilities of cultivating neurodivergent lifeworlds. In certain key respects, attending to Sedgwick's interest in the nondualistic promise and potentiality of texture and touch alongside Baggs's evocative account of her practice of crocheting as a "new perseveration" is suggestively resonant with other counter-cartographies of neurodivergence surfaced in this book. I have attempted to trace how an alternative trajectory opened up by the concept of neurodiversity might circumvent or surpass those elements within it that are constrained by the logics within which a concept of neurodiversity can gain cultural intelligibility—including the concept's potentially unwitting collusion with liberal and neoliberal paradigms of inclusion.

Fernand Deligny has been crucial for my articulation of this project, in part because of just how aslant he was from almost all of the influential theoretical traditions in which the performative has figured, including structuralism and poststructuralism; Marxism; psychoanalysis; behaviorism; cognitivism; and ultimately the most recent regime of neuronal ideology. At several points in his writings, Deligny "describes his retreat in the Cévennes as an attempt to *destitute* language."[10] In a similar way, reading Sedgwick alongside Baggs suggests how the counter-cartographies of neurodivergence I have traced operate by way of a *destitution* of autism and other clinical categories of neurological difference, seeking instead plural, provisional, and "nonce" aesthetic registers: modes of evacuating apparatuses of psychiatric and neuronal power in ways that allow different, and perhaps even playful, uses of them.[11]

Deligny's project represents an important historical precursor to some of the ideas about autism and neurological difference as "modes of being" that have been even more lushly evoked and articulated by Baggs and Sedgwick, among many others. These projects invite us to become especially alert to the ways that autistic and neurodivergent artists, writers, filmmakers, and others have destituted the performative force of clinical categories, turning to different aesthetic registers and terrains. Pursuing these questions requires navigating toward other terrains and precincts—both real and, in the case of the final example I turn to in these concluding pages, imagined. To do so, let us turn toward a final a counter-cartography of neurodivergence: an imaginative, speculative project that maps the existence of a subterranean network known as the global Shy Underground, where shyness is not always and immediately approached as a problem or a failure of proper, neurotypical relationality and sociality. Instead, it is seen as a mode of aesthetic self-fashioning, one that occupies a destituent relationship to the psychopolitical (and increasingly neuropolitical) regimes of modernity and that operates within and beyond the discursive regime of the diagnostic.

The World Is Our Corner

How might the emerging concepts of neurodiversity and neurodivergence contribute to our understanding of a critical genealogy of shyness? Shyness indexes recessive, recalcitrant, inscrutable, ambivalent, and otherwise vexed attitudes toward sociality, so it is an especially interesting category to explore in light of the recent attention, in critical scholarship on disability and neurodiversity, to how sociality itself has come to function as a compulsory norm.[12]

How is it that shyness has transmuted from a term evoking the quieter repertoires and softer textures through which the idiosyncrasies of a personality might be expressed into a designation for concerning behavior that has increasingly come to be viewed as a menacing indication of something far more dangerous: an excessive or abnormal inwardness that at its most extreme is personified by the figures of the school shooter or suicide bomber?[13] What might be characterized as a dramatic shift in the meaning and status of shyness can be situated within a much longer genealogy of psychiatric power that stretches back not only to mid-twentieth-century debates over psychiatry's status as a legitimate field of expertise but also to nineteenth-century criminology's construction of the "mental defective as someone who is dangerous."[14] The nineteenth-century category of the *work-shy*, for example, was invented as a designation that municipalities applied to vagrants, criminals, and "mental defectives" who were either incapable of or irredeemably resistant to integration into the workforce. (Like many other eugenic-era concepts, "work-shy" would go on to become a quasi-legal category adopted by the Nazi regime for its own genocidal eugenic ends.)

In *Shyness: How Normal Behavior Became a Sickness,* literary critic Christopher Lane traces the way shyness was brought under the umbrella of psychiatric expertise. Lane reveals how behavior that British psychiatrists in the 1960s began to refer to with the quasi-diagnosis of "social phobia" made its first appearance in the 1980 revision to the American Psychiatric Association's *DSM,* which jettisoned the psychoanalytic frameworks that had predominated in previous versions of the manual in favor of a biopsychiatric approach to the diagnosis and treatment of mental disorders. The consequence "of this biomedical turn in psychiatry," Lane writes, "is a growing consensus that traits once attributed to mavericks, skeptics, or mere introverts are psychiatric disorders that drugs should eliminate."[15] Indeed, the biomedicalization of psychiatry cannot be understood apart from the rapidly expanding market for psychopharmaceutic drugs that developed alongside psychiatry's much-contested bid for scientific legitimacy over the latter half of the twentieth century.

The reverberations of this history can be felt in the ways that shyness and social phobia are evoked in the diagnostic and para-diagnostic language used to identify ASDs. While shyness most explicitly appears in the current edition of the *DSM* as a symptom of anxiety disorder, and hence is separate from the entry on the much-debated diagnostic criteria for autism, changes in clinical and cultural understandings of autism have followed a parallel trajectory to the process by which shyness became medicalized.[16] Autism is still steadfastly characterized, within the clinical literature, in terms of excessive impairments in social functioning: an "inability to relate to others in the 'ordinary way,'" to cite Leo Kanner's 1943 article "Autistic Disturbances of Affective Contact," often credited with originating the modern clinical conception of autism as a diagnostic category.[17]

To be sure, many subsequent decades of research, writing, and activism—to say nothing of the quotidian acts of neurodivergent resistance and survival necessary to navigate a world that is hostile to both shyness and autism—have revealed just how shallow and misleading such initial accounts of autism were in their efforts to describe autistic sociality, which manifests in ways that are as wildly varied and heterogeneous as every other "disordered" aspect of human behavior that has been brought underneath autism's diagnostic umbrella.

Yet what if the conditions that have allowed shyness to be viewed with persistent and increasing suspicion—as the potentially pathological expression of a dangerous anti-sociality—might in fact contain the seeds of possibility for shyness to be reclaimed or resignified, even to become the grounds for revolutionary political movements and aesthetic strategies? How might shyness become the basis for what Foucault would call a "counterdiscourse" that emerges when those who are diagnosed or pathologized begin to speak back in the language used to pathologize and diagnose them?[18] How might such a counterdiscourse contain possibilities for shyness to be resignified and retrofitted by locating hidden points of tactical subterfuge and covert resistance? How, then, might the concepts of neurodiversity and neurodivergence contribute to our understanding of a critical genealogy of shyness?

The global Shy Underground project began its life as a small book by London-based writer, artist, and activist Hamja Ahsan published by the Book Works, an independent artists' press, in 2017 and entitled *Shy Radicals: The Antisystemic Politics of the Militant Introvert*.[19] Informed by the DIY aesthetics of zine culture, *Shy Radicals* draws together imagined communiqués, covert interviews, and hidden histories of a global insurgency movement calling itself the Shy Underground, which dreams of establishing the Shy People's Republic of Aspergistan, "an independent Pan-Shyist state representing the interests of all Shy, Introvert and Autistic Spectrum peoples" where "civic privilege will only be granted to the voice of the unheard." The first section of the book consists of a "draft constitution of the Shy People's Republic of Aspergistan," which we read is to be created as "a revolutionary vanguard state guided by anti-systemic Introvert ideology."[20] There is a deft poetic sensibility at work: Aspergistan's flag consists of an ellipsis set against a black background, "symbolizing silence and the depths of the ocean" (23). The national flower is the root: "Shy Radicals acknowledge the privileging of the blooming flower image to be part of the systemic enforcement of Extrovert normativity" (23). Aspergistan's national motto—"The World Is Our Corner"—would soon come to adorn the very real flags that the artist made and started distributing to be flown from very real buildings where his work was beginning to be exhibited. Written in the key of Jorge Luis Borges crossed with Tao Lin, *Shy Radicals* presents itself as a sort of guidebook to Aspergistan, an imagined territory that is gradually turning not so imaginary. Subsequent sections of the book contain various historical and contemporary documents culled from what appears to be a secretive, global Shy Underground movement, whose members, organized in cells scattered across the globe, we learn, seek to reclaim for their lineage a whole canon of the proto–Shy Radicals; these include "Rosa Parks, Blaise Pascal, Emily Dickinson, Wednesday Addams, and Lisa Simpson" (63). Other touchstones are Richey James Edwards and Kurt Cobain; medieval Persian Sufi poet Attar of Nishapur; and filmmaker Satyajit Ray.

Hamja Ahsan was born in 1981 in London's Tooting neighborhood. His parents had immigrated to London from Bangladesh in the 1960s. Though he was raised as a somewhat observant Muslim and attended

Figure 14. Flag of the Shy People's Republic of Aspergistan. The flag's words read, "The world is our corner." Installation view from the 33rd Ljubljana Biennial of Graphic Arts, *Crack Up—Crack Down* (Mousse Publishing, Ljubljana, 2019). Photo by Hamja Ahsan. Courtesy of the International Centre of Graphic Arts (MGLC) Archive.

madrassa as a child, his parents were part of what he describes as an "aspirational class" of South Asian immigrants to the former colonial metropole for whom religious observance was less important. He hated secondary school, which he regarded as the worst six years of his life, and attempted suicide at seventeen, "which I regarded as a tribute to the school." Ahsan continues: "I just hated the particular form of sociality associated with secondary school. . . . I saw how the forms of hierarchy in school worked, quite led by corporate marketing. If you didn't wear Nike, Reebok or Adidas shoes, you were seen as a degenerate, and you would be bullied. A lot of it was around gender. I was always being effeminate, I was always called gay. I had longer hair because I used to like dark music."[21]

Though diagnosed as bipolar at age eighteen, Ahsan early on cultivated a more idiosyncratic and subversive understanding of his own neurodivergence, primarily through the intense attachments he developed as teenager to certain extravagantly gloomy male rock musicians of the early 1990s. An early obsession was Richey James Edwards, the morose and self-destructive front man of Welsh alternative band Manic Street Preachers. When he was thirteen, Ahsan used his father's office photocopier to make his first zine, called *Nausea,* inspired by Edwards and his bandmates. Ahsan was drawn to the Manic Street Preachers because of the way the band was "on one hand about socialism and class struggle but on the other hand always describing problems with alcoholism, eating disorders, depression, suicide."

The passionate fanzine community that Ahsan discovered through the Manic Street Preachers was part of a larger ecology of a noncommercial, amateur, and self-published zine-making subculture whose anti-capitalist commitments still followed the aggressively oppositional, working-class origins of punk subculture. The DIY ethos of making zines, which is inseparable from the underground networks of renegade publishing and exchange that sustain it, belongs to what José Esteban Muñoz has described as the "punk rock commons": a distinctive way of being in common with others that defines punk as an anti-genre—not in the sense that punk "refuses genre, but more like it's a genre of refusal."[22] The zine subcultures that Ahsan discovered provided a new idiom for understanding the politics of mental health as being connected to longer histories of radical social critique and artistic experimentation that could inform something like a Shy Underground network, forged through covert and improvisatory circuits of publication and exchange and united by a refusal to accede to the mandates of extrovert supremacy.

While readers may be given pause by Ahsan's humorous provocations with diagnostic nomenclature, which imagine a whole alternative geopolitics out of clinical syndromes, *Shy Radicals* and the projects that it has subsequently generated can also be read as a manifesto in defense of shyness and introversion that fully embraces what Remi Yergeau has called the "neuroqueer potentials for narrating and claiming the abject, the antisocial, the asocial."[23] In line with the utopian, surrealist, and speculative traditions from which it draws, Aspergistan is an intricately constructed fictional world that also functions as a biting critique of the present. The global reach of Ahsan's imagined network of Shy Underground cells possesses an uncanny echo of the global influence and authority exerted by the *DSM*—which is not just confined to psychiatric practitioners but extends its capillary reach throughout the official institutions of our society like schools, courtrooms, and prisons.

The distinctive set of cultural references that the Shy Radicals movement would take up were shaped in response to a very different set of personal and political circumstances. In July 2006, British police arrived at Ahsan's family's flat in Tooting. Shockingly, and seemingly out of nowhere, they arrested his brother, poet and translator Syed Talha Ahsan. The family would learn that Talha was being detained in connection with charges that the counterterrorism arm of the U.S. Department of Justice was bringing against Babar Ahmad, the leader of a small Salafist reading group that Talha had attended as a bookish high school student in search of opportunities to understand his Muslim faith. Caught up in the expanded miasmas of international law through which the post-9/11 U.S. security state sought to wage the global war on terror, they were charged with providing marginal "material support" for a website alleged to have disseminated messages from militant jihadist groups based in Chechnya. Even though, as lawyers from the British Centre of Constitutional Rights noted, the "Crown Prosecution Service stated on multiple occasions that there was insufficient evidence to charge the pair with any criminal offence under U.K. law," both were extradited in 2012 despite never having previously set foot in the United States (justified on the legal pretext that one of the website's internet domain addresses had been traced to a server located in Connecticut).[24] After spending two years imprisoned at the high-security Northern Correctional Institution, Talha agreed to a plea deal on lesser charges and was released to return to the United Kingdom in 2014. Over the course of his nearly decade-long ordeal, Talha ended up serving one of the longest periods of detention without trial in modern British history, much of it spent in solitary confinement.

Talha Ahsan's Asperger syndrome diagnosis played an important role in his legal defense strategy and in the subsequent attention brought to the case. Briefings filed on his behalf included a statement from a psychiatrist who had examined him and declared that "by virtue of his Asperger's syndrome and depressive disorder, (Talha) is an extremely vulnerable individual who, from a psychiatric perspective, would be more appropriately placed in a specialist service for adults with autistic disorders and co-morbid mental health problems, with a level of security dictated by his risk assessment."[25] Talha Ahsan's case highlights how a medical discourse of diagnosis is in turn linked to the militarized apparatuses of the post-9/11 security state. Indeed, the Shy Radicals project urgently intervenes at an often overlooked point of intersection between neurodiversity and the ethnic and racial politics of the U.S.-driven global war on terror, which drastically expanded the surveillance and criminalization of Muslim communities across the globe. In Talha's legal case, the construction of shyness or introversion as a pathological or even dangerous symptom was compounded by the deeply racialized and Islamophobic logic that undergirds the contemporary field of counterterrorism. The role of psychiatric expertise in the consolidation of an increasingly medicalized understanding of terrorism as "a symptom of the deviant psyche, the psyche gone awry, or the failed psyche" cannot be overlooked; nor can its emergence within a geopolitical context in which Islam and Muslim cultures are persistently characterized as pathologically "backward," uncivilized, and even monstrous.[26]

Shy Radicals offers a bracing vision of how shyness, introversion, and other forms of inwardness that might not rise to the threshold of clinical diagnosis might in fact become the basis for an otherwise—in this case, an underground revolutionary movement fueled by insurgent cultural practices and forms of the militant introvert in the face of an extrovert-supremacist world. Another indication of the seriousness and urgency of the Shy Radicals project, despite its surface-level insouciance, concerns the way that it implicitly invokes the Islamic virtue of modesty, al-ḥayāʾ,

which is often translated as "shyness." The concept of al-ḥayā᾿ has a rich and complex history within Islamic thought that stretches far beyond the scope of the present discussion. Both Islamic and secular sources recognize al-ḥayā᾿ as a property said to be possessed by the Prophet Muhammad himself. Yet al-ḥayā᾿ has also been important to recent debates about Islam's relationship to secular modernity. For instance, anthropologist Saba Mahmood argues that how al-ḥayā᾿ structures the relationship between the expression of faith and bodily comportment for many Muslims problematizes bedrock understandings "about the role embodied behavior plays in the constitution of the subject" in Western, liberal, and feminist theoretical frameworks.[27]

Yet when in *Shy Radicals* Ahsan has one Amy Littlewood—"the longest detained-without-trial Shy Radicals political prisoner"—compare diagnostic taxonomy manuals to "an aviary of exotic birds" (54), he seems to be invoking a potent counterpoint to how autism was invoked in his brother's legal case. "I, Otherstani," a 2013 poem that Talha wrote while in prison in the United States, was in part inspired by a famous parable by twelfth-century Sufi mystic Attar of Nishapur, which tells the story of a gathering of the birds of the world who assemble to select a leader from among themselves. "I, Otherstani" describes a "world divided into Hereistan and Thereistan," in which "a geometry of death weaves a map across a terrain/each calls mine."

So where is Otherstan?
It is between the gaps of words, the hollows between syllables
Its rivers are no better than running noses.[28]

The Shy Underground reimagines the language and iconography of radical liberation movements of the past to ask how the tactics they adopted might be reconstituted in defense of those Otherstanis who seek to dwell in "between the gaps of words" or in the "hollows between syllables." Otherstan and Aspergistan are imaginative responses to a divided world in which shyness is no longer just a euphemism for the quieter repertoires and softer textures through which the idiosyncrasies of a personality can be expressed but a potentially ominous behavioral symptom—the troubling sign of an abnormal, excessive, even dangerous tendency toward introversion.

The first pages of what would become the Shy Radicals project were written while Ahsan was in the midst of spearheading the public campaign to secure his brother's release. While searching for ways to help Talha endure the harrowing conditions of his long imprisonment, Ahsan had come across a guide to surviving solitary confinement written by Bonnie Kerness, a Quaker activist and prison watch coordinator for the American Friends Service Committee. In an interesting parallel to the ethos of punk zine culture, the guidebook circulates through underground networks of information distribution to reach its intended audience, passing from one prisoner to another in defiance of the knowledge-deadening designs of the carceral institution.

Inspired by Kerness's guidebook, the first section of *Shy Radicals* is presented in the form of a transcript of an interview with Amy Littlewood. The interview, we are told, was conducted in the presence of her human rights lawyer by a journalist who "has chosen to remain anonymous." Littlewood is an Australian national who refuses to claim her citizenship status, instead "declaring herself to be a citizen of the 'Aspergistan homeland state'" (54). Her responses to the anonymous journalist's questions offer a riveting account of the origins and development of the Shy Radicals movement, presenting a kind of fun-house mirror version of the forking historical trajectories taken by radical social movements after the 1960s. "The medics pathologize our peoples," she says, "but we should instead, as the Socialist Patient's Collective advised, use our illness as our weapon" (57). Littlewood's militant defense of shyness requires drawing strategic lines of alliance and solidarity across various forms of difference: "Divide and rule is their game. First, the authorities attempted to divide us into various pathologies: Asperger's syndrome, social anxiety disorder, depression. But we are all one. We suffer as one. We fight as one. And then it was 'extremist' introverts and 'moderate' introverts. They want to depoliticize Shyness as a purely 'cultural phenomenon' or a medical pathology. . . . They want us to accept the taxonomies of their diagnostic manuals like an aviary of exotic birds. But shyness is a political position" (56).

The global network of the Shy Underground movement that Hamja Ahsan imagined is starting to manifest itself in the world beyond the pages of the published book thanks to a growing network of readers who recognize a place for themselves in the project's vision of a radical shy, introvert, and autistic alliance that upends and unsettles seemingly sedimented axes of identity and belonging: "Shy Radicals is not just about revolutionary empowerment and a defense strategy for the Shy people, but a revolutionary remapping of the totem of identity politics" (138). This has allowed Shy Radicals to continue on as a collaboratively generated, constantly evolving project, one that has now taken on a certain formal resemblance to the networked, distributed, and modulating character of the internet. Ahsan considers the circulation of new ideas, images, and DIY art and writing projects aligned with the Shy Underground to be an integral extension of the work itself. For the 2019 edition of the Ljubljana Biennial of Graphic Arts, curated by art collective Slavs and Tatars, Ahsan created a referendum modeled on the ballot used for the Brexit vote that invited visitors to the exhibition to cast their votes on whether Ljubljana should formally secede from Slovenia to join the Shy People's Republic. (The vote tally was overwhelmingly in favor; Ahsan was awarded the Biennial's grand prize.) The @ShyRadicals Instagram account is full of images uploaded and tagged by a far-flung global network of partisans and fellow travelers of the Shy Underground movement. Many send selfies giving the salute of the Shy Introfada—"curling fist in front of mouth"—which is at once a tribute to and a sly détournement of the gestural iconography associated with the Black Power and other militant anticolonial liberation movements of the 1960s and 1970s.

This project of speculatively mapping (while also generating) the territory of Aspergistan has continued to evolve and take on new inventive forms. Ahsan's contribution to the 2023 edition of the international art exhibition *Documenta* consisted of a series of LED signs advertising a set of competing fried chicken franchises affixed to public buildings throughout Kassel, the small German city that has hosted *Documenta* every five years since 1955. (Unfortunately, the fried chicken shops themselves were unrealized.) Thus, in addition to posting LED signs for Kaliphate Fried Chicken ("Feeding the Ummah Since 1924"), the Popular Front for the Liberation of Fried Chicken, and Fanon Fried Chicken ("Fast Food for the Wretched of the Earth"), Ahsan also included a sign for Aspergistan Midnight Wings (24 hours). As Ahsan notes of this piece, "Many see the rise of chicken shops, especially in the U.K. but also in other western European countries, as the rise of Islamification. . . . But what these places actually offer are spaces that are beyond borders, beyond nation states, beyond ethnicities and beyond languages. Fried chicken has the power to do that."[29] While certainly Ahsan's efforts to map the imaginary terrain of Aspergistan, he observes, "is fiction that's supposed to make people laugh, every single discussion that occurs afterward is always deadly serious."[30] In line with the mélange of speculative, utopian, and surrealist traditions from which it draws, Aspergistan is an intricately constructed fictional world that also functions as a biting critique of the present.

In a 2019 interview, Hamja Ahsan observed that "if we generally had an autism liberation movement, I believe it would liberate others in the process."[31] The urgency of creating a movement that would be capacious enough to include the most marginalized, discounted, and disenfranchised among its adherents is intriguing. As the historical instances I have traced in the previous chapters suggest, there have also been countermaneuvers, evasions, and everyday resistances that have taken shape in the eddies of these histories of attempts to compel neurotypicality. The archive under consideration here has unfurled mainly outside conventional channels of social recognition and political legitimation and beyond the glare of what is conventionally understood to be oppositional, political, or resistant in the usual ways that these stances are typically defined and adjudicated. Rather, I have sought to emphasize an archive that could sustain an account of the performative that bridges the importance of art and aesthetic practice with attempts to shape the behavior of autistic and other neurodivergent people.

This has largely not been an account of performative force of the kind that functions by mounting a frontal resistance to power, or that uncritically adopts the terms and the battle terrain produced by the dominant ordering of the sensorium according to a rubric that will gradually come to be nameable as neurotypical. Instead, many of the most important parts of this book's argument emerge from instances that are indirect and imperceptible. The examples that I have turned to in this book implicitly challenge and call into question the parameters of what we mean by performance as action or consequential behavior. These projects reject the medicalizing or pathologizing perspectives that define neurovariation in terms of debilitation or lack, endeavoring instead to ask how such variations actually engender other possibilities for thinking about neurodivergence as a mode of being. Their authors suggest that even as such relational styles and engagements may remain inscrutable or inaccessible to the neurotypical perspective of the ordinary way, they are nonetheless worthy of critical attention. Rather, I have attempted to be alert to the ways that autistic and neurodivergent artists, writers, filmmakers, and others have *destituted* the performative force of clinical categories, turning to different aesthetic registers to repurpose them.

Just as the cartographic tracings of Deligny's network that were not undertaken as part of a finished or already elaborated project, this too is a performativity of the errant, but one that still maintains a sense of experimentation and openness toward an institution to come, always on the verge of arriving but definitionally resistant to any solidification or realization in the present. "Otherwise said," writes Deligny of his group's tiny encampment in the mountainous desert, "this small, completely minuscule part of the earthly globe where the children whose wandering trajectories we trace walk and run, does not claim to seed the entire surface and does not at all tend toward a globality where the ideological absolute could be found."[32]

Turning back to the imaginary cartography of Aspergistan, we might ask whether, in the age of neurological personhood and neuronal ideology, the curled fist of the Shy Introfada might silently signal the vanguard of a new terrain of destituent struggle. Could attending to the radically anti–"extrovert supremacism" of the militant introvert that is called for by the denizens of the Shy Underground be one of the defining struggles of today? Though *Shy Radicals* does not definitively answer this question, it does, in the most rigorous aesthetic traditions of speculative and critical hope, crystallize something about how it feels to be alive right now. Shy Radicals suggests a pathway for a neurodivergent politics that might be recast as a destituent struggle, one that deactivates the forms of compulsory sociality that structure the Extrovert-supremacist world. As such, we underestimate the quietly subversive and subterranean revolutionary potential of shy power at our peril. "Our silence and reclusiveness means that our message cannot be misused or instrumentalized," the Japanese Hikikomori delegation to the Shy Underground network warns in their missive to the group. "We cannot be stopped."[33]

Acknowledgments

Crucial support enabling the completion of this project was provided by the Henry Merritt Wriston Award and a Cogut Institute Faculty Fellowship at Brown University, and the Emerging Faculty Leaders Award from the Institute for Citizens and Scholars. Archival research that came to form the basis for this book was made possible thanks to a Mellon Postdoctoral Fellowship at the Wolf Humanities Center at the University of Pennsylvania and a Mellon/ACLS Dissertation Completion Fellowship. I would like to acknowledge the help of the librarians and archivists at L'Institut Mémoires de l'édition contemporaine (IMEC).

An important milestone in the development of the eventual form that this book was to take was a symposium at Brown University, organized with the help of students in my seminar "Neurodiversity: Science, Politics and Culture" and the support of the Department of Theatre Arts and Performance Studies, the Pembroke Center, and the Cogut Institute for the Humanities. I am especially grateful to the symposium's participants—Remi Yergeau, Cyrée Jarelle Johnson, Hamja Ahsan, Ly Xīnzhèn M. Zhǎngsūn Brown, Jina B. Kim, Diana Paulin, and Nic John Ramos—for sharing their catalyzing work. My thanks as well to Javier Téllez, Jonathan Berger, Lia Gangitano, the International Centre of Graphic Arts in Ljubljana, Mitchell-Innes & Nash and the Estate of William Pope.L, and Sandra Alvarez de Toledo and Anaïs Masson at Editions L'Arachnéen. Danielle M. Kasprzak, Leah Pennywark, and the team at the University of Minnesota Press guided the book's pathway to publication with great skill, care, and patience.

The ideas in this study are inseparable from conversations and encounters with many people I have had over the course of writing it. The heart of this project emerged under the mentorship of José Esteban Muñoz, who was the first person to see how my inchoate ideas might cohere into a contribution to and from performance studies. José's imprint on my thinking and impact on my life suffuse everything I write; his absence is still keenly felt every day. I am also thankful to Tavia Nyong'o, André Lepecki, Karen Shimakawa, Barbara Browning, Ann Pellegrini, Richard Schechner, Diana Taylor, and other faculty members in the Department of Performance Studies at New York University. Many of the trajectories of thinking and writing that shaped this book were first opened up to me by Patricia Clough, Licia Fiol-Matta, Alexander Galloway, Faye Ginsburg, Gayatri Gopinath, Elizabeth Grosz, Heather Love, Avital Ronell, and Gus Stadler. I deeply benefited, along the way, from the chance to learn from Jennifer Doyle, Lisa Duggan, Jasbir Puar, Juana María Rodríguez, and Karen Tongson, as well as Sally Bachner, Howard Needler, Khachig Tölölyan, John Vincent, Fred Schenk, and Makoto Ogura.

This book was strengthened by ongoing discussions with many scholars of disability, autism, and neurodiversity, and I would particularly like to acknowledge D. L. Adams, Tanja Aho, Patrick Anderson, Liat Ben-Moshe, Michael Bérubé, La Marr Jurelle Bruce, Mel Y. Chen, Jina B. Kim, Georgina Kleege, Petra Kuppers, Micki McGee, Mara Mills, Diana Paulin, Therí Pickens, Emily Lim Rogers, Sami Schalk, Yvonne Schmidt, Susan Schweik, Jess Waggoner, and Cynthia Wu. I am grateful to Julie Dind, Marlon Miguel, Sarah Moses, Laura Odello, Peter Szendy, and David Wills for their assistance with matters of translation.

Many wonderful colleagues at Brown contributed to the welcoming intellectual community that helped nurture this book, including Leticia Alvarado, Amanda Anderson, Jayna Brown, Sarah dAngelo, J. Dellecave, Spencer Golub, Alani Hicks-Bartlett, Bonnie Honig, Julia Jarcho, Jasmine Johnson, Lynne Joyrich, Jacques Khalip, Jennifer Lambe, Brian Lander, Kym Moore, Madison Moore, Sawako Nakayasu, Laura Odello, Emily Owens, Kevin Quashie, Rebecca Schneider, Holly Shaffer, Sydney Skybetter, Peter Szendy, Thea Quiray Tagle, Sarah Thomas, Debbie Weinstein, Sarah Wilbur, and Patricia Ybarra. It is also a pleasure to acknowledge the graduate students I've had the privilege of working with, and from whom I have learned so much, including Cecilia Azar, Amber Hawk Swanson (who also offered critical assistance with image permissions),

Yeong Ran Kim, Mohammad Mehdi Kimiagari, Courtney Lau, Marlon Jiménez Oviedo, J. D. Stokely, Mariahadessa Ekere Tallie, and Brett Zehner. Julie Dind, my first doctoral advisee, provided indispensable assistance, interlocution, and expertise not only with translation questions but also on everything related to our shared interest in Fernand Deligny, and our mutual belief in his relevance for thinking through new modes and articulations of autism as a way of being.

My work on this project has taken place alongside and in the company of many friends and compatriots in performance studies, including Sareh Afshar, Katie Brewer-Ball, Joshua Chambers-Letson, J. DeLeon, Adrienne Edwards, Joshua Javier Guzmán, Raquel Gutiérrez, Vivian Huang, Karen Jaime, Summer Kim Lee, Deb Levine, Christine Mok, Coleman Nye, Ethan Philbrick, Alex Pittman, Leticia Robles-Moreno, Sandra Ruiz, Shanté Paradigm Smalls, Jeanne Vaccaro, Alexandra Vazquez, Shane Vogel, and Hentyle Yapp. I am also grateful for the intellectual comradeship of John Andrews, Marcus Anthony Brock, Lauren DiGiulio, Sarah Kessler, Marci Kwon, Greta LaFleur, Meredith Lee, Katie Lennard, Amber Musser, Jamie Parra, Judy Rodríguez, Poulomi Saha, Avgi Saketopoulou, Robyn Schroeder, Aarti Sethi, Althea Sricar, Eric Stanley, Magda Szcześniak, Damon Young, Gillian Young, and Genevieve Yue.

The friendships I've been fortunate to develop with artists Ron Athey, Nao Bustamante, Vaginal Davis, Stosh Fila, and Julie Tolentino have enabled me to cultivate an aesthetic and political imagination capacious enough to conceptualize a project like this one simply by letting me spend time with them. The life-sustaining companionship of Ari M. Brostoff, Dan Drake, Allison Hughes, Peter Oleksik, Russell Perkins, Christine Stulik, Dennis Webber, Margaret Trissel, Coco Joly, Susannah Hyland, and Solomon Trissel Hyland has been essential. I must also thank Arden Handler, Suzi Naiburg, and Diana Lidofsky for their indispensable support through the writing process.

My family—Marc Hilton and Judith Aronson, Ezra Hilton, Orly Henry, and Margalit and Jonah—has been steadfastly encouraging throughout this long and sometimes arduous journey. Hugo the irrepressable schnauzer arrived late on the scene, bearing boundless quantities of joy that carried me over the finish line. Finally: this book would quite literally not exist without Iván Ramos. I am thankful for the thinking we have done and the life we have made together.

Notes

Introduction

1. Téllez, "Filmmaker Javier Téllez."

2. Javier Téllez, interview with the author, New York City, October 2017.

3. At one time considered one of the most progressive mental health institutions in Latin America, Bárbula occupies a significant if largely overlooked place within the transnational geographies of psychiatric thought. The hospital was founded in the 1951 by Cristóbal Masia, a student of radical Catalan psychiatrist François Tosquelles, director of the Saint-Alban psychiatric hospital in France. Tosquelles proposed a radically new vision of mental health treatment that sought to address the social basis of psychological suffering by reimaging the social dynamics of the clinical institution, including doctors, other staff, and patients. See Robcis, *Disalienation.*

4. Rancière, *Aesthesis,* x.

5. Rancière, *Politics of Aesthetics,* 13.

6. Rancière, 13.

7. Téllez in Faguet, "Sueño de la razón," 50.

8. Gloria Anzaldúa writes of this continent-spanning territorial dividing line between the United States and Mexico as "una herida abierta [an open wound] where the Third World grates against the first and bleeds." Anzaldúa, *Borderlands,* 25.

9. Téllez, "Madness Is the Language." See also, e.g., Levinas, *Otherwise than Being.*

10. *Neurodiversity* continues to be a term in active circulation within autism self-advocacy, disability, and mental health communities and discourses, even as the word *neurodivergence,* originally proposed by writer and autism activist Kassiane A. Asasumasu, has more recently come to prominence, especially in online discussions. The latter term has tended to be used to indicate a wider

range of conditions, experiences, and diagnostic taxonomies. It also offers a preferable adjective, *neurodivergent,* to use in contrast to the term *neurotypical.* See Asasumasu, Radical Neurodivergence Speaking (blog).

11. Malabou, *What Should We Do with Our Brain?*

12. See Fleche, "Echoing Autism."

13. Kaplan, "Afterword," 303–4.

14. See Kittay, "When Caring Is Just."

15. McGee, "Neurodiversity."

16. Ogilvie, "Living between the Lines," 16.

17. Deligny, *Arachnean,* 79. I have drawn from Burk and Porter's published English translation of Deligny's *L'Arachnéen et autres textes* as well as the original French texts published in Deligny's *Oeuvres.* My discussion also incorporates unpublished material, including typed and handwritten manuscripts and personal correspondence, that I viewed in Deligny's archives at L'Institut Mémoires de l'édition contemporaine (IMEC) in France. Translations from these original French sources are my own unless otherwise indicated.

18. See also Yergeau, *Authoring Autism;* and J. J. Kahn, "On Evasion."

19. American Psychiatric Association, *Diagnostic and Statistical Manual, Fifth Edition.*

20. "Surface of emergence" is a concept from Foucault, *Archeology of Knowledge.*

21. On the historical emergence of autism as distinct clinical category, the following sources are especially illuminating: Eyal, *Autism Matrix;* Hacking, *Social Construction of What?;* McDonaugh, "Autism and Modernism"; Nadesan, *Constructing Autism;* Silberman, *NeuroTribes;* Silverman, *Understanding Autism.*

22. Sinclair, "Don't Mourn for Us."

23. Singer, "Why Can't You Be Normal."

24. Singer, "There's a Lot in a Name."

25. Singer.

26. Blume, "Neurodiversity." See also Savarese and Savarese, "Superior Half of Speaking," and Jaarsma and Welin, "Autism as a Natural Human Variation."

27. On debility and capacity as affect-laden categories for conceptualizing the distribution of vulnerability and risk within and beyond liberal regimes of the "normal," see Puar, "Cost of Getting Better"; and Puar, *Right to Maim.*

28. Wallace, "Are You On It?"

29. "Muskie" is quoted in Savarese and Savarese, "Superior Half of Speaking."

30. Bleuler, *Dementia Praecox.*

31. Kanner, "Autistic Disturbances," 242.

32. Kanner, "Irrelevant and Metaphorical Language," 242.

33. Eyal, "For a Sociology of Expertise," 868.

34. See Eyal, *Autism Matrix,* 76–82.

35. See Bettelheim, *Empty Fortress.*

36. See Friedan, *Feminine Mystique,* 413–16.

37. Nadesan, *Constructing Autism,* 109.

38. The hypothesis that autistic people lack a Theory of Mind has become widely known in connection with the research of cognitive psychologist Simon Baron-Cohen, who lays out the theory in its most comprehensive form in *Mindblindness.* "Mindblindness" is a term that has been increasingly criticized by many autistic writers and self-advocates when used to describe the condition. Nonetheless, it continues to circulate in wider public discussions of autism and certain other mental disorders. For autistic and neurodivergent critiques of mindblindness, see Blackburn et al., "Discussion about Theory of Mind"; and Yergeau, "Clinically Significant Disturbance."

39. Markram, Rinaldi, and Markram, "Intense World Syndrome," 77.

40. See Mottron, Dawson, and Soulières, "Enhanced Perception."

41. Baron-Cohen, "Systemizing Quotient," 358.

42. Rodas, *Autistic Disturbances,* 59.

43. Straus speculates about whether "due to its lack of secure biological basis, autism might eventually follow the path of neurasthenia and hysteria into quaintness and irrelevance." Straus, *Autism as Culture,* 465.

44. McGuire, *War on Autism,* 44.

45. Yergeau, *Authoring Autism,* 32.

46. See, e.g., Mouridsen et al., "Mortality and Causes of Death."

47. Foucault, *"Society Must Be Defended,"* 241. In the same lecture, Foucault offers the concept of the statistical mortality rate as one of his key examples of the new technologies of biopower that emerged in the latter part of the eighteenth century, which inaugurate a shift in the target of governance from the individual to the "population." The transition from individual to population is characterized by a shift from the governance of "man-as-body" (sovereign power) to the governance of "man-as-species" (disciplinary power and biopower).

48. Clare, *Brilliant Imperfection,* 48.

49. On the legal cases taken against the Rotenberg Center, see Ahern, *Torture not Treatment.*

50. Adams and Erevelles, "Unexpected Spaces," 361.

51. Scott, "Evidence of Experience," 773.

52. The most sustained discussions of psychiatric power are contained in the lectures from 1973 to 1975, the period during which Foucault was also engaged in writing *Discipline and Punish.* These lectures are collected in *Psychiatric Power* and *Abnormal.*

53. Foucault, *Psychiatric Power,* 202.

54. Canguilhem, *The Normal and the Pathological,* 277.

55. Foucault, *Abnormal,* 50.

56. This point will become central to the account of biopower developed in Foucault's *History of Sexuality, Vol. 1.*

57. It is worth considering why this is so. Lynne Huffer notes that for the first several decades of his scholarly reception in the United States critics tended to concentrate on only a few of the books that were published and translated during Foucault's lifetime (most notably *History of Sexuality, Vol. 1,* and *Discipline and Punish,* and, to a lesser extent, *The Archeology of Knowledge* and *The Order of Things*). For this reason, the wider context and full scope of Foucault's insights were frequently reduced and simplified, even as they became foundational for entirely new areas of critical research. Huffer maintains that such limited and partial readings of Foucault have even led to outright misrepresentations of his positions—particularly regarding his controversial arguments about the unpredictable and diffuse character of power; the historical contingency of modern taxonomies of sexual identity; and the bleak prospects for individual or collective political resistance that his work has seemed, for some, to represent. Thus, Foucault's influence across the humanities and social sciences—while extensive and lasting—has been based on a partial and incomplete view of his ideas. See Huffer, *Mad for Foucault.* Jasbir Puar offers a related point regarding the separate and sometimes contradictory ways that Foucault's work was taken up during the first decades of his posthumous reception. Puar notes that in their readings of *History of Sexuality, Vol. 1,* queer theorists focused on the critiques of psychoanalysis and the repressive hypothesis found in the book's first half, while postcolonial and critical race scholars tended to draw from the account of biopower formulated in its latter pages to emphasize the racial and ethnic stratifications endemic to the biopolitical management of human life. Puar writes that we "can trace the genealogic engagements of *The History of Sexuality* as a splitting: scholars of race and postcoloniality taking up biopolitics, while queer scholars work with dismantling the repressive hypothesis." (She adds: "These are tendencies, not absolutes.") Arguably this schism is no longer as pervasive, due in part to the transnational turn within queer studies as well as the field's increasing engagement with questions of disability and bodily capacity. See Puar, *Terrorist Assemblages,* 34.

58. See Davis, "Constructing Normalcy."

59. Garland-Thomson, *Figuring Physical Disability,* 8.

60. Lazzarato, "Concepts of Life."

61. Rose and Abi-Rached, *Neuro;* Connolly, *Neuropolitics;* Malabou, *What Should We Do with Our Brain?*

62. Bergson, *Matter and Memory,* 30.

63. Sedgwick and Frank, "Shame in the Cybernetic Fold," 105.

64. Malabou, *What Should We Do with Our Brain?,* 47.

65. Malabou, 68.

66. See Malabou, *New Wounded.*

67. Slaby and Gallagher, "Critical Neuroscience."

68. Pitts-Taylor, "Plastic Brain," 639.

69. Cromby, Newton, and Williams, "Neuroscience and Subjectivity," 224.

70. Lazzarato, "Concepts of Life."

71. Terranova, "Futurepublic."

72. Han, *Burnout Society,* 23; emphasis added.

73. Skott-Myhre and Taylor, "Autism: Schizo of Postmodern Capital," 39.

74. Skott-Myhre and Taylor, 45; emphasis added. Erin Manning similarly considers autism and neurodiversity as minor or minoritarian modes of perception and selfhood in *The Minor Gesture,* among other works.

75. Cooter, "Neural Veils," 148.

76. Cooter, 151–52.

77. See Harvey, *Brief History of Neoliberalism.*

78. On disability and the austerity politics of neoliberalism, see Mitchell and Snyder, *Biopolitics of Disability.*

79. Spade, *Normal Life,* 20.

80. See Povinelli, *Economies of Abandonment,* and Ferguson, *Reorder of Things,* for two scholarly accounts that inform this project's understanding of liberalism's incorporative approach to difference. In disability studies, analyses of the vexations of liberal inclusion include Ben-Moshe, *Decarcerating Disability;* J. Kim, "Toward a Crip-of-Color Critique"; Puar, *Right to Maim;* Samuels, *Fantasies of Identification;* and Schalk, *Black Disability Politics.*

81. Mitchell and Snyder, "Disability as Multitude," 184.

82. Taylor, "The Right Not to Work."

83. Cowen, "Economic and Rational Choice Approach."

84. High-functioning autism is commonly, if not universally, used interchangeably with Asperger syndrome. Yet as demonstrated by the controversies surrounding proposals to eliminate Asperger syndrome from the most recent revision to the *DSM,* whether the wide range of abilities, impairments, and behaviors that have come to be associated with autism can be attributed to a single, biologically discrete disorder remains far from settled within biomedical and psychiatric research.

85. Kim, "Decoding the High Functioning Label."

86. Quoted in Baggs, "Putting Autism on Trial."

87. Murray, "Autism Functions."

88. Murray.

89. Deligny, *Nous et l'innocent,* 43: "Qu'en serait-il d'un *mode de relation* qui ne serait pas utile à la société, pas utilisable, pas utilisé? Un mode de relation hors function?" (What would it be like to have a mode of relation that would not be useful to society, not usable, not used? A nonfunctioning mode of relation?) Bertrand Ogilvie suggests that Deligny constantly found himself struggling with a contradiction identified by Georges Bataille, who asked "how to form the project of exiting from all projects?" Ogilvie, "Living between the Lines," 15. See Bataille, *Inner Experience.*

90. Deligny, *Nous et l'innocent,* 79.

91. Deligny, *Arachnean,* 149.

92. Deligny, 86.

93. Deligny, *Arachnéen et autres textes,* 31.

94. Deligny, *Arachnean,* 52.

95. See especially Carlson, *Affect, Animals, Autists,* which provides an account of how the human/nonhuman distinction has been a key theme within theatrical representations of autism. Her study is complementary to my own in many respects. See also Anne Fleche, "Echoing Autism."

96. Performance, as Michael Trask observes, has become one of the most significant and contested terms in social theory in the post–World War II period. This status has led it to become ever more firmly fixed and institutionalized within the "knowledge factory" of the university through the establishment of academic departments and degree programs in performance studies, and with performance and performativity being taken up as conceptual terms and frameworks in an ever-widening variety of academic fields, including anthropology, art history, robotics, economics, and quantum physics. See Trask, *Camp Sites;* see also Pickering, *Mangle of Practice.* In the genealogy of speech act theory and performativity, this trajectory can be traced from J. L. Austin's 1954 lectures, published in 1975 as *How to Do Things with Words,* through Judith Butler's writing on excitable speech acts. The theoretical work around performativity and its influence on more traditional scholarship of the performing arts has not been without controversy or contestation (see, e.g., Manning's entry on "Performance" in *Keywords in American Studies*). Shannon Jackson's *Professing Performance* and Erika Fischer-Lichte's *Transformative Power of Performance* illuminate key aspects of these debates as they have played out within academic field formations of theatre and performance studies in the United States and Europe. Diana Taylor's *Performance* offers an account of performance theory grounded in the decolonial politics and aesthetics of the Hemispheric Americas. An account of performativity as a mode of racialized "doing" is offered by José Esteban Muñoz in "Feeling Brown, Feeling Down" and elsewhere.

97. Conquergood, "Performance Studies," 146.

98. McGrath, *Naming Adult Autism,* 196.

99. Rodas, *Autistic Disturbances,* 34.

100. J. J. Kahn, "On Evasion."

101. Benveniste, "Analytical Philosophy and Language," 236–38.

102. Felman, *Scandal,* 65.

103. The etymological derivation of *function* is from the classical Latin functiō-, which itself is traced to the Latin verb fungor (discharge, observe, perform), and includes now-obsolete usages for the observance of religious rituals and the payment of taxes. See "Function," *Oxford English Dictionary,* www.oed.com.

104. Murray, "Autism Functions/The Function of Autism."

105. Murray.

106. Invisible Committee, *Now.*

107. Invisible Committee, 78–79.

108. Invisible Committee, 81.

109. Cited in Invisible Committee, 83.

110. Ogilvie, "Living between the Lines," 16.

111. Deligny, *Arachnean,* 145.

112. Deligny is referring to several passages in Guattari's essay "La place du signifiant dans l'institution," published in English as "The Role of the Signifier in the Institution" in *Molecular Revolution,* that lay out a theory of language within institutions (including psychiatric institutions) as the "collective enunciation" of a group. Drawing on his years spent as a staff psychiatrist at La Borde, Guattari offers an account of collective enunciation as the way that "signs and things engage one another independently of the subjective control that agents of individual utterance claim to have over them. . . . A collective agency of utterance is then in a position to *deprive* [destituer] the spoken word of its function as imaginary support to the cosmos. It replaces it with a collective voice that combines machinic elements of all kinds—human, semiotic, technological, scientific, etc. The illusion of specific utterance by a human subject vanishes, and can be seen as having been merely a side-effect of the statements produced and manipulated by political and economic systems." Guattari, *Molecular Revolution,* 76.

113. Deligny, "Le croire et le craindre," in *Oeuvres,* 1162. The original reads: "Destituer—la parole—n'implique-t-il pas la nécessité d'instituer 'autre chose'?"

114. Pinchevski, "Bartleby's Autism," 54.

115. Pinchevski, 39.

116. Pinchevski, 52.

117. Deligny, "A comme asile," 30; translation by me and Julie Dind.

1. Feral Performatives

1. Itard, *Historical Account,* 10 (page numbers appear parenthetically subsequently). This chapter cites the 1802 English translation of Itard's book, published a year after the French original, which first appeared as *De l'éducation d'un homme sauvage* in 1801.

2. See Simpson, "From Savage to Citizen," 561–74.

3. Eyal, *Autism Matrix,* 151. See also Lovaas, "Development," and Lovaas et al., "Some Generalizations."

4. Yergeau, *Authoring Autism,* 112.

5. Frith, *Autism,* 35.

6. Collins, *Not Even Wrong.*

7. See Haraway, *Simians, Cyborgs, and Women,* 164. See also Hacking, *Social Construction of What?,* 311.

8. Mitchell and Snyder, "Compulsory Feral-ization," 631.

9. White, *Tropics of Discourse,* 154.

10. White, 154.

11. Kant, "Answer to the Question," 17. Notably for the historical debate about the relationship between "nervous sensibility" and "intellect" discussed below,

Kant continues: "This immaturity is self-incurred when its cause does not lie in a lack of intellect, but rather in a lack of resolve and courage to make use of one's intellect without the direction of another." Kant's own writing on insanity and his philosophical classification of mental disorders as an outgrowth of the conflict between reason and the "passions" would be taken up in the French psychiatric tradition of "moral treatment" advanced by Philippe Pinel and Jean-Étienne Dominique Esquirol, largely thanks to the intermediary influence of Scottish physician Alexander Crichton, who had studied advances in medical psychology in Germany. Crichton's *An Inquiry into the Nature and Origins of Mental Derangement,* which Pinel encountered on its publication in 1798, "confirmed Pinel's belief that his reliance on observation of the patient's feelings, as expressed in words, gestures, moods, and attitudes toward others, offered a reliable—indeed, the only reliable—path toward a diagnosis of mental illness in the living patient." Weiner, "Mind and Body," 361–62.

12. Benzaquén, *Encounters with Wild Children,* 9.

13. Simplican, *Capacity Contract,* 47.

14. Itard, *Historical Account,* 144.

15. Itard, 144.

16. Itard refers to Alexander Crichton as well as English physician Francis Willis, who was charged with managing King George III's struggles with mental illness in the 1780s; both were cited by Pinel in his highly influential *Traité médico-philosophique sur l'aliénation mentale* (1800) as predecessors for his own approach to psychological therapy as "moral treatment," which emphasized the therapeutic value of writing case histories through close observation and conversation with patients and rejected earlier treatments of insanity like bleeding and purging as antiquated and cruel. See Weiner, "Mind and Body," 354.

17. Sheldon, *Child to Come,* 630.

18. A genealogy of the modern psychiatric surveillance of childhood is sketched in Foucault's 1973–74 lectures on psychiatric power. The lecture dated January 16, 1974, contains an illuminating discussion of Itard. See Foucault, *Psychiatric Power,* 202–31.

19. Foucault, *Psychiatric Power,* 223.

20. Foucault, 203.

21. Foucault, 204.

22. Foucault, 205; he quotes here from Esquirol, *Des Maladies mentale.*

23. Foucault, *Psychiatric Power,* 221.

24. Gillain, *François Truffaut,* 236.

25. Gillain, 239.

26. Cited in Andrew, "Every Teacher Needs a Truant," 237.

27. Andrew, 231.

28. Cited in de Baecque and Toubiana, *Truffaut,* 261.

29. Fernand Deligny, letter to François Truffaut, 16 November 1968.

30. Mitchell and Snyder, "Compulsory Feral-ization," 629.

31. *L'Autre côté de la parole,* unpublished manuscript, IMEC Fonds Deligny, DGN 5, p. 1.

32. This biographical summary is indebted to the extensive "Chronologie" compiled by Sandra Alvarez de Toledo, the editor of Fernand Deligny's *Oeuvres,* 1821–31.

33. In Deligny, *Oeuvres,* 1822.

34. Deligny, "A comme asile."

35. Dosse, *Gilles Deleuze and Félix Guattari,* 72.

36. Miguel, "Le matérialisme concret," 133; my translation.

37. For a collection of Deligny's writings on cinema and the image that also situates his work within the history of film and traditions of minor media, see Deligny, *Camering.*

38. Astruc, "Birth of the New Avant-Garde," 158. In this essay, Astruc defines auteurism in cinema as having "gradually become a language . . . a form in which and by which an artist can express his thoughts, however abstract they may be, or translate his obsessions exactly as he does in the contemporary essay or novel" (158).

39. Andrew, "Malraux, Bazin," 162.

40. Sontag, "Artaud," xxxv–vi.

41. Astruc, "Birth of the New Avant-Garde."

42. Fernand Deligny, "La caméra outil pédagogique," in Deligny, *Camérer,* 22–27; my translation. A slightly different English translation appears in Deligny, *Camering,* 70.

43. Merleau-Ponty, "Indirect Language."

44. Deligny, *Oeuvres,* 1744; my translation.

45. Sontag, "Artaud," xxxvi.

46. See Deligny and Truffaut, "Correspondence."

47. Conley, *Cartographic Cinema,* 150.

48. Though a number of subsequent scholars and commentators have referred to Yves as autistic, Deligny himself does not describe him as such. Typically Deligny says that Yves was "débile profonde," and he is also described as "psychotic." Deligny's shift to a specific interest in autism is typically dated to the beginning of his work with Janmari in 1966, several years after the footage that would become *Le moindre geste* was shot. (My thanks to Julie Dind for noting this important detail.) The lack of terminological clarity in these discussions is indicative of the extent to which diagnostic language was in a state of flux during this period; autism was often diagnosed interchangeably with childhood schizophrenia among other disorders until the early 1980s.

49. Andrew, "Malraux, Bazin," 162. See also Deligny, *Oeuvres,* 213.

50. D. Kahn, *Noise Water Meat,* 348.

51. See Mitchell and Snyder, *Narrative Prosthesis.*

52. See Guattari, "Cinéma."

53. Genosko, *Félix Guattari,* 135.

54. Getino and Solanas, "Toward a Third Cinema," 275.

55. Daney, *Cinema House,* 180–81. This text was originally published in 1976.

56. Andrew, "Every Teacher Needs a Truant," 221.

57. Andrew, 230.

58. Quoted in Andrew, 232.

59. Andrew, "Every Teacher Needs a Truant," 233.

60. Lovaas, "Development," 621. See Eyal, *Autism Matrix,* 151. Lovaas noted the "striking similarity" of ABA to Itard's methods with Victor as early as 1973: see Lovaas et al., "Some Generalizations," 163.

61. Yergeau, *Authoring Autism,* 103.

2. (Un)making Asylum

1. Beck, *Life of the Theatre,* 67.

2. James, "Living Theatre," 475.

3. Martin, *Theater Is in the Street,* 75.

4. In Martin, 75.

5. See Rostagno, Beck, and Malina, *We, the Living Theatre,* 29–36; and Beck, *Life of the Theatre,* 173–75.

6. Sagura, "Nous avons tant Aimé Gourgas."

7. Alvarez de Toledo, "Introduction," 673.

8. Dosse, *Gilles Deleuze and Félix Guattari,* 633.

9. "Asylum," *Oxford English Dictionary,* accessed July 2023, https://doi.org/10.1093/OED/2658640832.

10. The body of historical scholarship on the central role of the asylum system and moral treatment in the development of psychiatric science and medicine in the nineteenth century is vast, with much of the literature organized around specific national contexts. See, e.g., Goldstein, *Console and Classify;* Grob, *Mental Institutions in America;* Melling and Forsythe, *Insanity, Institutions and Society;* Rothman, *Discovery of the Asylum;* Scull, *Psychiatry and Its Discontents;* and Wright, "Getting Out of the Asylum."

11. Scull, *Psychiatry and Its Discontents,* 43.

12. Foucault, *History of Madness,* 479.

13. Delingy, "A comme asile," 12. This and all subsequent quotations from "A comme asile" ("A for Asylum") are translated by Julie Dind and me. Deligny seems to have been working on "A for Asylum" between 1983 and 1984. In 1999, three years after Deligny's death, Paris publisher Dunod released *A comme asile,* a book that included the titular essay and a second text from the same period, "In Praise of Asylum," as well as the complete text of *The Innocent and Us,* a selection of Deligny's writing assembled by Isaac Joseph and originally released by publisher Maspero in 1975. Taken together, "A for Asylum," "In Praise of Asylum," and *The Innocent and Us* provide a kind of constellated self-portrait of Deligny's attempt to forge a mode of communal life in the course of his work

alongside—or, as Deligny would say, in close proximity to—children and young adults diagnosed as autistic.

14. Delingy, "A comme asile," 7.

15. This chapter's understanding of deinstitutionalization as a complex historical phenomenon that has operated at many levels of social reality—from the spatial and institutional to the micropolitics of subjectivity—has been especially informed by Ben-Moshe, *Decarcerating Disability.*

16. See Robcis, *Disalientation.*

17. Deleuze and Guattari, *Thousand Plateaus,* 296.

18. Garcin-Marrou, "Portrait de Félix Guattari," 139; my translation.

19. Garcin-Marrou, 139.

20. Oury, "Hospital Is Ill," 34.

21. Krtolica and Sibertin-Blanc, "Children Estranged from Language," 214.

22. Deligny, "A comme asile," 29.

23. Krtolica and Sibertin-Blanc, "Children Estranged from Language," 215.

24. Rodenbeck, *Radical Prototypes,* 160.

25. See Turner, *Ritual Process.*

26. Fonds Deligny, IMEC, "Cahiers de L'immuable," DGN 30, handwritten notes. The original text reads: "Les gestes symbolique qui correspondent à certaines mouvements du corps sont adaptables du point de vue de la sélection. La signification de ces mouvements varie beaucoup d'une culture à l'autre."

27. Deligny, *Arachnean,* 144.

28. See Balibar, "Structuralism."

29. Deligny to Althusser, September 1976, in *Correspondance des Cévennes,* 564–65; my translation. The phrase "individual always already subject" is a quotation from Althusser, "Ideology."

30. Althusser's 1971 "Ideology and Ideological State Apparatuses" was initially published in French in 1970 as "Idéologie et appareils idéologiques d'état." It later appeared in Althusser, *Positions* (1976).

31. Althusser, "Ideology," 173; emphasis in original.

32. Althusser, 174.

33. Althusser and Balibar, *Reading Capital,* 124.

34. Althusser, "Ideology," 175.

35. Balibar, "Althusser's Dramaturgy," 4.

36. Althusser, "On Brecht and Marx," 146.

37. Bargu, "Althusser's Materialist Theater," 85.

38. Butler, *Excitable Speech,* 2.

39. Butler, 5.

40. Butler, 49.

41. Bargu, "Althusser's Materialist Theater," 85.

42. On the significance of *Titicut Follies* for the development of both the political and aesthetic possibilities of observational cinema see Barnouw, *Documentary;* Chanan, *Politics of Documentary;* Grant, *Voyages of Discovery;* Nichols, *Introduction;* and Winston, *Claiming the Real.*

43. Grant, *Voyages of Discovery,* 1–2.

44. Armstrong, "Wiseman's Realm," 20.

45. Pearson, "Follies."

46. Bridgewater State Hospital's predecessor on the site, the Bridgewater Almshouse, opened in 1854. It was one of three almshouses that the Commonwealth of Massachusetts established in 1852 on the recommendation of the Board of Commissioners of Alien Passengers to address the burgeoning numbers of "helpless poor" starting in the 1840s, a trend that increased in urgency with the large wave of Irish immigration to the northeastern part of the United States. See O'Connell, "Caring for the Sick and Poor."

47. Wiseman in Baumann, "Entretien avec Frederick Wiseman," 66; my translation.

48. Baumann, "Entretien avec Frederick Wiseman," 66.

49. Goffman, *Asylums,* 23.

50. Quoted in Grant, *Voyages of Discovery,* 31.

51. Chanan, *Politics of Documentary,* 255.

52. Mamber, *Cinema Verite,* 291; Grant, *Voyages of Discovery.*

53. Goffman, *Asylums,* 319.

54. See Deligny, *Correspondance des Cévennes,* 994–95; my translation. The book in question is Gauchet and Swain, *La pratique de l'esprit humain,* published in English as *Madness and Democracy.*

55. In French, the sentence can also be rendered as: "And if he has not, who denied him understanding?" Both entendre (to hear) and entendement (understanding) find their etymology from the Latin intendere, literally "to stretch toward."

56. Deligny, letter to Marcel Gauchet, November 21, 1982, in *Correspondance des Cévennes,* 1003; my translation. Deligny also seems to have had on his mind some of the key lines of argument found in Karl Marx's early writings on the "objectification" of the human senses as a process of "estrangement," or alienation, from nature. For instance, in the *Economic and Philosophical Manuscripts of 1844,* Marx writes: "The individual *is the social being.* His life, even if it may not appear in the direct form of a *communal* life in association with others—is therefore an expression and confirmation of *social life.* [. . .] In his *consciousness of species* man confirms his real *social* life and simply repeats his real existence in thought, just as conversely the being of the species confirms itself in species-consciousness and exists for *itself* in its generality as a thinking being" (138; emphasis in original).

57. Alvarez de Toledo, "Untopicality."

58. *The Autistic Subject: On the Threshold of Language* by psychoanalyst Leon S. Brenner is a recent example of an attempt to produce a Lacanian account of autism. See also Maleval, *L'Autiste et sa voix;* and Laurent, *La bataille de l'autisme.*

59. Deligny, letter to Marcel Gauchet, November 21, 1982, in *Correspondance des Cévennes,* 1001; my translation.

60. Alvarez de Toledo, "Untopicality."
61. Ogillvie, "Living Between the Lines," 11.
62. Deligny, *Arachnean,* 145.
63. Deligny, 155.
64. Wiame, "Reading Deleuze and Guattari," 54.
65. Krtolica and Sibertin-Blanc, "Children Estranged from Language," 215.
66. Muñoz, "Ephemera as Evidence," 10.
67. Muñoz, 10.
68. Foucault, *Discipline and Punish.*
69. Deligny, *Arachnean,* 149.
70. Deligny, "A comme asile," 55.
71. See Berger, *Disarticulate.*
72. Masschelein and Verstraete, "Living in the Presence of Others," 1197.
73. Hudak, "When Nothing Happens," 98.
74. Deligny, "A comme asile," 21.
75. Deligny, *Oeuvres,* 707; my translation.
76. Deligny, 707.
77. See Kuppers et al., "Mad Methodologies."
78. Masschelein and Verstraete, "Living in the Presence of Others," 1189.

3. Map, Crawl, Wander, Trace

1. Maxwell, "William Pope.L," 150.
2. Peabody, "'Reassurance Project,'" 195.
3. Pope.L, "Notes on Crawling Piece," 66.
4. Maxwell, "William Pope.L," 150.
5. Lepecki, *Exhausting Dance,* 97.
6. Glissant, *Poetics of Relation,* 190.
7. Bradley, "Introduction," 130.
8. Foucault defines psychiatric power as "a positive technique of intervention and transformation" that emerged in the nineteenth century in tandem with the development of psychiatry as a distinct medical science. Foucault, *Abnormal,* 53.
9. See Eyal, *Autism Matrix;* and Metzl, *Protest Psychosis.*
10. Samuels, *Fantasies of Identification;* Davis, *Enforcing Normalcy;* Schweik, *Ugly Laws.*
11. See Hogarth, "Medical Science, Racial Ideology, and Practice, to Reconstruction."
12. Bruce, *How to Go Mad,* 17.
13. Elman, "Policing at the Synapse."
14. See Travers, Tincani, and Krezmien, "Multiyear National Profile"; and Mandell et al., "Race Differences."
15. Skida et al., "Disparate Access."
16. I alternate between referring to Avonte Oquendo by his first name and referring to him by his last name to foreground how the performative force of

the proper name itself was mobilized by politicians and policymakers in their decision to call the bill "Avonte's Law."

17. Kolker, "Boy Who Ran."

18. Avonte's Law Act of 2014, S.2386, 113th Cong. Full text available at https://www.congress.gov/bill/113th-congress/senate-bill/2386.

19. Kevin and Avonte's Law of 2017, S.2070. This is a quote from the text of the bill when it was introduced on November 2, 2017, which may be found at https://www.congress.gov/bill/115th-congress/house-bill/4221.

20. Browne, *Dark Matters,* 16.

21. Povinelli, *Economies of Abandonment,* 20.

22. Povinelli, "Defining Security in Late Liberalism," 28.

23. See especially Foucault, *Security, Territory, Population.*

24. Eyal, *Autism Matrix,* 30.

25. See Trent, *Inventing the Feeble Mind.*

26. Eyal, *Autism Matrix,* 78.

27. Metzl, *Protest Psychosis,* xxi.

28. Broderick, "Autism as Rhetoric." See also Broderick and Ne'eman, "Autism as Metaphor."

29. See, e.g., abfh, "Autism Speaks' Eugenic Agenda."

30. Spencer, "Why Parents of Children."

31. See Berrington, "Reporter's Guide."

32. Robison, "I Resign My Roles."

33. See, e.g., Autism Speaks, "Autism Speaks' President Liz Feld."

34. Nikolas Rose and Joelle M. Abi-Rached use the term "neuromolecular gaze" to describe an epistemological shift in the biomedical and psychiatric study of the human mind that occurred with the solidification of neuroscience as an interdisciplinary paradigm for representing the brain in terms that are at once molecular and physically "reductive." The shift that they and other sociologists of science have traced has had far-reaching consequences for social, political, and ethical understandings of human personhood. See Rose and Abi-Rached, "Birth."

35. Simon, "Speaking Truth and Power," 40.

36. Wagner, "Performance," 68. Wagner is partly drawing from Krauss's important essay "Video," 51.

37. Wagner, "Performance," 68.

38. Fiske, "Surveilling the City," 81.

39. Browne, "Race and Surveillance," 72.

40. See especially Fleetwood, *Troubling Vision.*

41. Hartman, *Scenes of Subjection,* 20.

42. Butler, "Endangered/Endangering," 16.

43. Butler, 17.

44. Clinical definitions and scientific understandings of autism and ASDs remain remarkably unsettled and contentious topics of debate. On the historically

contingent and variable meanings of autism, see especially Eyal, *Autism Matrix;* Silberman, *NeuroTribes;* Nadesan, *Constructing Autism;* and Straus, "Autism as Culture."

45. Stimming, also referred to in the clinical literature on autism as "stereotypy" or "self-stimulatory behavior," is defined as the repetitive or perseverative movement of the body (such as vestibular rocking, hand flapping, or rubbing the skin). See Hervas, "Stereotypic Behavior."

46. Yergeau, "Clinically Significant Disturbance."

47. See Anderson et al., "Occurrence and Family Impact."

48. McIlwain, "Day My Son Went Missing."

49. A 2014 article in the *British Journal of Psychiatry* discusses "electronic monitoring as an aid to security and public safety in a forensic setting." The authors of the study, all clinical psychiatrists, provide a measured endorsement of the practice of using "active" GPS tracking devices to monitor psychiatric patients "as part of a comprehensive protocol for risk management and recovery." While they acknowledge that such interventions "may be cause for ethical concerns and controversy" and further note that "The evidence for electronic monitoring has failed to keep pace with increased use and development of technology," the authors nonetheless conclude that the practice of attaching—even "voluntarily"—nonremovable devices would allow medical and police authorities to monitor the movements of individuals with specific psychiatric disorders in potentially beneficial ways. See Tully, Hearn, and Fahy, "Can Electronic Monitoring," 83–85.

50. CDC, "ICD-9-CM Code for Wandering."

51. ASAN et al., "Joint Letter to CDC."

52. ASAN et al., emphasis added.

53. Rancière, *Dissensus,* 37.

54. Lepecki, "Choreopolice and Choreopolitics," 19.

55. See Autism Unites, http://autismunites.org.

56. Elman, "Policing at the Synapse."

57. Kant, "Answer to the Question," 533.

58. Kotef, *Movement,* 5.

59. Kawash, *Dislocating the Color Line,* 80.

60. Cervenak, *Wandering,* 20.

61. See, e.g., Barrett, *Racial Blackness,* 90–93. On the trope of fugitivity in slave narratives, see Kawash, *Dislocating the Color Line.* For accounts of fugitivity and escape as modalities of Black performance, see especially Brooks, *Bodies in Dissent;* Moten, *In the Break;* and DeFrantz and Gonzalez, eds., *Black Performance Theory.*

62. Moten, "Case of Blackness," 179.

63. Moten, 179.

64. Moten, 179.

65. I thank Tavia Nyong'o for suggesting this formulation of the issue in question.

66. Higashida, *Reason I Jump*, 94–95.
67. Conley, "Mapping in the Folds," 127.
68. Conley, 127.
69. Nancy, *Pleasure of Drawing*, 92.
70. Lynch, *Image of the City.*
71. Jameson, "Cognitive Mapping," 349.
72. Colin McCabe, "Preface," xiv
73. Gerlach, "Lines, Contours and Legends," 34.
74. Gerlach, 34.
75. Williams, *Autism and Sensing*, 62.
76. Pope.L, "An Interview with Artist Pope.L," 221–22.
77. Pope.L., 221–22.
78. Pope.L, *My Kingdom for a Title*, 154.
79. Pope.L, "An Interview with Artist Pope.L," 221.

4. The Missing Voice

1. Bascomb, *Loud Hands.*

2. The notion of the voice as the bearer of a "phonic substance" that both supports and exceeds its function as the material/sonic carrier of meaning within speech has an extensive intellectual lineage, extending from Roman Jakobson and the Prague School of Linguistics to more recent theoretical reflections on the voice by contemporary thinkers including Mladen Dolar and Fred Moten. This chapter is especially indebted to a deconstructive strand of this line of thinking that understands the voice as what Fred Moten, in the context of his theorization of Black performance as the "resistance of the object," calls "an irruption of phonic substance that cuts and augments meaning." Moten, *In the Break*, 14. See also Dolar, *Voice and Nothing More;* Jakobson, *Child Language, Aphasia and Phonological Universals;* and Jakobson, *Six Lectures on Sound and Meaning.*

3. Baggs, *In My Language.* Here I am informed by Amber Musser's interest in how masochism can "reveal the sensations that become attached to difference." Musser, *Sensational Flesh*, 1.

4. "FC" is a broadly used designation to describe techniques that enable persons with language and speech impairments to communicate using either assistive technology or another person acting as a mediator.

5. Annemarie Jagose has suggested that "the more valuable insight afforded by Foucault's call to bodies and pleasures is the recognition that one's relation to the disciplinary system of sexuality is necessarily articulated with regard to historically specific and bounded sites of contestation." Jagose, *Orgasmology*, 182.

6. Participant Inc., "Jonathan Berger."

7. Participant Inc.

8. Participant Inc.

9. McQuaid, "Labor of Love."

10. Quoted in Heilman, "I Am in Here."

11. Utter, "Jonathan Berger."
12. See Schuler and Prizant, "Echolalia."
13. Kanner, "Autistic Disturbances," 242.
14. Baggs, *In My Language.*
15. Baggs.
16. CNN, "American Morning."
17. Wolman, "Truth about Autism."
18. Antze, "On the Pragmatics of Empathy," 313.
19. Coté, "Technics and the Human Sensorium."
20. Manning, "Shape of Enthusiasm," 87–88.
21. Manning, *Relationscapes,* 221.
22. Though it is slightly more cautious than Manning, a similar risk arises in Steven Shaviro's brief invocation of autistic perception in his book on speculative realism, *The Universe of Things.* Shaviro writes: "We might well describe such non-correlational thought as *autistic*—provided that we use this term in a non-pejorative and non-medicalized sense. As the neurodiversity movement helps us understand, autistic modes of thought should not be stigmatized as deficient just because they are entirely *different* from neurotypical ones. Contrary to popular (and sometimes medical) prejudice, people along the autistic spectrum are not solipsists, and they are not lacking in empathy. . . . Autistics are fully immersed in the world, immanently and without relations of phenomenological intentionality. In consequence, they seem to be less incorrigibly 'correlationist' in their basic attunement to the world than neurotypicals are." Shaviro, *Universe of Things,* 132.
23. The party, along with the story of Tsang's complex relationship with the owners and patrons of the Silver Platter, is the subject of Tsang's 2011 film *Wildness.*
24. Tsang, "I Dislike the Word Visibility."
25. "Haptic," *Oxford English Dictionary,* accessed March 17, 2015, https://www.oed.com/view/Entry/84082?redirectedFrom=haptic&.
26. Deleuze, *Francis Bacon,* 155.
27. Martin Jay offers an intellectual genealogy of ocularcentrism in *Downcast Eyes.*
28. Marks, *Skin,* 171–72.
29. Here I am informed by Eugenie Brinkema's discussion of the cinematic formalization of affect by way of a reading of Janet Leigh's tears (or are they merely drops of water?) in a famous shot from Hitchcock's film *Psycho.* See Brinkema, *Forms of the Affects.*
30. Diamond, "Brechtian Theory/Feminist Theory," 89.
31. Revermann, "Brecht and Greek Tragedy," 221.
32. Brecht, *Mother Courage,* 55.
33. Vork, "Silencing Violence," 37.
34. Mitchell and Snyder, *Narrative Prosthesis.*

35. Vork, "Opening Acts," 79.
36. Quayson, *Aesthetic Nervousness,* 24.
37. Solga, *"Mother Courage,"* 342.
38. Solga, 342.
39. Diamond, *Unmaking Mimesis,* 53.
40. Austin, *How to Do Things with Words.*
41. Butler, "Critically Queer," 19.
42. Puchner, "Manifesto = Theatre," 463.
43. Lewiecki-Wilson, "Rethinking Rhetoric," 161.
44. Cartwright, *Moral Spectatorship,* 166.
45. Cartwright, 159–60.
46. Tsang, "I Dislike the Word Visibility."
47. Groner, "Sex as 'Spock,'" 274.
48. Blackman is quoted in Walters, *Rhetorical Touch,* 119.
49. Grandin, *Thinking in Pictures,* 90.
50. Grandin, *Emergence,* 108.
51. Groner, "Sex as 'Spock,'" 265.
52. Baggs, "About Mel Baggs."

Coda

1. Baggs, "Crocheting and Dancing."
2. Sedgwick, *Touching Feeling,* 13–14.
3. Sedgwick, "Making Things, Practicing Emptiness," 69.
4. Sedgwick, 79.
5. Sedgwick, "Affect Theory," 156.
6. Sedgwick, 157–58. Sedgwick is quoting from Blackburn et al., "Discussion about Theory of Mind."
7. Sedgwick, "Affect Theory," 160.
8. Sedgwick, 160.
9. Sedgwick, *Epistemology of the Closet,* 85.
10. Deligny, *Oeuvres,* 1161.
11. Giorgio Agamben has written of what he describes as a destituent position with respect to the ontological structure of politics itself. Agamben describes this as "the capacity to *deactivate*" the apparatuses through which subjectivity is produced and render its effects inoperative—but to do so in a way "without simply destroying it." Rather, he continues, destituence works "by liberating the potentials that have remained inactive" within something—"a power, a function, a human operation"—"in order to allow a different use of them." Agamben, *Use of Bodies,* 273. Agamben's striking figuration for distituent power in some ways echoes of his discussion in an earlier work that "humanity will play with law just as children play with disused objects, not in order to restore them to their canonical use but to free them from it for good." Agamben, *State of Exception,* 64.

12. The concept of compulsory sociality is developed in Dolmage, *Disability Rhetoric,* 114–15; Rodas, "On the Spectrum"; and Yergeau, *Authoring Autism,* 27. Compulsory sociality extends on the influential account of disability as a violation of "compulsory able-bodiedness" proposed by Robert McRuer and Abby Wilkerson. McRuer notes that this idea is itself indebted to Adrienne Rich's formulation of the lesbian as a figure that defies and exposes the social force of "compulsory heterosexuality." See McRuer, "Compulsory Able-Bodiedness."

13. Ly Xīnzhèn M. Zhǎngsūn Brown addresses the growing prevalence of popular media narratives linking autism to violence, particularly as such narratives are perennially intensified in the United States and elsewhere after mass shootings (largely by white men), in a post on the blog Autistic Hoya. Brown, "I Am Autistic."

14. Foucault, *Psychiatric Power,* 220.

15. Lane, *Shyness,* 208.

16. American Psychiatric Association, *DSM.* According to a 2009 study in the *Journal of Anxiety Disorders,* "Shyness and social anxiety are known to be conceptually and empirically related and have often been used interchangeably in the extant literature even though they have, in part, different meanings. . . . Although social anxiety and shyness reflect the process of affective (e.g., nervousness), cognitive (e.g., fear of evaluation) and behavioral (e.g., awkward social responses) uneasiness in social situations, temperamental shyness is presumed to be an enduring trait-like characteristic of one's personality." Brunet et al., "Shyness and Face Scanning," 909. The authors of this study draw their understanding of shyness from a book-length study published by the American Psychological Association: Beidel and Turner, *Shy Children.*

17. Kanner, "Autistic Disturbances," 242.

18. Foucault discusses the formation of a "reverse" discourse that took place in the latter half of the nineteenth century as "homosexuality began to speak on its own behalf, to demand that its legitimacy or 'naturality' be acknowledged, often in the same vocabulary, using the same categories by which it was medically disqualified. There is not, on the one side, a discourse of power, and opposite it, another discourse that runs counter to it. Discourses are tactical elements or blocks operating in the field of force relations; there can exist different and even contradictory discourses within the same strategy; they can, on the contrary, circulate without changing their form from one strategy to another, opposing strategy." Foucault, *History of Sexuality,* 101–2.

19. H. Ahsan, *Shy Radicals.*

20. H. Ahsan, 17. Subsequent citations are provided parenthetically.

21. Unless other citation is provided, quotations from Hamja Ahsan are from interviews with the author that took place June–July 2020.

22. Muñoz, "Wildness," 655.

23. Yergeau, *Authoring Autism,* 62.

24. The circumstances at issue in the case of Syed Talha Ahsan and his codefendant, Babar Ahmad, are detailed in evidence submitted to the House of

Lords Select Committee, which notes that the case illustrates the "dangers of granting extra-territorial jurisdiction of the U.S.'s more punitive system to the U.K." See written evidence to the House of Lords Select Committee (EXL0049) filed by David Bermingham, Dr. Nisha Kapoor, Julia O'Dwyer, Arun Kundnani with Centre of Constitutional Rights (USA), Islamic Human Rights Commission and Frances Webber of Institute of Race Relations. See Azmy et al., "Evidence from U.S. Experts."

25. This quotation appears in a press release issued by a human rights group: Scotland Against Criminalising Communities, "May Shows Contempt."

26. Puar and Rai, "Monster, Terrorist, Fag," 123–24.

27. Mahmood, *Politics of Piety,* 155.

28. T. Ahsan, "I, Otherstani."

29. H. Ahsan, "Hamja Ahsan."

30. Sutton, "Hamja Ahsan Discusses."

31. Hamja Ahsan, "Interviews: Hamja Ahsan," *Art Forum,* September 24, 2019, www.artforum.com/interviews/hamja-ahsan-discusses-shy-radicals-and-extrovert-supremacy-80790.

32. Deligny, "Cartes prises et cartes tracées" in *L'Arachnéen et autres textes,* 138; my translation.

33. H. Ahsan, *Shy Radicals,* 37.

Bibliography

abfh. "Autism Speaks' Eugenic Agenda." Whose Planet Is It Anyway? (blog), October 22, 2007. http://autisticbfh.blogspot.com/2007/10/autism-speaks-eugenic-agenda.html.

Adams, D. L., and Nirmala Erevelles. "Unexpected Spaces of Confinement: Aversive Technologies, Intellectual Disability, and 'Bare Life.'" *Punishment and Society* 19, no. 3 (2017): 348–65.

Agamben, Giorgio. *State of Exception.* Translated by Kevin Attell. Chicago: University of Chicago Press, 2005.

Agamben, Giorgio. *The Use of Bodies.* Translated by Adam Kosko. Stanford, Calif.: Stanford University Press, 2004.

Ahern, Laurie. *Torture not Treatment: Electric Shock and Long-Term Restraint in the United States on Children and Adults with Disabilities at the Judge Rotenberg Center.* Washington, D.C.: Mental Disability Rights International, 2010.

Ahsan, Hamja. "Hamja Ahsan: 'I'm Trying to Reclaim Fried Chicken for Muslims.'" Profile by Indlieb Farazi Saber. *Middle East Eye,* September 9, 2022. https://www.middleeasteye.net/discover/british-muslim-hamja-ahsan-artist-fried-chicken-shop.

Ahsan, Hamja. *Shy Radicals: The Antisystemic Politics of the Militant Introvert.* London: Book Works, 2017.

Ahsan, Talha. "I, Otherstani." *Skin Deep,* February 7, 2020. https://skindeepmag.com/articles/otherstani-a-world-without-borders-imaged-from-behind-bars.

Althusser, Louis. "Idéologie et appareils idéologiques d'état." *La Pensée,* no. 151 (June 1970): 3–38.

Althusser, Louis. "Ideology and Ideological State Apparatuses (Notes towards an Investigation)." In *Lenin and Philosophy and Other Essays,* translated by Ben Brewster, 127–86. New York: Monthly Review, 1971.

Althusser, Louis. "On Brecht and Marx." Translated by Max Statkiewicz. In *Louis Althusser,* edited by Warren Montag, 136–39. New York: Palgrave Macmillan, 2003.

Althusser, Louis. *Positions.* Paris: Les Éditions Sociales, 1976.

Althusser, Louis, and Étienne Balibar. *Reading Capital.* Translated by Ben Brewster. London: Verso, 2009.

Alvarez de Toledo, Sandra. "Cartes et légendes: Documents: 1968–1979." In *Oeuvres,* by Fernand Deligny, edited by Sandra Alvarez de Toledo, 1053–83. Paris: Éditions L'Arachnéen, 2007.

Alvarez de Toledo, Sandra. "Introduction: *Nous et l'innocent.*" In *Oeuvres,* by Fernand Deligny, edited by Sandra Alvarez de Toledo, 673–84. Paris: Éditions L'Arachnéen, 2007.

Alvarez de Toledo, Sandra. "The Untopicality of Fernand Deligny." Translated by Émilie Chevrier. Éditions L'Arachnéen website, 2007, https://www.editions-arachneen.fr/catalogue/oeuvres/. Translation of "L'inactualité de Fernand Deligny." In *Oeuvres,* by Fernand Deligny, edited by Sandra Alvarez de Toledo, 21–37. Paris: Éditions L'Arachnéen, 2007.

American Psychiatric Association. *Diagnostic and Statistical Manual of Mental Disorders, Fifth Edition.* Washington, D.C.: American Psychiatric Association, 2013.

Anderson, Connie, J. Kiely Law, Amy Daniels, Catherine Rice, David S. Mandell, Louis Hagopian, and Paul A. Law. "Occurrence and Family Impact of Elopement in Children with Autism Spectrum Disorders." *Pediatrics* 130, no. 5 (2012): 870–77.

Andrew, Dudley. "Every Teacher Needs a Truant: Bazin and *L'Enfant Sauvage.*" In *A Companion to François Truffaut,* edited by Dudley Andrew and Anne Gillain, 221–41. Hoboken, N.J.: Wiley-Blackwell, 2013.

Andrew, Dudley. "Malraux, Bazin, and the Gesture of Picasso." In *Opening Bazin: Postwar Film Theory and Its Afterlife,* edited by Herve Joubert-Laurencin and Dudley Andrew, 153–66. Oxford: Oxford University Press, 2010.

Antze, Paul. "On the Pragmatics of Empathy in the Neurodiversity Movement." In *Ordinary Ethics: Anthropology, Language, and Action,* edited by Michael Lambek, 310–27. New York: Fordham University Press, 2010.

Anzaldúa, Gloria. *Borderlands/La Frontera: The New Mestiza.* San Francisco: Aunt Lute, 1999.

Armstrong, Dan. "Wiseman's Realm of Transgression: *Titicut Follies,* the Symbolic Father, and the Spectacle of Confinement." *Cinema Journal* 29, no. 1 (1989): 20–35.

(ASAN) Autistic Self Advocacy Network et al. "Joint Letter to CDC on Proposed ICD-9-CM Wandering Code." April 4, 2011. https://autisticadvocacy.org/2011/04/joint-letter-on-proposed-wandering-code/.

Asasumasu, Kassiane A. Radical Neurodivergence Speaking (blog), 2010–18. http://timetolisten.blogspot.com/.

Astruc, Alexandre. "The Birth of the New Avant-Garde: La Caméra-Stylo." In *Film and Literature: An Introduction and Reader,* edited by Timothy Corrigan, 181–85. Upper Saddle River, N.J.: Prentice Hall, 1998.

Austin, J. L. *How to Do Things with Words.* Cambridge, Mass.: Harvard University Press, 1975.

Autism Speaks. "Autism Speaks' President Liz Feld Talks Avonte's Law on ABC New York." January 25, 2015. https://www.autismspeaks.org/news/news-item/autism-speaks039-president-liz-feld-talks-avonte039s-law-abc-new-york.

Azmy, Baher, Sally Eberhardt, Pardiss Kebriaei, Arun Kundnani, William P. Quigley, Laura Rovner, Saskia Sassen, and Jeanne Theoharis. "Evidence from U.S. Experts to the House of Lords Select Committee on the Extradition Law: Written Evidence (EXL0049)," September 12, 2014. http://data.parliament.uk/writtenevidence/committeeevidence.svc/evidencedocument/extradition-law-committee/extradition-law/written/12515.pdf.

Baggs, Mel. "About Mel Baggs." Ballastexistenz (blog), April 5, 2007. https://ballastexistenz.wordpress.com/2007/04/05/what-pdd-nos-officially-means/.

Baggs, Mel. "Crocheting and Dancing." Ballastexistenz (blog), April 30, 2014. https://ballastexistenz.wordpress.com/2014/04/30/expressions-of-posautivity/.

Baggs, Mel. *In My Language.* YouTube video, 8:36. January 14, 2007. https://www.youtube.com/watch?v=JnylM1hI2jc.

Baggs, Mel. "Putting Autism on Trial: An Interview with [Mel] Baggs." Interview by Donna Williams. Polly's Pages (aka "Donna Williams") (blog), July 3, 2007. http://blog.donnawilliams.net/2007/07/03/putting-autism-on-trial-an-interview-with-amanda-baggs/.

Balibar, Étienne. "Althusser's Dramaturgy and the Critique of Ideology." *differences* 26, no. 3 (2015): 1–22.

Balibar, Étienne. "Structuralism: A Destitution of the Subject?" *differences* 14, no. 1 (2003): 1–21.

Bargu, Banu. "Althusser's Materialist Theater: Ideology and Its Aporias." *differences* 26, no. 3 (2015): 81–106.

Barnouw, Erik. *Documentary: A History of the Non-fiction Film.* Oxford: Oxford University Press, 1993.

Baron-Cohen, Simon. *Mindblindness: An Essay on Autism and Theory of Mind.* Cambridge, Mass.: MIT Press, 1997.

Baron-Cohen, Simon. "The Systemizing Quotient: An Investigation of Adults with Asperger Syndrome or High-Functioning Autism, and Normal Sex Differences." *Philosophical Transactions of the Royal Society of London B* 358, no. 1430 (2003): 361–74.

Barrett, Lindon W. *Racial Blackness and the Discontinuity of Western Modernity.* Champaign: University of Illinois Press, 2013.

Bascomb, Julia, ed. *Loud Hands: Autistic People, Speaking.* Washington, D.C.: Autistic Self Advocacy Network, 2012.

Bataille, Georges. *Inner Experience.* Translated by Leslie Anne Boldt. Albany: State University of New York Press, 1988.

Baumann, Fabien. "Entretien avec Frederick Wiseman: *Titicut Follies* est une comédie musicale!" *Positif,* no. 581 (July–August 2009): 66–68.

Beck, Julian. *The Life of the Theatre: The Relation of the Artist to the Struggle of the People.* New York: Limelight, 1991.

Beidel, Deborah C., and Samuel M. Turner. *Shy Children, Phobic Adults: Nature and Treatment of Social Anxiety Disorder.* 2nd ed. Washington, D.C.: American Psychological Association, 2007.

Ben-Moshe, Liat. *Decarcerating Disability: Deinstitutionalization and Prison Abolition.* Minneapolis: University of Minnesota Press, 2020.

Benveniste, Émile. "Analytical Philosophy and Language." In *Problems in General Linguistics,* vol. 1, translated by Mary E. Meek, 236–38. Coral Gables, Fla.: University of Miami Press, 1971.

Benzaquén, Adriana S. *Encounters with Wild Children: Temptation and Disappointment in the Study of Human Nature.* Montreal: McGill-Queen's University Press, 2006.

Berger, James. *The Disarticulate: Language, Disability, and the Narratives of Modernity.* New York: NYU Press, 2014.

Bergson, Henri. *Matter and Memory.* Translated by N. M. Paul and W. S. Palmer. Cambridge, Mass.: Zone, 1991.

Berrington, Lucy. "A Reporter's Guide to the Autism Speaks Debacle." *Psychology Today* (blog), November 14, 2013. https://www.psychologytoday.com/blog/aspergers-alive/201311/reporters-guide-the-autism-speaks-debacle.

Bettelheim, Bruno. *The Empty Fortress: Infantile Autism and the Birth of the Self.* New York: Free Press, 1967.

Blackburn, Jared, Katja Gottschewski, Elsa George, and Niki L. "A Discussion about Theory of Mind: From an Autistic Perspective." Proceedings of Autism Europe's 6th International Congress. https://web.archive.org/web/20080207092942/http://www.autistics.org/library/AE2000-ToM.html.

Bleuler, Eugen. *Dementia Praecox oder Gruppe der Schizophrenien: Handbuch der Psychiatrie.* Leipzig: Deuticke, 1911.

Blume, Harvey. "Neurodiversity: On the Neurological Underpinnings of Geekdom." *Atlantic,* September 1998. https://www.theatlantic.com/magazine/archive/1998/09/neurodiversity/305909/.

Bradley, Rizvana. "Introduction: Other Sensualities." *Women and Performance* 24, nos. 2–3 (2014): 129–33.

Brenner, Leon. *The Autistic Subject: On the Threshold of Language.* London: Palgrave Macmillan, 2020.

Brinkema, Eugenie. *The Forms of the Affects.* Durham, N.C.: Duke University Press, 2014.

Broderick, Alicia A. "Autism as Rhetoric: Exploring Watershed Rhetorical Moments in Applied Behavior Analysis Discourse." *Disability Studies Quarterly* 31, no. 3 (2011). http://dsq-sds.org/article/view/1674/1597.

Broderick, Alicia A., and Ari Ne'eman. "Autism as Metaphor: Narrative and Counter-narrative." *International Journal of Inclusive Education* 12, nos. 5–6 (2008): 459–76.

Brooks, Daphne A. *Bodies in Dissent: Spectacular Performances of Race and Freedom, 1850–1910.* Durham, N.C.: Duke University Press, 2006.

Brown, Ly Xīnzhèn M. Zhǎngsūn. "I Am Autistic, and I Am Obsessed with Violence." Autistic Hoya (blog), 2013. https://www.autistichoya.com/.

Browne, Simone. *Dark Matters: On the Surveillance of Blackness.* Durham, N.C.: Duke University Press, 2015.

Browne, Simone. "Race and Surveillance." In *The Routledge Handbook of Surveillance Studies,* edited by Kirstie Ball, Kevin Haggerty, and David Lyon, 72–80. New York: Routledge, 2014.

Bruce, La Marr Jurelle. *How to Go Mad without Losing Your Mind: Madness and Black Radical Creativity.* Durham, N.C.: Duke University Press, 2021.

Brunet, Paul M., Jennifer J. Heisz, Catherine J. Mondloch, David I. Shore, and Louis A. Schmidt. "Shyness and Face Scanning in Children." *Journal of Anxiety Disorders* 23, no. 7 (2009): 909–14.

Butler, Judith. "Critically Queer." *GLQ* 1 (1993): 17–32.

Butler, Judith. "Endangered/Endangering: Schematic Racism and White Paranoia." In *Reading Rodney King, Reading Urban Uprising,* edited by Robert Gooding-Williams, 15–22. New York: Routledge, 1993.

Butler, Judith. *Excitable Speech.* New York: Routledge, 1997.

Canguilhem, Georges. *The Normal and the Pathological.* Translated by Carolyn R. Fawcett. New York: Zone, 1991.

Carlson, Marla. *Affect, Animals, and Autists: Feeling around the Edges of the Human in Performance.* Ann Arbor: University of Michigan Press, 2018.

Cartwright, Lisa. *Moral Spectatorship: Technologies of Voice and Affect in Postwar Representations of the Child.* Durham, N.C.: Duke University Press, 2008.

(CDC) Centers for Disease Control and Prevention. "ICD-9-CM Code for Wandering." Effective October 1, 2011. https://www.alzra.org/wp-content/uploads/2011/10/ICD-9-CM-Code-for-Wandering.pdf.

Cervenak, Sarah Jane. *Wandering: Philosophical Performances of Racial and Sexual Freedom.* Durham, N.C.: Duke University Press, 2014.

Chanan, Michael. *The Politics of Documentary.* London: British Film Institute, 2007.

Clare, Eli. *Brilliant Imperfection: Grappling with Cure.* Durham, N.C.: Duke University Press, 2017.

CNN. "American Morning." CNN transcripts, February 22, 2007. https://transcripts.cnn.com/show/ltm/date/2007-02-22/segment/01.

Collins, Paul. *Not Even Wrong: A Father's Journey into the Lost History of Autism.* New York: Bloomsbury, 2005.

Conley, Tom. *Cartographic Cinema.* Minneapolis: University of Minnesota Press, 2006.

Conley, Tom. "Mapping in the Folds: Deleuze 'Cartographe.'" *Discourse* 20, no. 3 (1998): 123–38.

Connolly, William. *Neuropolitics: Thinking, Culture, Speed.* Minneapolis: University of Minnesota Press, 2002.

Conquergood, Dwight. "Performance Studies: Interventions and Radical Research." *TDR* 46, no 2 (2002): 145–56.

Cooter, Roger. "Neural Veils and the Will to Historical Critique: Why Historians of Science Need to Take the Neuro-Turn Seriously." *Isis* 105, no. 1 (2014): 145–54.

Coté, Mark. "Technics and the Human Sensorium: Rethinking Media Theory through the Body." *Theory and Event* 13, no. 4 (2010). https://muse.jhu.edu/pub/1/article/407142.

Cowen, Tyler. "An Economic and Rational Choice Approach to the Autism Spectrum and Human Neurodiversity." GMU Working Paper in Economics No. 11-58. Department of Economics, George Mason University, December 22, 2011. https://dx.doi.org/10.2139/ssrn.1975809.

Crichton, Alexander. *An Inquiry into the Nature and Origin of Mental Derangement, Comprehending a Concise System of the Physiology and Pathology of the Human Mind, and a History of the Passions and Their Effects.* London: Cadell and Davies, 1798.

Cromby, John, Tim Newton, and Simon J. Williams. "Neuroscience and Subjectivity." *Subjectivity* 4 (2011): 215–26.

Daney, Serge. *The Cinema House and the World, 1. The "Cahiers du Cinéma" Years, 1962–1981.* Translated by Christine Pichini. South Pasadena, Calif.: Semiotext(e), 2022.

Davis, Lennard J. "Constructing Normalcy: The Bell Curve, the Novel, and the Invention of the Disabled Body in the Nineteenth Century." In *The Disability Studies Reader,* 2nd ed., edited by Lennard Davis, 3–16. New York: Routledge, 2006.

Davis, Lennard J. *Enforcing Normalcy: Disability, Deafness, and the Body.* New York: Verso, 1995.

de Baecque, Antoine, and Serge Toubiana. *Truffaut.* Translated by Catherine Temerson. New York: Knopf, 1999.

DeFrantz, Thomas F., and Anita Gonzalez, eds. *Black Performance Theory.* Durham, N.C.: Duke University Press, 2014.

Deleuze, Gilles. *Francis Bacon: The Logic of Sensation.* Translated by Daniel W. Smith. Minneapolis: University of Minnesota Press, 2005.

Deleuze, Gilles, and Félix Guattari. *A Thousand Plateaus: Capitalism and Schizophrenia.* Translated by Brian Massumi. Minneapolis: University of Minnesota Press, 1987.

Deligny, Fernand. "A comme asile." In *A comme asile suivi de Nous et l'innocent,* 7–60. Paris: Dunod, 1999.

Deligny, Fernand. *L'Arachnéen et autres textes.* Paris: Éditions L'Arachnéen, 2009.

Deligny, Fernand. *The Arachnean and Other Texts.* Translated by Drew Burk and Catherine Porter. Minneapolis: Univocal, 2015.

Deligny, Fernand. *Camérer: À propos d'images.* Edited by Sandra Alvarez de Toledo, Anaïs Masson, Marlon Miguel, and Marina Vidal-Naquet. Paris: Éditions L'Arachnéen, 2021.

Deligny, Fernand. *Camering: Fernand Deligny on Cinema and the Image.* Edited with an introduction by Marlon Miguel. Postface by Elena Vogelman. Translated by Sarah Moses. Leiden, the Netherlands: Leiden University Press, 2022.

Deligny, Fernand. *Correspondance des Cévennes, 1968–1996.* Paris: Éditions L'Arachnéen, 2018.

Deligny, Fernand. *Nous et l'innocent.* Paris: Maspero, 1976.

Deligny, Fernand. *Oeuvres.* Edited by Sandra Alvarez de Toledo. Paris: Éditions L'Arachnéen, 2007.

Deligny, Fernand, and François Truffaut. "Correspondence." *1895: Revue de l'association française de recherche sur l'histoire du cinema* 42 (2004): 77–110.

Diamond, Elin. "Brechtian Theory/Feminist Theory: Toward a Gestic Feminist Criticism." *TDR* 32, no. 1 (1988): 82–94.

Diamond, Elin. *Unmaking Mimesis: Essays on Feminism and Theatre.* London: Routledge, 1997.

Dolar, Mladen. *A Voice and Nothing More.* Cambridge, Mass.: MIT Press, 2006.

Dolmage, Jay Timothy. *Disability Rhetoric.* Syracuse, N.Y.: Syracuse University Press, 2004.

Dosse, François. *Gilles Deleuze and Félix Guattari: Intersecting Lives.* Translated by Deborah Glassman. New York: Columbia University Press, 2010.

Elman, Julie Passanante. "Policing at the Synapse: Ferguson, Race, and the Disability Politics of the Teen Brain." *Somatosphere,* May 4, 2015. http://somatosphere.net/2015/05/policing-at-the-synapse-ferguson-race-and-the-disability-politics-of-the-teen-brain.html.

Esquirol, Jean-Étienne Dominique. *Des Maladies mentale: Considérées sous les rapports médical, hygiénique et médico-légal.* Paris: J.-B. Baillière, 1838.

Eyal, Gil. *The Autism Matrix.* London: Polity, 2011.

Eyal, Gil. "For a Sociology of Expertise: The Social Origins of the Autism Epidemic." *American Journal of Sociology* 118, no. 4 (2013): 863–907.

Faguet, Michèle. "El sueño de la razón produce monstruos: On the Work of Javier Téllez." *Afterall* 18 (Summer 2008): 46–53.

Felman, Shoshana. *The Scandal of the Speaking Body: Don Juan with J. L. Austin, or Seduction in Two Languages.* Translated by Catherine Porter. Stanford, Calif.: Stanford University Press, 2002.

Ferguson, Roderick. *The Reorder of Things: The University and Its Pedagogies of Minority Difference.* Minneapolis: University of Minnesota Press, 2012.

Fischer-Lichte, Erika. *The Transformative Power of Performance: A New Aesthetics.* Translated by Saskya Iris Jain. London: Routledge, 2008.

Fiske, John. "Surveilling the City: Whiteness, the Black Man, and Democratic Totalitarianism." *Theory, Culture and Society* 15, no. 2 (1998): 67–88.

Fleche, Anne. "Echoing Autism: Performance, Performativity, and the Writings of Donna Williams." *TDR* 41, no. 3 (1997): 107–21.

Fleetwood, Nicole. *Troubling Vision: Performance, Visuality, and Blackness.* Chicago: University of Chicago Press, 2011.

Foucault, Michel. *Abnormal: Lectures at the Collège de France, 1974–75.* Edited by Valerio Marchetti and Antonella Salomoni. Translated by Graham Burchell. New York: Picador, 2003.

Foucault, Michel. *The Archeology of Knowledge.* Translated by A. M. Sheridan Smith. New York: Pantheon, 1982.

Foucault, Michel. *Discipline and Punish: The Birth of the Prison.* Translated by Alan Sheridan. New York: Vintage, 1995.

Foucault, Michel. *History of Madness.* Edited by Jean Khalfa. Translated by Jonathan Murphy and Jean Khalfa. London: Routledge, 2006.

Foucault, Michel. *History of Sexuality, Vol. 1: An Introduction.* Translated by Robert Hurley. New York: Vintage, 1990.

Foucault, Michel. *The Order of Things: An Archaeology of the Human Sciences.* Translated by Alan Sheridan. New York: Vintage Books, 1994.

Foucault, Michel. *Psychiatric Power: Lectures at the Collège de France, 1973–1974.* Edited by Jacques Lagrange and Arnold I. Davidson. Translated by Graham Burchell. New York: Picador, 2006.

Foucault, Michel. *Security, Territory, Population: Lectures at the Collège de France, 1977–1978.* Edited by Michel Senellart. Translated by Graham Burchell. New York: Palgrave, 2007.

Foucault, Michel. *"Society Must Be Defended": Lectures at the Collège de France, 1975–1976.* Edited by Mauro Bertani and Alessandro Fontana. Translated by David Macey. New York: Picador, 2003.

Friedan, Betty. *The Feminine Mystique* (1963). New York: Norton, 2010.

Frith, Uta. *Autism: Explaining the Enigma.* London: Wiley-Blackwell, 2003.

Garcin-Marrou, Flore. "Portrait de Félix Guattari en auteur dramatique." *Chimères* 77, no. 2 (2012): 137–48.

Garland-Thomson, Rosemarie. *Figuring Physical Disability in American Culture and Literature.* New York: Columbia University Press, 1997.

Gauchet, Marcel, and Gladys Swain. *Madness and Democracy: The Modern Psychiatric Universe.* Translated by Catherine Porter. Princeton, N.J.: Princeton University Press, 1999.

Gauchet, Marcel, and Gladys Swain. *La pratique de l'esprit humain: L'institution asilaire et la révolution démocratique.* Paris: Gallimard, 1980.

Genosko, Gary. *Félix Guattari: A Critical Introduction.* London: Pluto, 2009.

Gerlach, Joe. "Lines, Contours and Legends: Coordinates for Vernacular Mapping." *Progress in Human Geography* 38, no. 1 (2014): 22–39.

Getino, Octavio, and Fernando Solanas. "Toward a Third Cinema." In *Film Theory: An Anthology,* edited by Toby Miller and Robert Stam, 265–86. Oxford: Blackwell, 2000.

Gillain, Anne. *François Truffaut: The Lost Secret.* Translated by Alistair Fox. Bloomington: Indiana University Press, 2013.

Glissant, Édouard. *Poetics of Relation.* Translated by Betsy Wing. Ann Arbor: University of Michigan Press, 1997.

Goffman, Erving. *Asylums: Essays on the Condition of the Social Situation of Mental Patients and Other Inmates.* New York: Anchor, 1961.

Goffman, Erving. *The Presentation of Self in Everyday Life.* New York: Anchor, 1959.

Goffman, Erving. *Stigma: Notes on the Management of Spoiled Identity.* Englewood Cliffs, N.J.: Prentice Hall, 1963.

Goldstein, Jan. *Console and Classify: The French Psychiatric Profession in the Nineteenth Century.* Chicago: University of Chicago Press, 2001.

Grandin, Temple. *Emergence: Labeled Autistic.* New York: Warner, 1996.

Grandin, Temple. *Thinking in Pictures: My Life with Autism.* New York: Vintage, 2006.

Grant, Barry Keith. *Voyages of Discovery: The Cinema of Frederick Wiseman.* Rev. ed. New York: Columbia University Press, 2023.

Grob, Gerald. *Mental Institutions in America: Social Policy to 1873.* New York: Free Press, 1973.

Groner, Rachael. "Sex as 'Spock': Autism, Sexuality, and Autobiographical Narrative." In *Sex and Disability,* edited by Robert McRuer and Anna Mollow, 263–84. Durham, N.C.: Duke University Press, 2012.

Guattari, Félix. "Le cinéma: Un art mineur." In *La revolution moléculaire,* 203–38. Paris: Recherches, 1977.

Guattari, Félix. *Molecular Revolution: Psychiatry and Politics* (1977). Translated by Rosemary Sheed. Harmondsworth: Penguin, 1984.

Hacking, Ian. *The Social Construction of What?* Cambridge, Mass.: Harvard University Press, 1999.

Han, Byung-Chul. *The Burnout Society.* Translated by Erik Butler. Stanford, Calif.: Stanford University Press, 2015.

Haraway, Donna. *Simians, Cyborgs, and Women: The Reinvention of Nature.* New York: Routledge, 1991.

Hartman, Saidiya. *Scenes of Subjection: Terror, Slavery, and Self-making in Nineteenth-Century America.* Oxford: Oxford University Press, 1997.

Harvey, David. *A Brief History of Neoliberalism.* Oxford: Oxford University Press, 2007.

Hervas, Amaia. "Stereotypic Behavior." In *Encyclopedia of Autism Spectrum Disorders,* 2nd ed., edited by Fred R. Volkmar. New York: Springer, 2021. https://link.springer.com/referencework/10.1007/978-1-4614-6435-8.

Higashida, Naoki. *The Reason I Jump: The Inner Voice of a Thirteen-Year-Old Boy with Autism.* Translated by KA Yoshida and David Mitchell. New York: Random House, 2013.

Hudak, Glenn M. "When Nothing Happens: Autos, Autism, and 'Disabled' Technology." *Philosophy of Education* 71 (2015): 96–104.

Huffer, Lynne. *Mad for Foucault: Rethinking the Foundations of Queer Theory.* New York: Columbia University Press, 2010.

Invisible Committee. *Now.* Translated by Robert Hurley. Cambridge, Mass.: MIT Press, 2017.

Itard, Jean-Marc. *De l'éducation d'un homme sauvage, ou des premiers développements physiques et moraux du jeune sauvage de l'Aveyron.* Paris: Goujon, 1801.

Itard, Jean-Marc. *An Historical Account of the Discovery and Education of a Savage Man.* London: Richard Philips, 1802.

Jaarsma, Pier, and Stellan Welin. "Autism as a Natural Human Variation: Reflections on the Claims of the Neurodiversity Movement." *Health Care Analysis* 20, no. 1 (2011): 20–30.

Jackson, Shannon. *Professing Performance: Theatre in the Academy from Philology to Performativity.* Cambridge: Cambridge University Press, 2004.

Jagose, Annemarie. *Orgasmology.* Durham, N.C.: Duke University Press, 2012.

Jakobson, Roman. *Child Language, Aphasia and Phonological Universals.* Berlin: De Gruyter, 1980.

Jakobson, Roman. *Six Lectures on Sound and Meaning.* Translated by John Mepham. Cambridge, Mass.: MIT Press, 1978.

James, Norman. "The Living Theatre: Its Use of the Stage." *Journal of Aesthetics and Art Criticism* 29, no. 4 (1971): 475–83.

Jameson, Fredric. "Cognitive Mapping." In *Marxism and the Interpretation of Culture,* edited by Cary Nelson and Lawrence Grossberg, 347–60. Champaign: University of Illinois Press, 1988.

Jay, Martin. *Downcast Eyes: The Denigration of Vision in Twentieth-Century French Thought.* Berkeley: University of California Press, 1994.

Kahn, Douglas. *Noise Water Meat: A History of Sound in the Arts.* Cambridge, Mass.: MIT Press, 1999.

Kahn, J. J. "On Evasion." *Art Papers,* Winter 2018–19. https://www.artpapers.org/on-evasion/.

Kanner, Leo. "Autistic Disturbances of Affective Contact." *Nervous Child* 2 (1943): 217–50.

Kanner, Leo. "Irrelevant and Metaphorical Language in Early Infantile Autism." *American Journal of Psychiatry* 103 (1946): 242–46.

Kant, Immanual. "An Answer to the Question: What Is Enlightenment?" (1784). In *Toward Perpetual Peace and Other Writings on Politics, Peace, and History: Immanuel Kant,* edited by Pauline Kleingeld, translated by David L. Colclasure, 17–23. New Haven, Conn.: Yale University Press, 2006.

Kaplan, Cora. "Afterword: Liberalism, Feminism, and Defect." In *"Defects": Engendering the Modern Body,* edited by Helen Deutsch and Felicity Nussbaum, 303–18. Ann Arbor: University of Michigan Press, 2000.

Kawash, Samira. *Dislocating the Color Line: Identity, Hybridity, and Singularity in African-American Narrative.* Palo Alto, Calif.: Stanford University Press, 1997.

Kim, Cynthia. "Decoding the High Functioning Label." Musings of an Aspie (blog), June 23, 2013. http://musingsofanaspie.com/2013/06/26/decoding-the-high-functioning-label/.

Kim, Jina. "Toward a Crip-of-Color Critique: Thinking with Minich's 'Enabling Whom?'" *Lateral* 6, no. 1 (2017). https://doi.org/10.25158/L6.1.14.

Kittay, Eva Feder. "When Caring Is Just and Justice Is Caring: Justice and Mental Retardation." In *The Subject of Care: Feminist Perspectives on Dependency,* edited by Eva Feder Kittay and Ellen K. Feder, 257–76. Lanham, Md.: Rowman & Littlefield, 2003.

Kolker, Robert. "The Boy Who Ran: The Life and Death of Avonte Oquendo." *New York Magazine,* March 30, 2014. https://nymag.com/intelligencer/2014/03/life-and-death-of-avonte-oquendo.html.

Kotef, Hagar. *Movement and the Ordering of Freedom: On Liberal Governances of Mobility.* Durham, N.C.: Duke University Press, 2015.

Krauss, Rosalind. "Video: The Aesthetics of Narcissism." *October* 1 (Spring 1976): 50–64.

Krtolica, Igor, and Guillaume Sibertin-Blanc. "The Children Estranged from Language: Fernand Deligny, in His Time, and against Lacan." *Psychoanalysis and History* 21, no. 2 (2019): 221–27.

Kuppers, Petra, Stephanie Heit, April Sizemore-Barber, V. K. Preston, Andy Hickey, and Andrew Wille. "Mad Methodologies and Community Performance: The Asylum Project at Bedlam." *Theatre Topics* 26, no. 2 (2016): 221–37.

Lane, Christopher. *Shyness: How Normal Behavior Became a Sickness.* New Haven, Conn.: Yale University Press, 2008.

Laurent, Éric. *La bataille de l'autisme: De la clinique à la politique.* Paris: Navarin, 2012.

Lazzarato, Maurizio. "The Concepts of Life and the Living in the Societies of Control." In *Deleuze and the Social,* edited by Martin Fuglsang and Bent Meier Sorensen, 171–90. Edinburgh: Edinburgh University Press, 2006.

Lepecki, André. "Choreopolice and Choreopolitics, or The Task of the Dancer." *TDR* 57, no. 4 (2013): 13–27.

Lepecki, André. *Exhausting Dance: Performance and the Politics of Movement.* London: Routledge, 2006.

Levinas, Emanuel. *Otherwise Than Being or Beyond Essence* (1974). Translated by Alphonso Lingis. Boston: Kluwer, 1978.

Lewiecki-Wilson, Cynthia. "Rethinking Rhetoric through Mental Disabilities." *Rhetoric Review* 22, no. 2 (2003): 156–67.

Lovaas, O. Ivar. "The Development of Treatment-Research Project for Developmentally Disabled and Autistic Children." *Journal of Applied Behavior Analysis* 26, no. 4 (1993): 617–30.

Lovaas, O. Ivar, Robert Koegel, James Q. Simmons, and Judith Stevens Long. "Some Generalizations and Follow-up Measures on Autistic-Children in Behavior Therapy." *Journal of Applied Behavior Analysis* 6, no. 1 (1973): 131–66.

Lynch, Kevin. *The Image of the City.* Cambridge, Mass.: MIT Press, 1960.

MacCabe, Colin. Preface to *The Geopolitical Aesthetic: Cinema and Space in the World System,* by Frederic Jameson. Bloomington: Indiana University Press, 1992.

Mahmood, Saba. *Politics of Piety: The Islamic Revival and the Feminist Subject.* Princeton, N.J.: Princeton University Press, 2011.

Malabou, Catherine. *The New Wounded: From Neurosis to Brain Damage.* Translated by Steven Miller. New York: Fordham University Press, 2012.

Malabou, Catherine. *What Should We Do with Our Brain?* Translated by Sebastian Rand. New York: Fordham University Press, 2008.

Maleval, Jean-Claude. *L'Autiste et sa voix.* Paris: Seuil, 2009.

Mamber, Stephan. *Cinema Verite in America: Studies in Uncontrolled Documentary.* Cambridge, Mass.: MIT Press, 1974.

Mandell, David S., John Listerud, Susan E. Levy, and Jennifer A. Pinto-Marin. "Race Differences in the Age at Diagnosis among Medicaid-Eligible Children with Autism." *Journal of the American Academy of Child and Adolescent Psychiatry* 41, no. 12 (2002): 1447–53.

Manning, Erin. *The Minor Gesture.* Durham, N.C.: Duke University Press, 2016.

Manning, Erin. *Relationscapes: Movement, Art, Philosophy.* Cambridge, Mass.: MIT Press, 2009.

Manning, Erin. "The Shape of Enthusiasm." *Parallax* 17, no. 2 (2011): 84–109.

Manning, Susan. "Performance." In *Keywords in American Studies,* edited by Bruce Burgett and Glenn Hendler. New York: NYU Press, 2007/2020. https://keywords.nyupress.org/american-cultural-studies/essay/performance/.

Markram, Henry, Tania Rinaldi, and Kamila Markram. "The Intense World Syndrome: An Alternative Hypothesis for Autism." *Frontiers in Neuroscience* 1, no. 1 (2007): 77–96.

Marks, Laura U. *The Skin of the Film: Intercultural Cinema, Embodiment, and the Senses.* Durham, N.C.: Duke University Press, 2000.

Marx, Karl. *Economic and Philosophical Manuscripts of 1844.* Edited by Dirk J. Struik, translated by Martin Milligan. New York: International Publishers, 1964.

Martin, Bradford D. *The Theater Is in the Street: Politics and Public Performance in 1960s America.* Boston: University of Massachusetts Press, 2004.

Masschelein, Jan, and Pieter Verstraete. "Living in the Presence of Others: Towards a Reconfiguration of Space, Asylum, and Inclusion." *International Journal of Inclusive Education* 16, no. 11 (2012): 1189–202.

Maxwell, Jessica. "William Pope.L Landscape + Object + Animal (review)." *Nka: Journal of Contemporary African Art* 28 (2011): 149–51.

McDonaugh, Patrick. "Autism and Modernism: A Genealogical Exploration." In *Autism and Representation,* edited by Mark Osteen, 99–116. New York: Routledge, 2008.

McGee, Micki. "Neurodiversity." *Contexts* 11, no. 12 (2012): 12–13.

McGrath, James. *Naming Adult Autism: Culture, Science, Identity.* Lanham, Md.: Rowman & Littlefield, 2017.

McGuire, Anne. *War on Autism: On the Cultural Logic of Normative Violence.* Ann Arbor: University of Michigan Press, 2016.

McIlwain, Lori. "The Day My Son Went Missing: Wandering Is a Major Concern for Parents of Children with Autism." *New York Times,* November 12, 2013. https://www.nytimes.com/2013/11/13/opinion/wandering-is-a-major-concern-for-parents-of-children-with-autism.html.

McQuaid, Cate. "Labor of Love." *Architecture Boston,* November 28, 2019. https://www.architects.org/stories/labor-of-love.

McRuer, Robert. "Compulsory Able-bodiedness and Queer/Disabled Existence." In *The Disability Studies Reader,* 2nd ed., edited by Lennard J. Davis, 301–8. New York: Routledge, 2006.

Melling, Joseph, and Bill Forsythe, eds. *Insanity, Institutions and Society: A Social History of Madness in Comparative Perspective.* London: Routledge, 1999.

Merleau-Ponty, Maurice. "Indirect Language and the Voices of Silence." In *Signs,* translated by Richard C. McCleary, 39–83. Evanston, Ill.: Northwestern University Press, 1964.

Metzl, Jonathan. *The Protest Psychosis: How Schizophrenia Became a Black Disease.* Boston: Beacon, 2009.

Miguel, Marlon. "Le matérialisme concret de Fernand Deligny: Vers une pensée du milieu humain." *Actuel Marx* 2, no. 62 (2017): 124–39.

Mitchell, David T., and Sharon L. Snyder. *The Biopolitics of Disability: Neoliberalism, Ablenationalism, and Peripheral Embodiment.* Ann Arbor: University of Michigan Press, 2015.

Mitchell, David T., and Sharon L. Snyder. "Compulsory Feral-ization: Institutionalizing Disability Studies." *PMLA* 120, no. 2 (2005): 627–34.

Mitchell, David T., and Sharon L. Snyder. "Disability as Multitude: Reworking Nonproductive Labor Power." *Journal of Literary and Cultural Disability Studies* 4, no. 2 (2010): 179–93.

Mitchell, David T., and Sharon L. Snyder. *Narrative Prosthesis: Disability and the Dependencies of Discourse.* Ann Arbor: University of Michigan Press, 2000.

Moten, Fred. "The Case of Blackness." *Criticism* 50, no. 2 (2008): 177–218.

Moten, Fred. *In the Break: The Aesthetics of the Black Radical Tradition.* Minneapolis: University of Minnesota Press, 2003.

Mottron, Laurent, Michelle Dawson, and Isabelle Soulières. "Enhanced Perception in Savant Syndrome: Patterns, Structure, and Creativity." *Philosophical*

Transactions of the Royal Society B: Biological Sciences 364, no. 1522 (2009): 1385–91.

Mouridsen, Svend E., Henrik Brønnum-Hansen, Bente Rich, and Torben Isager. "Mortality and Causes of Death in Autism Spectrum Disorders: An Update." *Autism* 12, no. 4 (2008): 403–14.

Muñoz, José Esteban. "Ephemera as Evidence: Introductory Notes to Queer Acts." *Women and Performance* 8, no. 2 (1996): 5–16.

Muñoz, José Esteban. "Feeling Brown, Feeling Down: Latina Affect, the Performativity of Race, and the Depressive Position." *Signs* 31, no. 3 (2006): 675–88.

Muñoz, José Esteban. "The Wildness of the Punk Rock Commons." *South Atlantic Quarterly* 117, no. 3 (2018): 653–58.

Murray, Stuart. "Autism Functions/The Function of Autism." *Disability Studies Quarterly* 30, no. 1 (2010). http://dsq-sds.org/article/view/1048/1229.

Musser, Amber. *Sensational Flesh: Race, Power, Masochism.* New York: NYU Press, 2014.

Nadesan, Majia Holmer. *Constructing Autism: Unravelling the "Truth" and Understanding the Social.* New York: Routledge, 2005.

Nancy, Jean-Luc. *The Pleasure of Drawing.* Translated by Philip Armstrong. New York: Fordham University Press, 2013.

Nichols, Bill. *Introduction to Documentary.* 3rd ed. Bloomington: Indiana University Press, 2017.

O'Connell, Lucille. "Caring for the Sick and Poor: The State Almshouse at Bridgewater, 1854–1887." *Bridgewater Review* 3, no. 1 (1984): 8–12.

Ogilvie, Bertrand. "Living between the Lines." In *The Arachnean and Other Texts,* by Fernand Deligny, translated by Drew Burk and Catherine Porter, 9–19. Minneapolis: Univocal, 2015.

Oury, Jean. "The Hospital Is Ill: Interview with Jean Oury." Conducted by David Reggio and Mauricio Novello. Translated by David Reggio. Edited by Peter Osborne. *Radical Philosophy* 143 (May–June 2007): 32–45.

Participant Inc. "Jonathan Berger, *An Introduction to Nameless Love.*" Press release, 2020. https://www.participantinc.org/seasons/season-18/an-introduction-to-nameless-love.

Peabody, Rebecca. "'The Reassurance Project': William Pope.L in the Archive." *Getty Research Journal* 4 (2012): 195–200.

Pearson, Jesse. "The Follies of Documentary Filmmaking." *Vice,* September 1, 2007. https://www.vice.com/en/article/pp3y4b/doc-v14n9.

Pickering, Andrew. *The Mangle of Practice: Time, Agency, and Science.* Chicago: University of Chicago Press, 1995.

Pinchevski, Amit. "Bartleby's Autism: Wandering Along Incommunicability." *Cultural Critique* 78 (Spring 2011): 27–59.

Pinel, Philippe. *Traité médico-philosophique sur l'aliénation mentale.* Paris: Cailleet Ravier, 1800.

Pitts-Taylor, Victoria. "The Plastic Brain: Neoliberalism and the Neuronal Self." *Health* 14, no. 6 (2010): 635–52.

Pope.L, William. "An Interview with Artist Pope.L." Conducted by Rizvana Bradley. *Women and Performance* 24, nos. 2–3 (2014): 220–23.

Pope.L, William. *My Kingdom for a Title.* New York: Mitchell-Ines & Nash/Los Angeles: New Documents, 2021.

Pope.L, William. "Notes on Crawling Piece. a.k.a. How Much Is that Nigger in the Window? (Summer 1991/Streets of New York City)." *Art Journal* 56, no. 4 (1997): 65–66.

Povinelli, Elizabeth. "Defining Security in Late Liberalism: A Comment on Pedersen and Holbraad." In *Times of Security: Ethnographies of Fear, Protest, and the Future,* edited by Martin Holbraad and Morten Axel Pedersen, 28–32. New York: Routledge, 2013.

Povinelli, Elizabeth. *Economies of Abandonment: Social Belonging and Endurance in Late Liberalism.* Durham, N.C.: Duke University Press, 2011.

Puar, Jasbir K. *The Right to Maim: Debility, Capacity, Disability.* Durham, N.C.: Duke University Press, 2017.

Puar, Jasbir K. "The Cost of Getting Better: Suicide, Sensation, Switchpoints." *GLQ* 18, no. 1 (2012): 149–58.

Puar, Jasbir K. *Terrorist Assemblages: Homonationalism in Queer Times.* Durham, N.C.: Duke University Press, 2007.

Puar, Jasbir K., and Amit S. Rai. "Monster, Terrorist, Fag: The War on Terrorism and the Production of Docile Patriots." *Social Text* 20, no. 3 (2002): 117–48.

Puchner, Martin. "Manifesto = Theatre." *Theatre Journal* 54, no. 3 (2002): 449–65.

Quayson, Ato. *Aesthetic Nervousness: Disability and the Crisis of Representation.* New York: Columbia University Press, 2007.

Rancière, Jacques. *Aesthesis: Scenes from the Aesthetic Regime of Art.* Translated by Zakir Paul. New York: Verso, 2013.

Rancière, Jacques. *Dissensus: On Politics and Aesthetics.* Translated by Steve Corcoran. New York: Continuum, 2010.

Rancière, Jacques. *The Politics of Aesthetics: The Distribution of the Sensible.* Translated by Gabriel Rockhill. London: Continuum, 2004.

Revermann, Martin. "Brecht and Greek Tragedy: Re-thinking the Dialectics of Utilising the Tradition of Theatre." *German Life and Letters* 69, no. 2 (2016): 213–32.

Robcis, Camille. *Disalientation: Politics, Philosophy, and Radical Psychiatry in Postwar France.* Chicago: University of Chicago Press, 2021.

Robison, John Elder. "I Resign My Roles at Autism Speaks." Look Me in the Eye (blog), November 13, 2013. http://jerobison.blogspot.com/2013/11/i-resign-my-roles-at-autism-speaks.html.

Rodas, Julia Miele. *Autistic Disturbances: Theorizing Autism Poetics from the DSM to Robinson Crusoe.* Ann Arbor: University of Michigan Press, 2018.

Rodas, Julia Miele. "On the Spectrum: Rereading Contact and Affect in *Jane Eyre*." *Nineteenth-Century Gender Studies* 4, no. 2 (2008). https://www.ncgs journal.com/issue42/PDFs/rodas.pdf.

Rodenbeck, Judith. *Radical Prototypes*. Cambridge, Mass.: MIT Press, 2012.

Rose, Nikolas, and Joelle Abi-Rached. "The Birth of the Neuromolecular Gaze." *History of the Human Sciences* 23, no. 1 (2010): 11–36.

Rose, Nikolas, and Joelle M. Abi-Rached. *Neuro: The New Brain Sciences and the Management of the Mind*. Princeton, N.J.: Princeton University Press, 2013.

Rostagno, Aldo, Julian Beck, and Judith Malina. *We, the Living Theatre*. Westminster, Md.: Ballantine Walden, 1970.

Rothman, David, *The Discovery of the Asylum: Social Order and Disorder in the New Republic*. Boston: Little, Brown, 1971.

Sagura, Jean. "Nous avons tant Aimé Gourgas." March 30, 2008. http://www .jeansegura.fr/gourgas.html.

Samuels, Ellen. *Fantasies of Identification: Disability, Gender, Race*. New York: NYU Press, 2014.

Savarese, Ralph James, and Emily Thornton Savarese. "The Superior Half of Speaking." *Disability Studies Quarterly* 30, no. 1 (2010). http://dsq-sds.org/article/view/1062/1230.

Schaefer, Joy. "Truffaut's *L'enfant sauvage* (The Wild Child, 1970): Evoking Autism and the Nascent 'Eugenic Atlantic.'" *Ought* 1, no. 1 (Fall 2019): 10–41.

Schalk, Sami. *Black Disability Politics*. Durham, N.C.: Duke University Press, 2022.

Schechner, Richard. *Between Theater and Anthropology*. Philadelphia: University of Pennsylvania Press, 1995.

Schechner, Richard. "Magnitudes of Performance." In *By Means of Performance: Intercultural Studies of Theater and Ritual*, edited by Richard Schechner and Willa Appel, 19–49. Cambridge: Cambridge University Press, 1990.

Schuler, Adriana L., and Barry M. Prizant. "Echolalia." In *Communication Problems in Autism*, edited by Eric Schopler and Gary B. Mesibov, 163–84. New York: Plenum, 1985.

Schweik, Susan M. *The Ugly Laws: Disability in Public*. New York: NYU Press, 2010.

Scotland Against Criminalising Communities. "May Shows Contempt for Human Rights, Justice and Muslims." Press release, October 16, 2012. http://www.sacc .org.uk/press/2012/may-shows-contempt-human-rights-justice-and-mus lims.

Scott, Joan W. "The Evidence of Experience." *Critical Inquiry* 17, no. 4 (1991): 773 –97.

Scull, Andrew. *Psychiatry and Its Discontents*. Oakland: University of California Press, 2019.

Sedgwick, Eve Kosofsky. "Affect Theory and Theory of Mind." In *The Weather in Proust*, edited by Jonathan Goldberg and Michael Moon, 144–63. Durham, N.C.: Duke University Press, 2011.

Sedgwick, Eve Kosofsky. *Epistemology of the Closet.* Berkeley: University of California Press, 1990.

Sedgwick, Eve Kosofsky. "Making Things, Practicing Emptiness." In *The Weather in Proust,* edited by Jonathan Goldberg and Michael Moon, 69–122. Durham, N.C.: Duke University Press, 2011.

Sedgwick, Eve Kosofsky. *Touching Feeling: Affect, Pedagogy, Performativity.* Durham, N.C.: Duke University Press, 2003.

Sedgwick, Eve Kosofsky, and Adam Frank. "Shame in the Cybernetic Fold: Reading Silvan Tomkins." In *Touching Feeling: Affect, Pedagogy, Performativity,* by Eve Kosofsky Sedgwick, 93–122. Durham, N.C.: Duke University Press, 2003.

Shaviro, Steven. *The Universe of Things: On Speculative Realism.* Minneapolis: University of Minnesota Press, 2014.

Sheldon, Rebecca. *The Child to Come: Life after the Human Catastrophe.* Minneapolis: University of Minnesota Press, 2016.

Silberman, Steve. *NeuroTribes: The Legacy of Autism and the Future of Neurodiversity.* New York: Random House, 2015.

Silverman, Chloe. *Understanding Autism: Parents, Doctors, and the History of a Disorder.* Princeton, N.J.: Princeton University Press, 2013.

Simon, Jonathan. "Speaking Truth and Power." *Law and Society Review* 36, no. 1 (2002): 37–44.

Simplican, Stacy Clifford. *The Capacity Contract: Intellectual Disability and the Question of Citizenship.* Minneapolis: University of Minnesota Press, 2015.

Simpson, Murray K. "From Savage to Citizen: Education, Colonialism and Idiocy." *British Journal of Sociology of Education* 28, no. 5 (2007): 561–74.

Sinclair, Jim. "Don't Mourn for Us." *Our Voice* 1, no. 3 (1993). https://philosophy.ucsc.edu/SinclairDontMournForUs.pdf.

Singer, Judy. "There's a Lot in a Name." Genius Within (blog), 2019. https://web.archive.org/web/20190906002405/https://www.geniuswithin.co.uk/blog/theres-a-lot-in-a-name-diversity-vs-divergence/.

Singer, Judy. "'Why Can't You Be Normal for Once in Your Life?' From a 'Problem with No Name' to the Emergence of a New Category of Difference." In *Disability Discourse,* edited by Mairian Corker and Sally French, 59–67. Buckingham, Pa.: Open University Press, 1999.

Skida, Russell J., Lori Poloni-Staudinger, Sarah Gallini, Ada B. Simmons, and Renae Peggins-Azziz. "Disparate Access: The Disproportionality of African American Students with Disabilities across Educational Environments." *Exceptional Children* 72, no. 4 (2006): 411–24.

Skott-Myhre, Hans A., and Christina Taylor. "Autism: Schizo of Postmodern Capital." *Deleuze Studies* 5, no. 1 (2011): 35–48.

Slaby, Jan, and Shaun Gallagher. "Critical Neuroscience and Socially Extended Minds." *Theory, Culture and Society* 32, no. 1 (2014): 33–59.

Solga, Kim. "*Mother Courage* and Its Abject: Reading the Violence of Identification." *Modern Drama* 46, no. 3 (2003): 339–57.

Sontag, Susan. "Artaud." In *Antonin Artaud: Selected Writings*, by Antonin Artaud, xvii–lix. New York: Farrar, Straus and Giroux, 1976.

Spade, Dean. *Normal Life: Administrative Violence, Critical Trans Politics, and the Limits of Law.* Durham, N.C.: Duke University Press, 2015.

Spencer, Brigianna. "Why Parents of Children with 'Medical Autism' Should Support Neurodiversity and the Anti-cure Movement." Kyriolexy (blog), December 14, 2012. https://speakingon.wordpress.com/2012/12/14/why-parents-of-children-with-medical-autism-should-support-neurodiversity-and-the-anti-cure-movement/.

Straus, Joseph N. "Autism as Culture." In *The Disability Studies Reader,* 4th ed., edited by Lennard J. Davis, 460–84. New York: Routledge, 2013.

Sutton, Kate. "Hamja Ahsan Discusses *Shy Radicals* and Extrovert Supremacy." *Artforum,* September 24, 2019. https://www.artforum.com/columns/hamja-ahsan-discusses-shy-radicals-and-extrovert-supremacy-244689/.

Taylor, Sunaura. "The Right Not to Work: Power and Disability." *Monthly Review* 55, issue 11 (March 2004). http://monthlyreview.org/2004/03/01/the-right-not-to-work-power-and-disability/.

Taylor, Diana. *Performance.* Durham, N.C.: Duke University Press, 2016.

Téllez, Javier. "Filmmaker Javier Téllez on That Time He Shot a Human Cannonball across the Border." Interview conducted by Iñaki Fernández de Retana. *Remezcla,* October 25, 2014. https://remezcla.com/features/film/javier-tellez-on-film-making-that-time-he-shot-a-human-cannonball-over-the-border/.

Téllez, Javier. "Madness Is the Language of the Excluded: An Interview with Javier Téllez." Conducted by Michèle Faguet and Cristobal Lehyt. *C Magazine* 92 (Winter 2006): 26–30.

Terranova, Tiziana. "Futurepublic: On Information Warfare, Bio-racism and Hegemony as Noopolitics." *Theory, Culture and Society* 24, no. 3 (2007): 125–45.

Trask, Michael. *Camp Sites: Sex, Politics, and Academic Style in Postwar America.* Stanford, Calif.: Stanford University Press, 2013.

Travers, Jason C., Matt Tincani, and Michael P. Krezmien. "A Multiyear National Profile of Racial Disparity in Autism Identification." *Journal of Special Education* 47, no. 1 (2011): 41–49.

Trent, James. *Inventing the Feeble Mind: A History of Mental Retardation in the United States.* Berkeley: University of California Press, 1995.

Tsang, Wu. "'I Dislike the Word Visibility': Wu Tsang on Sexuality, Creativity, and Conquering New York's Museums." Interview conducted by Chloe Wyma. *Blouin Art Info,* March 2, 2012. http://cliftonbenevento.com/wp-content/uploads/2011/08/TSA_Artinfo_Mar2012.pdf.

Tully, John, Dave Hearn, and Thomas Fahy. "Can Electronic Monitoring (GPS 'Tracking') Enhance Risk Management in Psychiatry?" *British Journal of Psychiatry* 205, no. 2 (2014): 83–85.

Turner, Victor. *The Ritual Process: Structure and Anti-structure.* Piscataway, N.J.: Transaction, 1995.

Utter, Mark. "Jonathan Berger Displays the Power of Love One Letter at a Time." Utter Communication Strategies (blog), December 22, 2019. https://www.utterenergy.org/blog/2019/12/22/jonathan-berger-displays-the-power-of-love-one-letter-at-a-time.

Vork, Robert. "Opening Acts: The Performance of Trauma in the Work of Shakespeare, Artaud, Brecht, and Cervantes." PhD diss., Emory University, 2013.

Vork, Robert. "Silencing Violence: Repetition and Revolution in *Mother Courage and Her Children.*" *Comparative Drama* 47, no. 1 (2013): 31–54.

Wagner, Ann. "Performance, Video, and the Rhetoric of Presence." *October* 91 (Winter 2000): 59–80.

Wallace, Benjamin. "Are You On It?" *New York Magazine,* October 28, 2012. http://nymag.com/news/features/autism-spectrum-2012-11/.

Walters, Shannon. *Rhetorical Touch: Disability, Identification, Haptics.* Columbia: University of South Carolina Press, 2014.

Weiner, Dora B. "Mind and Body in the Clinic: Philippe Pinel, Alexander Crichton, Dominique Esquirol, and the Birth of Psychiatry." In *The Languages of Psyche: Mind and Body in Enlightenment Thought,* edited by G. S. Rousseau, 331–402. Berkeley: University of California Press, 1990.

White, Hayden. *Tropics of Discourse: Essays in Cultural Criticism.* Baltimore, Md.: Johns Hopkins University Press, 1986.

Wiame, Aline. "Reading Deleuze and Guattari through Deligny's Theatres of Subjectivity: Mapping, Thinking, Performing." *Subjectivity* 9, no. 1 (2016): 38–58.

Williams, Donna. *Autism and Sensing: The Unlost Instinct.* London: Jessica Kingsley, 1998.

Winston, Brian. *Claiming the Real: The Griersonian Documentary and Its Legitimations.* London: British Film Institute, 1995.

Wolman, David. "The Truth about Autism: Scientists Reconsider What They *Think* They Know." *Wired,* February 2, 2008. https://www.wired.com/2008/02/ff-autism/.

Wright, David. "Getting Out of the Asylum: Understanding the Confinement of the Insane in the Nineteenth Century." *Social History of Medicine* 10 (1997): 137–55.

Yergeau, M. Remi. *Authoring Autism: On Rhetoric and Neurological Queerness.* Durham, N.C.: Duke University Press, 2018.

Yergeau, M. Remi. "Clinically Significant Disturbance: On Theorists Who Theorize Theory of Mind." *Disability Studies Quarterly* 33, no. 4 (2013). https://dsq-sds.org/index.php/dsq/article/view/3876/3405.

Index

LEON J. HILTON is assistant professor of theatre arts and performance studies at Brown University, where he is a faculty affiliate with the gender and sexuality studies program and the science and technology studies program.